Study Guide

Managerial Accounting
2005ℯ

Belverd E. Needles, Jr.
DePaul University

Susan V. Crosson
Santa Fe Community College, Florida

Houghton Mifflin Company   **Boston**   **New York**

Senior Sponsoring Editor: Bonnie Binkert
Senior Development Editor: Margaret Kearney
Senior Manufacturing Coordinator: Priscilla J. Bailey
Marketing Manager: Todd Berman

Printed in the U.S.A.

ISBN: 0-618-393854

123456789-VHG-08 07 06 05 04

Contents

To the Student

This study guide is intended to help you improve your performance in your first accounting course. It is designed for use with *Managerial Accounting* 2005© by Needles and Crosson.

Reviewing the Chapter

This section provides a concise but thorough summary of the essential points covered by the learning objectives in each corresponding chapter of the text. It also provides a review of key terms and, when appropriate, a summary of journal entries introduced in the text.

Self-Test

The self-test reviews the basic concepts introduced in the text chapter and helps you prepare for examinations based on the chapter's learning objectives.

Testing Your Knowledge

This section provides matching, short-answer, true-false, and multiple-choice questions to test your understanding of the concepts and vocabulary introduced in the text.

Applying Your Knowledge

Developing the ability to work problems is an essential part of learning acounting. In this section, you can exercise your ability to apply principles introduced in the text to "real-life" accounting situations. Many of these sections are followed by crossword puzzles that test your knowledge of key terms.

Answers

The study guide concludes with answers to all the questions, exercises, and puzzles that follow the chapter review. Answers are cross-referenced to the learning objectives in the text chapters.

CHAPTER 1　THE CHANGING BUSINESS ENVIRONMENT: A MANAGER'S PERSPECTIVE

REVIEWING THE CHAPTER

Objective 1: Distinguish management accounting from financial accounting and explain the role of management accounting in the management cycle.

1. **Management accounting** is the process of identifying, measuring, accumulating, analyzing, preparing, interpreting, and communicating information that management uses to plan, evaluate, and control an organization and to ensure that its resources are used and accounted for appropriately. The information that management accounting provides should be timely and accurate and support management decisions about pricing, planning, operations, and many other matters. The need for management accounting information exists regardless of the type of organization or its size.

2. Although both management accounting and financial accounting provide information essential to decision making, they differ in a number of ways. The primary users of management accounting information are people inside the organization—managers, as well as employees, who depend on the information to make informed decisions, to perform their jobs effectively, and to achieve their organization's goals. Financial accounting, on the other hand, uses the actual results of management decisions to prepare financial reports primarily for use by parties outside the organization—owners or stockholders, lenders, customers and governmental agencies. Whereas the format of management accounting reports is flexible, driven by the users' needs, financial accounting reports must conform to GAAP. The nature of the information in the reports also differs (historical or future-oriented in management accounting reports; historical and verifiable in financial accounting reports), as do the units of measure used and the frequency of the reports.

3. The management cycle involves four stages: planning, executing, reviewing, and reporting. Management accounting can provide an ongoing stream of relevant information that supports management decisions in each stage of this cycle.
   a. In the planning stage, managers use management accounting information to establish **strategic objectives** and **operating objectives** that support their company's **mission** and to formulate a comprehensive **business plan** for achieving those objectives. The business plan is usually expressed in financial terms in the form of budgets.
   b. In the executing stage, managers implement the business plan in ways that make optimal use of available resources. The information that management accounting provides about such matters as deliveries and sales is extremely useful in managing the **supply chain**—the path that leads from the supplier of the materials from which a product is made to the final consumer.
   c. In the reviewing stage, managers compare actual performance with planned performance and take steps to correct any problems.

d. The reports prepared in the final stage of the management cycle reflect the results of the efforts undertaken in the previous three stages. Any report, whether prepared for internal or external use, should present accurate information that is clear and useful to the reader. The key to preparing such a report is to apply the four *w*'s: who, what, why, and when.

Objective 2: Describe the value chain and its usefulness in analyzing a business.

4. The **value chain** conceives of each step in the manufacture of a product or the delivery of a service as a link in a chain that adds value to the product or service. These value-adding steps—research and development, design, supply, production, marketing, distribution, and customer service—are called **primary processes.** The value chain also includes **support services**—human resources, legal services, information services, and management accounting. Support services facilitate the primary processes but do not add value to the final product. Value chain analysis enables a company to focus on its **core competency.** It frequently results in the **outsourcing** of parts of the value chain that are not among a company's core competencies.

Objective 3: Identify the management tools used for continuous improvement and describe how they work to meet the demands of global competition and how management accounting supports them.

5. Several management tools have been developed to help firms compete in an expanding global market. They include the just-in-time (JIT) operating philosophy, total quality management (TQM), activity-based management (ABM), and the theory of constraints (TOC). All these methods are based on the concept of **continuous improvement**—that is, that management should never be satisfied with the status quo but should continue to seek better methods, better products or services, better processes, and better resources.

a. The **just-in-time (JIT) operating philosophy** requires that all resources—materials, personnel, and facilities—be acquired and used only as needed. Its objectives are to improve productivity and eliminate waste. Management accounting responds to a JIT environment by providing an information system that is sensitive to changes in production processes.

b. **Total quality management (TQM)** requires that all parts of a business work together to build quality into the firm's products or services. The **costs of quality** include both the costs of achieving quality and the costs of poor quality. Managers share accounting information about the magnitude and classification of costs of quality with their employees to stimulate improvement.

c. **Activity-based management (ABM)** identifies all major operating activities, determines the resources consumed by each of those activities and the cause of the resource usage, and categorizes the activities as value-adding or non-value-adding. **Value-adding activities** add value to a product or service, as perceived by the customer. **Nonvalue-adding activities** add cost to a product or service but do not increase its market value. ABM seeks to eliminate or reduce the cost of non-value adding activities. In assigning costs, ABM relies on **activity-based costing (ABC),** a management accounting practice that identifies all of an organization's major operating activities (both production and nonproduction), traces costs to those activities, and then assigns costs to the products or services that use the resources supplied by those activities.

d. According to the **theory of constraints (TOC),** limiting factors, or bottlenecks, occur during the production of any product or service, but by using management accounting information to identify such constraints, managers can focus attention and resources on them and achieve significant improvements. TOC thus helps managers set priorities on how they spend their time and other resources.

Objective 4: Explain the balanced scorecard and its relationship to performance measures.

6. **Performance measures** are quantitative tools that gauge an organization's performance in relation to a specific goal or an expected outcome. Performance measures may be either financial or nonfinancial.

a. Financial performance measures use monetary data to assess the performance of an organization or its segments. Examples of these measures include return on investment, net income as a percentage of sales, and the costs of poor quality as a percentage of sales.

b. Nonfinancial performance measures include the number of times an activity occurs or the time taken to perform a task. Examples are number of customer complaints, the time it takes to fill an order, number of orders shipped the same day, and the hours of inspection. Such performance measures are useful in reducing or eliminating waste and inefficiencies in operating activities.

7. Managers use performance measures in each stage of the management cycle. In the planning stage, they establish performance measures that will support the organization's mission and the objectives of its business plan. In the executing stage, performance measures guide and motivate the performance of employees and assist in assigning costs. In the reviewing stage, managers use the information that performance measures have provided to analyze significant differences between actual and planned performance and to improvise ways of improving performance. In the reporting stage, they use the results of performance measurement in preparing performance evaluations and in developing new budgets.

8. The **balanced scorecard** helps an organization measure and evaluate itself from a variety of viewpoints. It links the perspectives of an organization's four stakeholder groups—financial (owners, investors, and creditors), learning and growth (employees), internal business processes, and customers—with the organization's mission, objectives, resources, and performance measures. The balanced scorecard uses both financial and nonfinancial performance measures to assess whether the objectives of the four perspectives are being met.

9. To ensure its success, a company must compare its performance with that of similar companies in the same industry. **Benchmarking** is a technique for determining a company's competitive advantage by comparing its performance with that of its closest competitors. **Benchmarks** are measures of the best practices in an industry.

Objective 5: Prepare an analysis of nonfinancial data.

10. Using management tools like TQM and ABM and comprehensive frameworks like the balanced scorecard requires analysis of both financial and nonfinancial data. In analyzing nonfinancial data, it is important to compare performance measures with the objectives that are to achieved.

Objective 6: Identify the standards of ethical conduct for management accountants.

11. Conflicts between external parties (e.g., owners, creditors, governmental agencies, and the local community) can create ethical dilemmas for management and for management accountants, who have a responsibility to help management balance the interests of external parties. Throughout their careers, management accountants have an obligation to the public, their profession, the organizations they serve, and themselves to maintain the highest standards of ethical conduct. To provide guidance, the Institute of Management Accountants has issued standards of ethical conduct for practitioners of management accounting and financial management. These standards emphasize practitioners' responsibility in the areas of competence, confidentiality, integrity, and objectivity.

SELF-TEST

Test your knowledge of the chapter by choosing the best answer for each item below.

1. Management accounting information is needed in
   a. manufacturing companies only.
   b. large companies only.
   c. not-for-profit organizations only.
   d. all types and sizes of organizations.

2. When applied to a company's financial, production, and distribution data, management accounting procedures will
   a. guarantee the generation of a profit.
   b. satisfy requirements of the Internal Revenue Service.
   c. satisfy management's information needs.
   d. represent the union's basic collective bargaining agreement.

3. Which of the following statements is *false?*
   a. The primary users of financial accounting reports are parties outside the organization.
   b. Management accountants are not restricted to using historical data and can employ any unit of measure useful in a particular situation.
   c. The only restrictive guideline on financial accounting is that the accounting practice or technique used must produce accurate and useful information.
   d. Financial accounting typically records and reports on the assets, liabilities, equities, and net income of a company as a whole.

4. Which of the following is *not* a stage in the management cycle?
   a. Planning
   b. Executing
   c. Preparing financial statements
   d. Reviewing

5. Which of the following management philosophies evolved to help firms compete in a global market?
   a. Just-in-time operating philosophy
   b. Total quality management
   c. Activity-based management
   d. All of the above

6. Performance measures may be either financial or nonfinancial. Which of the following is *not* a financial performance measure?
   a. Number of customer complaints
   b. Return on equity
   c. Sales for the month
   d. Total costs of production

7. The standards of ethical conduct issued by the Institute of Management Accountants state that the management accountant has a responsibility in all of the following areas *except*
   a. compliance with IRS regulations.
   b. confidentiality.
   c. competence.
   d. objectivity.

TESTING YOUR KNOWLEDGE

Matching*

Match each term with its definition by writing the appropriate letter in the blank.

___f___ 1. Theory of constraints (TOC)

___b___ 2. Value-adding activity

___&c___ 3. Activity-based management (ABM)

___&g___ 4. Total quality management (TQM)

___e___ 5. Continuous improvement

___i___ 6. Management accounting

___ga___ 7. Balanced scorecard

___j___ 8. Nonvalue-adding activity

___d___ 9. Just-in-time (JIT) operating philosophy

___h___ 10. Activity-based costing (ABC)

a. A framework that uses both financial and non-financial performance measures to assess whether the objectives of a company's stakeholder groups are being met

b. Something that increases both product cost and desirability

c. A management tool that identifies and analyzes all major operating activities and seeks to eliminate those that do not add value to a product or service

d. A management approach that creates an environment in which materials, personnel, and facilities are acquired and used only as needed

e. The concept that management should never be satisfied with the status quo but should constantly seek better ways of doing things

f. A management tool that enables managers to identify limitations on production and to set priorities on their time and resources

g. A management approach that focuses on coordinating employees' efforts to achieve product or service excellence

h. A management accounting practice that traces costs to major operating activities and assigns the costs to the products that use the resources supplied by the activities

i. The field involved with providing useful information to managers for decision-making purposes

j. Something that increases product cost but does not enhance product desirability

Short Answer

Use the lines provided to answer each item.

1. What are the four traditional stages of the management cycle?

   Planning
   executing
   reviewing
   reporting

2. Briefly explain what is meant by a just-in-time operating philosophy.

   emphasizes the elimination of waste — personnel are hired & raw materials & facilities are purchased & used only as needed

---

Note to student: The matching quiz might be completed more efficiently by starting with the definition and searching for the corresponding term.

3. List the four areas emphasized by the standards of ethical conduct for management accountants.

Integrity
Competence
Confidentiality
Objectivity

4. Briefly explain the "four w's" of preparing a management report.

Who is report for
What information is needed
When is report due
Why is report being prepared

True-False

Circle T if the statement is true, F if it is false. Provide explanations for the false answers, using the blank lines at the end of the section.

T (F) **1.** The function of the management accountant is to make important decisions for the company.

(T) F **2.** Management accounting exists primarily for the benefit of people inside the company.

T (F) **3.** A management accountant for a not-for-profit or government organization relies more on financial accounting principles than on management accounting rules.

(T) F **4.** The business entity as a whole is the focal point of analysis in financial accounting.

(T) F **5.** The data that support management accounting reports often are subjective.

T (F) **6.** Financial accounting reports may be prepared whenever management requests them.

T (F) **7.** Avoiding conflicts of interest relates most closely to the ethical standard of confidentiality.

T (F) **8.** Enhancing one's professional skills relates most closely to the ethical standard of objectivity.

(T) F **9.** The just-in-time operating philosophy emphasizes the elimination of waste.

(T) F **10.** Performance measures may be either financial or nonfinancial.

(T) F **11.** Nonvalue-adding activities are prime targets for elimination.

(T) F **12.** Management accountants frequently use nonfinancial units in their analyses.

T (F) **13.** Planning is the second stage in the management cycle.

(T) F **14.** Activity-based management identifies activities as being value-adding or nonvalue-adding.

T (F) **15.** Activities that add value to a product, as perceived by the manufacturer, are known as value-adding activities.

7. integrity

6 regular, equal intervals

3 reverse is true

1 provide information for management to make decisions

8 competence

13 first stage

15 customer

Multiple Choice

Circle the letter of the best answer.

1. Developing skills on an ongoing basis relates most closely to which of the following standards of ethical conduct?
   a. Integrity
   b. Objectivity
   c. Confidentiality
   d. Competence

2. Refusing a gift that might influence one's actions relates most closely to which of the following standards of ethical conduct?
   a. Integrity
   b. Objectivity
   c. Confidentiality
   d. Competence

3. Management accounting and financial accounting do *not* differ with respect to
   a. the primary users of the accounting reports.
   b. the timeliness of the information presented in the reports.
   c. restrictive guidelines.
   d. the units of measurement used in analyses.

4. Which of the following adhere(s) to the concept of continuous improvement?
   a. Just-in-time operating philosophy
   b. Total quality management
   c. Activity-based management
   d. All of the above

5. The content of management accounting reports normally is dictated by
   a. the double-entry system.
   b. generally accepted accounting principles.
   c. users' needs.
   d. the need to present historical and verifiable data.

6. Management accounting reports and analyses are usually heavily subjective, which means that
   a. much of the data have been estimated.
   b. the reports and analyses ignore inflation.
   c. the data are verifiable.
   d. the units of measurement used are historical dollars.

7. Managers compare actual performance with expectations of performance at which stage of the management cycle?
   a. Planning
   b. Executing
   c. Reviewing
   d. Reporting

8. Which of the following is *not* based on nonfinancial data?
   a. Analysis of deliveries
   b. Operating budgets
   c. Customer surveys
   d. Analysis of labor hours worked

APPLYING YOUR KNOWLEDGE

Exercises

1. Each item in the lettered list below describes a characteristic of management accounting or financial accounting and falls into one of the categories in the numbered list that follows. Write the appropriate letter in the blanks beneath the columns for financial accounting and management accounting.

   a. Business entity as a whole
   b. No restrictions on reporting format other than the usefulness of the information presented
   c. Managers and employees
   d. Historical, objective, and verifiable
   e. Persons and organizations outside the business
   f. Whenever needed; might not be on a regular basis
   g. Double-entry system
   h. Various segments of the business entity
   i. Dollars at historical and market values
   j. Subjective and future-oriented for planning purposes, but objective and verifiable for decision making
   k. On a periodic and regular basis
   l. Not restricted to double-entry system; may use any appropriate system
   m. Adherence to GAAP
   n. Any useful monetary or physical measurement

	Financial Accounting	Management Accounting
1. Primary users of information	e	c
2. Accounting systems used	g	l
3. Restrictive guidelines	m	b
4. Units of measurement	i	n
5. Focal point of analysis	a	h
6. Frequency of reporting	k	f
7. Nature of information	d	j

2. Dom Lucia is the owner of Dom's Pizza Palace in upstate New York. The restaurant is always very busy. Over the years, Dom has developed the following measures of efficiency for his employees:

Number of Pizzas

Served per Hour	Employee Rating
Over 20	Excellent
17–19	Good
14–16	Average
10–13	Lazy
Under 10	The Pits

During March, Dom's generated the following information about labor hours:

Employee	Hours Worked	Number of Pizzas Served
P. Sanchez	130	2,860
S. Wang	140	2,520
R. Scotti	145	1,885
E. Butterfield	136	2,176
B. Jolita	168	3,192
B. Warner	154	2,310
G. Cohen	150	1,350

Using Dom's Rating scale, evaluate the performance of these employees.

Sanchez   22   excellent
Wang   18   good
Scotti   13   lazy
Butterfield 16   average
Jolita   19   good
Warner   15   average
Cohen   9   the pits

3. Sun Factory is implementing a total quality management system. It has found that the factors listed below have an impact on profits. Use an *a* to indicate that the costs related to each factor achieve quality and a *b* to indicate that they are the costs of poor quality.

1. Rework   b
2. Warranty repairs   b
3. Employee training   a
4. Inspection of materials   a
5. Customer complaints   b

CHAPTER 2 COST CONCEPTS AND COST ALLOCATION

REVIEWING THE CHAPTER

Objective 1: Describe how managers use information about costs in the management cycle.

1. Because costs affect profitability, having accurate and up-to-date cost information is important to managers in all types of for-profit organizations. During the management cycle, managers in manufacturing, retail, and service businesses use information about operating costs to plan, execute, review, and report on operating activities.
   a. In the planning stage, managers develop budgets and estimate selling prices for goods or services based on estimates of operating costs.
   b. In the executing stage, managers use cost information in several ways, including estimating the profitability of a product or service, deciding whether to drop a product line or service, and determining selling prices.
   c. In the reviewing stage, managers want to know about significant variances between estimated costs and actual costs. Such variances help them ascertain the reasons for cost overruns, which may enable them to avoid such problems in the future.
   d. In the reporting stage, managers expect to see financial statements that show the actual costs of operating activities, as well as performance reports that summarize the variance analyses done in the reviewing stage.

Objective 2: Explain how managers classify costs and how they use these cost classifications.

2. A single cost can be classified in several ways: by cost traceability, by cost behavior, by whether it is value-adding or nonvalue-adding, and by whether it is a product cost or a period cost.

3. By tracing costs to cost objects, such as products or services, managers can obtain a fairly accurate cost measurement on which to base decisions about pricing and about reallocating resources to other cost objects.
   a. **Direct costs** are costs that can be conveniently or economically traced to a specific cost object. The wages of production workers, which can be directly traced to an individual product, are an example.
   b. **Indirect costs** are costs that cannot be conveniently or economically traced to a cost object. Rivets used in the production of airplanes and glue used in the production of furniture are examples. Although difficult to trace, indirect costs must be included in the cost of a product or service; to do so, managers use a formula to assign them to a cost object.

4. Cost behavior is the way costs respond (or do not respond) to changes in volume or activity. A cost that changes in direct proportion to a change in productive output (or to any other measure of volume) is a **variable cost**. A **fixed cost** is one that remains constant within a defined range of activity or time period. By analyzing cost behavior, managers can calculate the number of units that must be sold to obtain a certain level of profit.

5. A **value-adding cost** is the cost of an activity that increases the market value of a product or service—that is, the value as perceived by the

customer. For example, if customers are willing to pay more for a product made of a better material, the company's cost of using that material in its product is a value-adding cost. A **nonvalue-adding cost** is the cost of an activity that adds cost to a product or service but does not increase its market value. Such a cost may, however, be necessary. For example, the accounting department is necessary for the operation of a business, but it does not add value to a business's product or service. By classifying costs as adding value or not adding value, managers can eliminate the costs of nonvalue-adding activities that are not essential to the business and try to reduce the costs of those that are essential.

6. For financial reporting purposes, managers classify costs as product costs or period costs.
   a. **Product costs** (also known as *inventoriable costs*) are costs assigned to inventory. They include the three elements of manufacturing cost: direct materials, direct labor, and manufacturing overhead. Product costs appear on the income statement as cost of goods sold and on the balance sheet as finished goods inventory.
   b. **Period costs** (also called *noninventoriable costs*) are the costs of resources used during the period that do not benefit future periods; selling and administrative expenses are an example. Period costs are classified as expenses in the period in which they are incurred and appear on the income statement as operating expenses.

Objective 3: Define and give examples of the three elements of product cost and compute the unit cost of a product.

7. The three elements of product cost are the costs of direct materials, direct labor, and manufacturing overhead. **Direct materials costs** are costs that can be conveniently and economically traced to specific products, such as the cost of the wood used in making a desk. **Direct labor costs** are the costs of the labor needed to make a product that can be conveniently and economically traced to specific units of the product (e.g., the wages of production workers). **Manufacturing overhead costs** (also called *factory overhead, factory burden,* or *indirect manufacturing costs*) are costs of production that cannot be practically or conveniently traced directly to an end product. They include the costs of indirect materials and indirect labor.
   a. **Indirect materials costs** are costs that are too insignificant to assign to direct materials—for example, the costs of nails, rivets, lubricants, and small tools.
   b. **Indirect labor costs** are labor costs for production-related activities that cannot be conveniently traced to a product, such as the costs of maintenance, inspection, engineering design, supervision, and materials handling.
   c. Other indirect manufacturing costs include the costs of building maintenance, property taxes, property insurance, rent, utilities, and depreciation on plant and equipment.

8. **Product unit cost** is the cost of manufacturing a single unit of product. It is computed either by dividing the total cost of direct materials, direct labor, and manufacturing overhead by the total number of units produced, or by determining the cost per unit for each element of the product cost and adding those per-unit costs. Product unit cost can be calculated by using the actual, normal, or standard costing methods.
   a. **Actual costing** uses the costs of direct materials, direct labor, and manufacturing overhead at the end of the accounting period, or when actual costs are known, to calculate the product unit cost.
   b. **Normal costing** can be used when the actual manufacturing overhead costs are not yet known. It combines *actual* direct materials and direct labor costs with *estimated* manufacturing overhead costs to calculate the product unit cost.
   c. **Standard costing** allows managers to use estimates (*standards*) of direct materials, direct labor, and manufacturing overhead costs to determine the product unit cost. Managers use standard costs as a benchmark for pricing decisions and for controlling product costs.

9. **Prime costs** are the primary costs of production; they are the sum of a product's direct materials costs and direct labor costs. **Conversion costs** are the costs of converting raw materials into finished goods; they are the sum of the direct labor and manufacturing overhead costs incurred in turning direct materials into a finished product.

Objective 4: Describe the flow of costs through a manufacturer's inventory accounts.

10. A manufacturer maintains a **Materials Inventory account,** a **Work in Process Inventory account,** and a **Finished Goods Inventory account.** The balance in the Materials Inventory account shows the cost of goods purchased but unused. The balance in the Work in Process Inventory account shows the costs assigned to partially completed

products. The balance in the Finished Goods Inventory account shows the costs of products completed but not yet sold.

11. Accountants track manufacturing costs and make changes in account balances by referring to the source documents that accompany the flow of costs through the production process.

    a. The purchasing process begins with a *purchase request* for materials. If the materials are not on hand, the purchasing department sends a *purchase order* to a supplier. A *receiving report* documents the arrival of the materials. The company then receives a *vendor's invoice* for payment for the materials. The costs of these materials increase the balance in the Materials Inventory account.

    b. As production begins, the storeroom clerk receives an authorized *materials request form* specifying which materials are to be sent to the production area. The cost of the direct materials transferred to production increases the balance of the Work in Process Inventory account, and the cost of the indirect materials transferred increases the balance of the Manufacturing Overhead account. The costs of both types of materials decrease the balance of the Materials Inventory account. *Time cards* are used to record production employees' hours; the cost of their labor increases the Work in Process Inventory account. A *job order cost card* records all costs incurred as the products move through production.

    c. The cost of completed products decreases the balance of the Work in Process Inventory account and increases the balance of the Finished Goods Inventory account. When a product is sold, a clerk prepares a *sales invoice*. A *shipping document* shows the quantity of goods shipped and gives a description of them. As products are sold, the balance in the Finished Goods Inventory account decreases, and the balance in the Cost of Goods Sold account increases.

12. **Manufacturing cost flow** is the flow of manufacturing costs (direct materials, direct labor, and manufacturing overhead) through the Materials Inventory, Work in Process Inventory, and Finished Goods Inventory accounts into the Cost of Goods Sold account. Manufacturing costs flow first into the Materials Inventory account, which is used to record the costs of materials when they are received and again when they are issued for use in production. As the production process begins, all manufacturing-related costs (direct materials, direct labor, and manufacturing overhead) are recorded in the Work in Process Inventory account. The total costs of direct materials, direct labor, and manufacturing overhead incurred and transferred to Work in Process Inventory during an accounting period are called **total manufacturing costs**. When products are completed, their costs move from the Work in Process Inventory account to the Finished Goods Inventory account. The **cost of goods manufactured** is the cost of all units completed and moved to finished goods storage. Costs remain in the Finished Goods Inventory account until the products are sold. They are then transferred to the Cost of Goods Sold account.

Objective 5: Compare how service, retail, and manufacturing organizations report costs on their financial statements and how they account for inventories.

13. A manufacturer prepares a **statement of cost of goods manufactured** so that the cost of goods sold can be summarized in the income statement. The example that follows illustrates the three steps involved in preparing a statement of cost of goods manufactured.

    a. First, the cost of direct materials used must be found.

Beginning balance, materials inventory	$100
Add direct materials purchased (net)	350
Cost of direct materials available for use	$450
Less ending balance, materials inventory	200
Cost of direct materials used	$250 (1)

    b. Second, total manufacturing costs must be computed.

Cost of direct materials used (computed in section **a**)	$ 250 (1)
Add direct labor costs	900
Add total manufacturing overhead costs	750
Total manufacturing costs	$1,900 (2)

    c. Third, the cost of goods manufactured must be computed.

Total manufacturing costs (computed in section **b**)	$1,900 (2)
Add beginning balance, work in process inventory	400
Total cost of work in process during the period	$2,300
Less ending balance, work in process inventory	700
Cost of goods manufactured	$1,600 (3)

14. When the figure for the cost of goods manufactured has been computed, it can be transferred to

the cost of goods sold section of the income statement, as follows:

Beginning balance, finished goods inventory	$1,250
Add cost of goods manufactured (computed in section **c**)	1,600 (3)
Total cost of finished goods available for sale	$2,850
Less ending balance, finished goods inventory	300
Cost of goods sold	$2,550

15. Because the operations of service, retail, and manufacturing organizations differ, their financial statements differ as well. Because a service organization sells services, not products, it has no inventory account on its balance sheet. The cost of sales on its income statement reflects the net cost of the services sold. A retail organization, which purchases products ready for resale, maintains only one inventory account on its balance sheet. Called the Merchandise Inventory account, it reflects the costs of goods held for resale. The cost of goods sold on a retail organization's income statement is simply the difference between the cost of goods available for sale and the ending merchandise inventory. A manufacturing organization, because it creates a product, maintains three inventory accounts on its balance sheet: Materials Inventory, Work in Process Inventory, and Finished Goods Inventory. Its cost of goods sold equals the cost of goods available for sale minus ending finished goods inventory.

Objective 6: Define *cost allocation* and explain how cost objects, cost pools, and cost drivers are used to assign manufacturing overhead costs.

16. Manufacturing overhead costs are indirect costs that must be collected and allocated in some manner. **Cost allocation** is the process of assigning a collection of indirect costs to a specific **cost object,** such as a product or service, using an allocation base known as a **cost driver.** A cost driver is an activity base representing a major business function, such as direct labor hours, direct labor costs, or units produced. As the cost driver increases in volume, it causes the **cost pool**—the collection of indirect costs assigned to a cost object—to increase in amount.

17. Allocating manufacturing overhead costs is a four-step process that corresponds to the four

stages of the management cycle. In the first step (the planning stage), managers estimate manufacturing overhead costs and calculate a **predetermined overhead rate** (in traditional settings) or an activity pool rate (in activity-based costing settings) at which they will assign overhead costs to products. In the second step (the executing stage), the *estimated* overhead costs are applied to the product's costs as units are manufactured. In the third step (the reviewing stage), the actual manufacturing overhead costs are recorded. In the fourth step (the reporting stage), the difference between the estimated and actual overhead costs is calculated and reconciled. The Cost of Goods Sold account is corrected if the amount of **overapplied overhead costs** or **underapplied overhead costs** is immaterial. If the amount is material, adjustments are made not only to the Cost of Goods Sold account, but also to the Work in Process Inventory and Finished Goods Inventory accounts.

18. Because managers use predetermined overhead rates to make pricing decisions and to control costs, the rates should be calculated as accurately as possible. The successful allocation of manufacturing overhead costs depends on two factors: a careful estimate of the total manufacturing overhead costs and a good forecast of the activity level of the cost driver.

Objective 7: Using the traditional method of allocating manufacturing overhead costs, calculate product unit cost.

19. The traditional approach to applying manufacturing overhead costs is to use a single predetermined overhead rate. The total manufacturing overhead costs constitute one cost pool, and a traditional activity base, such as direct labor hours, direct labor costs, or machine hours, is the cost driver.

20. The first step in calculating product unit cost when using the traditional method is to compute a predetermined overhead rate. The second step is to apply overhead costs to the products by multiplying the predetermined rate by the actual cost driver level. For example, assume that total manufacturing overhead is estimated at $100,000 and that the cost driver (direct labor hours) is estimated at 5,000 hours. Actual direct labor hours total 4,500. Of the 4,500 hours, 2,000 were spent on the production of 6,000 units of Product A, and 2,500 were spent on the production of 7,000

units of Product B. The predetermined overhead rate would be calculated as follows:

$$\frac{\$100,000}{5,000} = \$20 \text{ per Direct Labor Hour}$$

Manufacturing overhead would then be applied to both products as follows:

A: 2,000 D.L. Hours × $20 Rate = $40,000
B: 2,500 D.L. Hours × $20 Rate = $\underline{50,000}$
Total Applied $\underline{\underline{\$90,000}}$

Thus, manufacturing overhead cost per unit is

A: $\dfrac{\$40,000 \text{ Applied}}{6,000 \text{ Units}} = \$6.67 \text{ per Unit}$

B: $\dfrac{\$50,000 \text{ Applied}}{7,000 \text{ Units}} = \$7.14 \text{ per Unit}$

Objective 8: Using activity-based costing to assign manufacturing overhead costs, calculate product unit cost.

21. **Activity-based costing (ABC)** is a more accurate method of assigning overhead costs to products than the traditional method. It categorizes all indirect costs by activity, traces the indirect costs to those activities, and assigns activity costs to products using a cost driver related to the cause of the cost.

22. The first step in calculating product unit cost when using activity-based costing is to estimate the total manufacturing overhead costs and then group these costs into appropriate activity pools related to specific activities. After identifying the appropriate number of activity pools and a cost driver, estimated activity pool amounts and estimated cost driver levels must be determined. The next step is to calculate a predetermined activity cost rate for each activity pool, as shown in Table 1. The cost pool rate is the estimated activity pool amount divided by the estimated cost driver level. As shown in Table 2 (on the next page), manufacturing overhead costs are then applied to the products by using the cost driver levels for each cost driver multiplied by the appropriate rate.

23. The example in Table 2 shows that Product B's manufacturing overhead cost was lower than Product A's. The primary reason for this difference is that Product A requires more setups and inspections than Product B. The information about production requirements and the accuracy of the product unit cost that the ABC costing method yields provide managers with valuable insights.

Objective 9: Apply costing concepts to a service organization.

24. Because no products are manufactured in the course of providing services, service organizations have no materials costs. They do, however, have both direct labor costs and overhead costs, which are similar to those in manufacturing organizations. To determine the cost of performing a service, direct labor and service overhead costs are included in the computation.

TABLE 1

Activity Pool	Estimated Total Activity Pool Costs	Cost Driver	Estimated Total Cost Driver Level	Predetermined Activity Cost Rate
Setup	$10,000	Number of setups	100 setups	$100 per setup
Inspection	8,000	Number of inspections	400 inspections	$20 per inspection
Building	7,000	Machine hours	3,500 machine hours	$2 per machine hour
Packaging	$\underline{5,000}$ $\underline{\$30,000}$	Packaging hours	1,000 packaging hours	$5 per packaging hour

TABLE 2

Activity Pool	Activity Cost Rate	Actual Cost Driver Level	Product A Cost Applied	Actual Cost Driver Level	Product B Cost Applied
Setup	$100	70	$ 7,000	30	$ 3,000
Inspection	20	250	5,000	150	3,000
Building	2	1,500	3,000	2,000	4,000
Packaging	5	300	1,500	700	3,500
Total			$16,500		$13,500
÷ by Number of units			1,000		2,000
= Manufacturing overhead cost per unit			$16.50		$6.75

Test your knowledge of the chapter by choosing the best answer for each item below.

1. Manufacturing overhead costs include all of the following *except*
   a. direct labor.
   b. indirect labor.
   c. indirect materials.
   d. other indirect manufacturing costs.

2. Total product cost includes
   a. direct labor.
   b. indirect labor.
   c. manufacturing overhead.
   d. all of the above.

3. Which of the following statements is *false?*
   a. Service organizations do not maintain inventory levels.
   b. Service organizations use accounting information to make better decisions.
   c. A service organization's income statement reports cost of sales rather than cost of goods sold.
   d. A service organization's balance sheet includes an inventory account called Cost of Service.

4. Which of the following documents starts the purchasing process?
   a. Purchase order
   b. Purchase request
   c. Materials request
   d. Vendor's invoice

5. All manufacturing costs incurred and assigned to products currently in production are classified as
   a. work in process inventory costs.
   b. materials inventory costs.
   c. finished goods inventory costs.
   d. costs of goods sold.

6. Given estimated total manufacturing overhead costs of $100,000, estimated total direct labor hours (the cost driver) of 10,000, and units produced of 6,000, the predetermined overhead rate under the traditional approach to allocating overhead is
   a. 10 percent.
   b. 6 percent.
   c. $6.
   d. $10.

7. If the beginning balance in the Materials Inventory account was $4,200, the ending balance was $3,940, and $21,560 of materials were used during the month, what was the cost of the materials purchased during this period?
   a. $21,600
   b. $21,820
   c. $21,790
   d. $21,300

8. At Price Company, the month-end cost of goods sold was $393,910, the beginning finished goods inventory was $40,410, and the ending finished goods inventory was $42,900. What was the total cost of completed goods transferred to finished goods inventory during the month?
   a. $396,400
   b. $391,120
   c. $391,420
   d. $393,400

9. Underapplied manufacturing overhead results when
   a. actual manufacturing overhead is less than estimated manufacturing overhead.
   b. applied overhead is less than actual manufacturing overhead.
   c. applied overhead is greater than actual manufacturing overhead.
   d. the cost of indirect materials is less than estimated.

10. A key difference between the activity-based costing (ABC) and traditional costing methods is that
    a. the traditional costing method uses multiple activity pools.
    b. ABC uses multiple activity pools.
    c. ABC uses a single activity pool.
    d. ABC uses a single cost driver.

TESTING YOUR KNOWLEDGE

Matching*

Match each term with its definition by writing the appropriate letter in the blank.

_h_ **1.** Time card

_c_ **2.** Manufacturing overhead costs

_b_ **3.** Direct materials

_a_ **4.** Indirect materials

_g_ **5.** Direct labor costs

_d_ **6.** Indirect labor costs

_j_ **7.** Cost driver

_k_ **8.** Cost pool

_m_ **9.** Standard costing

_f_ **10.** Total product costs

_o_ **11.** Work in Process Inventory account

_l_ **12.** Finished Goods Inventory account

_e_ **13.** Cost of goods manufactured

_n_ **14.** Total manufacturing costs

_i_ **15.** Cost allocation

a. Materials that cannot be conveniently and economically traced to specific products

b. Materials that can be conveniently and economically traced to specific products

c. All indirect manufacturing costs

d. Wages, salaries, and related costs that cannot be conveniently and economically traced to specific products

e. The total cost charged to completed units during a period

f. Direct labor, direct materials, and manufacturing overhead costs

g. Wages, salaries, and related costs that can be conveniently and economically traced to specific products

h. A record of the number of hours worked by an employee

i. The assignment of a cost to a specific cost object

j. An activity that causes the activity pool to increase in amount

k. A collection of overhead costs or other indirect costs related to a cost object

l. An account that holds the costs assigned to all completed units that have not yet been sold

m. A method of cost measurement that uses the estimated costs of direct materials, direct labor, and manufacturing overhead to calculate a product unit cost

n. Total costs charged to production during a period

o. An account that records all manufacturing costs incurred and assigned to partially completed units of product

Short Answer

Use the lines provided to answer each item.

1. List the three types of inventory accounts that manufacturers maintain.

Materials Inventory
Work in Process Inventory
Finished Goods Inventory

2. What are the three main components of manufacturing costs?

Direct Materials
Direct Labor
Manufacturing Overhead

**Note to student:* The matching quiz might be completed more efficiently by starting with the definition and searching for the corresponding term.

3. When is a materials cost considered a direct materials cost?

When conveniently & economically traced to specific units of the product

4. List four ways in which managers use information about costs.

Profit or loss determination
Product pricing
Inventory valuation
Planning & cost control

5. Show how the cost of direct materials used is computed.

   Materials inventory, beginning
+ *Materials purchased*
= *Cost of direct material available for use*
− *Materials inventory, ending*
= *Cost of direct materials used*

6. Indicate the way in which total manufacturing costs are computed.

   Direct materials
+ *Direct labor*
+ *Manufacturing overhead*
= *Total manufacturing costs*

7. Show how the cost of goods manufactured is computed.

   Total manufacturing costs
+ *Work in process inventory, beginning*
= *Total cost of work in process during the year*
− *Work in process inventory, ending*
= *Cost of goods manufactured*

8. Explain how a predetermined overhead rate is computed.

Divide the cost pool of total estimated overhead costs by the total estimated cost driver level

9. What is overapplied manufacturing overhead?

manufacturing overhead costs applied to production during the period are greater than the actual manufacturing overhead costs

10. What is cost of goods manufactured?

The cost of all units completed & moved to finished goods storage during an accounting period

True-False

Circle T if the statement is true, F if it is false. Provide explanations for the false answers, using the blank lines at the end of the section.

(T) F   1. A product cost should not appear in the income statement until the period in which the product is sold.

(T) F   2. The Work in Process Inventory account does not contain any period costs (expenses).

(T) F   3. Activity-based costing uses multiple cost pools.

(T) F   4. *Factory burden* is another term for manufacturing overhead.

(T) F   5. The Materials Inventory account decreases as materials are used in production.

T (F)   6. Most of the product costs incurred by a manufacturer are also incurred by a service organization.

(T) F   7. Number of inspections is an example of a cost driver used in ABC costing.

T (F)   8. A purchase order is prepared before a purchase request.

T (F) **9.** The costs of factory supervision are classified as direct labor.

T (F) **10.** The statement of cost of goods manufactured must be prepared after the income statement.

(T) F **11.** To compute the cost of goods sold for a manufacturer, the beginning balance of Finished Goods Inventory must be known.

(T) F **12.** Cost of goods manufactured minus total manufacturing costs equals the change in Work in Process Inventory during a period.

T (F) **13.** Cost of goods manufactured must be computed before total manufacturing costs.

(T) F **14.** Cost of direct materials used must be computed before cost of goods manufactured.

(T) F **15.** Activity-based costing calculates a more accurate product cost than the traditional costing method.

(T) F **16.** An increase in the amount of an activity pool indicates that the cost driver has increased.

T (F) **17.** The smaller a cost object, the easier it is to trace manufacturing costs to the object.

T (F) **18.** Depreciation on plant and equipment is a direct cost.

9. indirect labor

10. reverse the order

13. reverse the order

6. service firm has no direct materials cost

8. reverse the order

17. harder

18. indirect material cost

Multiple Choice

Circle the letter of the best answer.

1. Which of the following is a direct materials cost?
   a. The cost of glue used in making a bookcase
   b. A janitor's salary
   c. The cost of legs used in making a chair
   d. The cost of rags used in cleaning a machine

2. Documents relating to materials must be processed in a specific order. Which of the following lists those documents in their proper order?
   a. Materials request, purchase request, purchase order, receiving report
   b. Purchase order, purchase request, receiving report, materials request
   c. Purchase request, purchase order, receiving report, materials request
   d. Receiving report, purchase order, materials request, purchase request

3. Which of the following would probably be considered a period cost?
   a. Salaries of salespeople
   b. Wages of an assembly-line worker
   c. Freight in
   d. Materials used in the manufacture of a product

4. Which of the following documents does a purchasing department send to a vendor?
   a. Purchase request
   b. Materials request
   c. Receiving report
   d. Purchase order

5. Which of the following documents does a store-room clerk receive before releasing materials to production?
   a. Materials request
   b. Purchase request
   c. Job order cost card
   d. Purchase order

6. "Activities" in activity-based costing are analogous to
   a. cost objects.
   b. activity pools.
   c. cost drivers.
   d. manufacturing overhead.

7. Activity pools in activity-based costing are
   a. usually fewer in number than in traditional costing.
   b. used to accumulate costs.
   c. the products being manufactured.
   d. the same as overapplied manufacturing overhead costs.

8. How many cost drivers does the traditional costing method typically use?
   a. One
   b. Two
   c. Three
   d. Four

9. In which stages of the management cycle do managers use product cost information?
   a. Planning
   b. Executing
   c. Reviewing
   d. All of the above

APPLYING YOUR KNOWLEDGE

Exercises

1. Kue Corporation has provided the following data for 20xx:

Cost of goods manufactured	$450,000	$75,000
Finished goods, Jan. 1	75,000	450,000
Finished goods, Dec. 31	80,000	$525,000
Direct materials, Jan. 1	92,000	80,000
Direct materials, Dec. 31	70,000	$445,000
Work in process, Jan. 1	55,000	
Work in process, Dec. 31	64,000	

In the space provided at the right, compute the cost of goods sold.

2. Using the data below, calculate the activity cost rates, costs applied to Product A and Product B, total costs applied, and the overhead cost per unit.

Activity Pool	Estimated Total Activity Pool Costs	Cost Driver	Estimated Total Cost Driver Level	Predetermined Activity Cost Rate
Setup	$10,000	Number of setups	200 setups	$ 50
Inspection	6,000	Number of inspections	300 inspections	$ 20
Building	8,000	Machine hours	4,000 machine hours	$ 2
Packaging	4,000	Packaging hours	1,000 packaging hours	$ 4
	$28,000			

		Product A		Product B	
Activity Pool	Activity Cost Rate	Actual Cost Driver Level	Cost Applied	Actual Cost Driver Level	Cost Applied
Setup	$ 50	70	$ 3500	30	$ 1500
Inspection	20	250	5000	150	3000
Building	2	1,500	3000	2,000	4000
Packaging	4	300	1200	700	2800
Total	$ 76		$ 12,700		$ 11,300
÷ by Number of units			1,000		2,000
= Manufacturing overhead cost per unit			$ 12.70		$ 5.65

3. Using the following data, prepare a statement of cost of goods manufactured for Specialty Company in the form provided below:

Depreciation, factory building and equipment	$ 31,800
Direct labor	142,900
Factory insurance	2,300
Factory utilities expense	26,000
Finished goods inventory, Jan. 1	82,400
Finished goods inventory, Dec. 31	71,000
General and administrative expenses	163,000
Indirect labor	42,800
Net sales	855,100
Other factory costs	12,600
Materials inventory, Jan. 1	8,700
Materials inventory, Dec. 31	32,600
Materials purchased (net)	168,300
Selling expenses	88,500
Work in process inventory, Jan. 1	34,200
Work in process inventory, Dec. 31	28,700

Specialty Company
Statement of Cost of Goods Manufactured
For the Year Ended December 31, 20xx

Direct materials used		
Materials inventory, Jan 1, 2004	$ 8700	
Direct materials purchased	168300	
Cost of direct materials available for use	$177,000	
Less materials inventory, December 31, 2004	32,600	
Cost of direct materials used		$144,400
Direct labor		142,900
Manufacturing overhead		
Indirect labor	$42,800	
Factory insurance	2300	
Factory utilities expense	26,000	
Depreciation, factory building & equipment	31,800	
Other factory costs	12,600	
Total manufacturing overhead costs		115,500
Total manufacturing costs		$402,800
Add work in process inventory, Jan 1, 2004		34,200
Total cost of work in process during the year		$437,000
Less work in process inventory, Dec 31, 2004		28,700
Cost of goods manufactured		$408,300

4. Classify the costs of each of the following as direct materials (DM), direct labor (DL), or manufacturing overhead (OH) costs:

<u>OH</u> **a.** Sandpaper

<u>DL</u> **b.** Worker who assembles a product

<u>OH</u> **c.** Worker who cleans machinery and sets it up

<u>DM</u> **d.** Steel plates used in production

<u>OH</u> **e.** Glue and nails

<u>DL</u> **f.** Worker who sands a product before it is painted

<u>DM</u> **g.** Wheels attached to a product

<u>OH</u> **h.** Depreciation of machinery

<u>OH</u> **i.** Paint used to touch up finished products

Crossword Puzzle
for Chapters 1 and 2

PURCHASE ORDER
INDIRECT
DEBIT
COST OF
PLAN
PERIOD
NAIL
WHO
DRIVER
DIRECT
STANDARD
TOTAL
PRODUCT COST
RATE
REQUISITION
RECEIVING
WORK IN PROCESS
OVERHEAD
FINISHED
TIME
RENT

ACROSS

4. Document sent to a supplier (2 words)
7. Not traceable to specific products
8. Normal inventory account balance
10. _____ goods manufactured (2 words)
12. What managers do as they begin the management cycle
13. _____ (noninventoriable) cost
14. An indirect material
16. Audience for a management report
18. Activity that increases a cost pool
19. Traceable to specific products
20. _____ (estimated) cost
21. The "T" of "TQM"

DOWN

1. Expenditure traceable to goods (2 words)
2. Predetermined overhead _____
3. Order, as materials
5. _____ report (prepared when goods arrive)
6. Partially completed goods (3 words)
9. Indirect manufacturing costs
11. _____ goods (ready-for-sale inventory)
15. Employee _____ cards
17. Example of 9-Down

CHAPTER 3 COSTING SYSTEMS: JOB ORDER COSTING

REVIEWING THE CHAPTER

Objective 1: Discuss the role information about costs plays in the management cycle and explain why unit cost is important.

1. The role of the management accountant is to develop a management information system that provides managers with the cost information they need. Information about costs is essential at each stage of the management cycle.

2. During the planning stage, managers use cost information to set performance expectations, estimate product or service costs, and establish selling prices. During the executing stage, they use cost information to make decisions about controlling costs, managing the company's volume of activity, ensuring quality, and negotiating prices. During the reviewing stage, managers analyze actual and targeted total and unit costs to evaluate performance and adjust planning and decision-making strategies. During the reporting stage, they use unit costs to prepare financial statements and internal performance reports.

Objective 2: Distinguish between the two basic types of product costing systems and identify the information each provides.

3. A **product costing system** is a set of procedures used to account for an organization's product costs. A product costing system should provide timely and accurate unit cost information for pricing, cost planning and control, inventory valuation, and financial statement preparation. The two basic types of product costing systems are the job order costing system and the process costing system.

4. Companies that make large, unique, or special-order products (e.g., ships, wedding invitations, or custom-made drapes) typically use a **job order costing system**. Such a system traces the costs of direct materials, direct labor, and manufacturing overhead to a specific batch of products or a specific **job order** (i.e., a customer order for a specific number of specially designed, made-to-order products). Job order costing measures the cost of each complete unit and summarizes the cost of all jobs in a single Work in Process Inventory account that is supported by job order cost cards. A **job order cost card** is the document on which all costs incurred in the production of a particular job order are recorded.

5. Companies that produce large amounts of similar products or liquid products or that have long, continuous production runs of identical products typically use a **process costing system.** Makers of paint, breakfast cereal, and paper would use such a system. A process costing system first traces the costs of direct materials, direct labor, and manufacturing overhead to processes, departments, or work cells and then assigns the costs to the products manufactured by those processes, departments, or work cells. Process costing uses several Work in Process Inventory accounts, one for each process, department, or work cell.

6. Few production processes are a perfect match for a job order costing or process costing system. The typical product costing system therefore combines parts of job order costing and process costing to create a hybrid system designed specifically for a company's production process.

Objective 3: Explain the cost flow in a manufacturer's job order costing system.

7. A job order costing system is designed to gather the costs of materials, labor, and manufacturing overhead for a specific order or batch of products. It provides timely, accurate cost information and facilitates the smooth and continuous flow of that information. This cost flow, along with the job order cost cards and the subsidiary ledgers for materials and finished goods inventories, is the core of the job order costing system. Because a job order costing system emphasizes cost flow, it is important to understand how costs are incurred, recorded, and transferred within the system.

a. The purchase of materials or supplies is recorded by increasing Materials Inventory and decreasing Cash or increasing Accounts Payable.

b. When materials or supplies are issued into production, Work in Process Inventory is increased for the direct materials portion, Manufacturing Overhead is increased for the indirect materials portion, and Materials Inventory is reduced.

c. The total cost of wages earned during the period is debited to the Factory Payroll account. The factory payroll is distributed to the production accounts by increasing the Work in Process Inventory for direct labor, increasing Manufacturing Overhead for indirect labor, and decreasing Factory Payroll for the amount of direct labor.

d. Manufacturing overhead costs, other than indirect materials and indirect labor, increase the Manufacturing Overhead account and decrease an appropriate account, such as Cash or Accounts Payable.

e. Manufacturing overhead is applied to specific jobs by increasing the Work in Process Inventory account and reducing the Manufacturing Overhead account.

f. Upon the completion of a job, Finished Goods Inventory is increased, and Work in Process Inventory is decreased.

g. When finished goods are sold, the sale is first recorded by increasing Cash or Accounts Receivable and increasing Sales for the total sales price. Cost of Goods Sold is then recog-

nized and Finished Goods Inventory is reduced for the cost attached to the goods sold.

h. At the end of the period, an adjustment must be made for under- or overapplied overhead.

Objective 4: Prepare a job order cost card and compute a job order's product unit cost.

8. In a job order costing system, all manufacturing costs are accumulated in one Work in Process Inventory account. Job order cost cards are used to connect those costs to specific jobs. Each job has its own job order cost card, which becomes part of the subsidiary ledger for the Work in Process Inventory account. The job cost card includes the costs of direct materials used, direct labor, and manufacturing overhead assigned to the job. When the job is completed, the product unit cost is computed by dividing the total costs for the job by the number of goods units produced.

Objective 5: Apply job order costing to a service organization.

9. Many service organizations use job order costing to compute the cost of rendering services. Because service organizations do not manufacture products, their materials costs are usually negligible.

10. Job order cost cards are used to track the costs of labor, materials and supplies, and service overhead for each job. To cover these costs and earn a profit, many service companies base jobs on **cost-plus contracts**, which require the customer to pay all costs plus a predetermined amount of profit.

11. When a job is finished, the costs on the completed job order cost card become the cost of services. The cost of services is adjusted at the end of the accounting period for the difference between the applied and actual service overhead costs.

Objective 6: Distinguish between job order costing and project costing.

12. **Projects** are broader and more complex than jobs. They require a multidisciplinary approach to the development and delivery of a product or service. Examples include the construction of a large-scale retail and residential complex and the development of a computer software program.

13. In contrast to job order costing, which focuses on a specific job order, project costing links many different job orders and processes by transferring costs from one job or process to another, collecting and summarizing costs in a variety of ways, and providing appropriate internal controls.

SELF-TEST

Test your knowledge of the chapter by choosing the best answer for each item below.

1. Which of the following companies is *most* likely to use a job order costing system?
   a. Jet aircraft manufacturer
   b. Paint manufacturer
   c. Soft drink producer
   d. Oil-refining company

2. An approach to product costing that assigns all manufacturing costs to specific job orders or batches of products is
   a. job order costing.
   b. process costing.
   c. total costing.
   d. activity-based costing.

3. The document used for tracking product costs in a job order costing system is a job order
   a. materials receiving report.
   b. cost card.
   c. request form.
   d. materials request card.

4. A job order cost card does *not* include costs for
   a. manufacturing overhead.
   b. direct materials used.
   c. direct materials purchased.
   d. direct labor.

5. During February, gross pay was $36,400 for direct labor and $45,600 for indirect labor. How much labor cost should have been entered directly into the Work in Process Inventory account during the month?
   a. $36,400
   b. $45,600
   c. $0
   d. $82,000

6. Job order costing in a service organization differs from job order costing in a manufacturing organization in that
   a. a job order cost card is not used.
   b. no overhead is applied.
   c. services cannot be inventoried.
   d. service costs include direct labor.

7. For complex tasks that require multiple departments, experts, and procedures, which costing technique is *most* appropriate?
   a. Job order costing
   b. Process costing
   c. Full costing
   d. Project costing

8. In which step(s) of the management cycle is product cost information useful?
   a. Planning
   b. Executing
   c. Reviewing
   d. All of the above

9. Project costing is used by companies that
   a. develop computer software programs.
   b. bottle soft drinks.
   c. produce made-to-order draperies.
   d. process milk.

10. In the planning stage of the management cycle, managers use product cost information to
    a. evaluate performance.
    b. make changes to improve quality.
    c. forecast product costs.
    d. determine whether production goals have been achieved.

TESTING YOUR KNOWLEDGE

Matching*

Match each term with its definition by writing the appropriate letter in the blank.

_c_   **1.** Cost-plus contract

_g_   **2.** Project costing

_f_   **3.** Process costing system

_b_   **4.** Job order costing system

_d_   **5.** Job order cost cards

_e_   **6.** Job order

_a_   **7.** Manufacturing Overhead account

a. An accounting record that contains indirect manufacturing costs incurred and applied

b. The accounting method used by a manufacturer of one-of-a-kind or special-order products

c. An arrangement that requires a customer to pay for all costs incurred on a job plus a predetermined amount of profit

d. Records of the accumulation of job costs

e. A customer order for a specific number of special-order products

f. The accounting method used by a manufacturer of a large number of similar products

g. A broad, complex, multidisciplinary approach to the production of a good or delivery of a service

Short Answer

Use the lines provided to answer each item.

1. What are a service organization's three job costs ?

Labor

Materials & supplies

Service overhead

2. What are the three components of work in process inventory?

Direct materials

Direct labor

Manufacturing overhead

3. After all data have been recorded on a job order cost card, how is product unit cost computed?

Total costs on job order cost card ÷ divide by the number of good units produced

4. List three products for which a job order costing system should be used.

jet planes, ferries, trains — large, unique, special-order products

---

*Note to student: The matching quiz might be completed more efficiently by starting with the definition and searching for the corresponding term.

True-False

Circle T if the statement is true, F if it is false. Provide explanations for the false answers, using the blank lines below.

(T) F   **1.** A manufacturer that mass-produces toys would be likely to use a process costing system.

(T) F   **2.** A job order costing system uses a single Work in Process Inventory account.

T **(F)**   **3.** Indirect manufacturing costs bypass Work in Process Inventory and are charged directly to Finished Goods Inventory.

(T) F   **4.** As soon as work begins on a job, a job order cost card is created.

T **(F)**   **5.** The product unit cost can be calculated before a job is completed.

(T) F   **6.** When overhead costs are applied to specific jobs, Work in Process Inventory increases, and Manufacturing Overhead decreases.

T **(F)**   **7.** When goods are shipped to a customer, Cost of Goods Sold increases, and Work in Process Inventory decreases.

(T) F   **8.** A manufacturer of custom-made clothing would probably use a job order costing system.

(T) F   **9.** The cost information needed to compute product unit cost can be found on the completed job order cost cards.

(T) F   **10.** Product cost information is used in all stages of the management cycle.

T **(F)**   **11.** Product costing in a service organization is exactly the same as in a manufacturing organization.

T **(F)**   **12.** A project costing system is the same as a process costing system.

(T) F   **13.** A brewery would probably use a process costing system.

---

3 Indirect costs charged to Work in Process through applied overhead

5. Job must be complete & all costs recorded on card

7 Finished Goods Inventory decreases

---

11 Services have no physical product to be inventoried & valued

12 project costing links many different job orders, & processes by transferring costs from one job or process to another, collecting & summarizing costs in a variety of ways & providing appropriate internal controls

Multiple Choice

Circle the letter of the best answer.

1. A job order costing system would most likely be used by a manufacturer of
   a. paper clips.
   b. gasoline.
   c. supersonic jets.
   d. electric clocks.

2. In a job order costing system, which of the following does *not* require an increase in Manufacturing Overhead?
   a. Indirect materials
   b. Applied overhead
   c. Depreciation expense
   d. Indirect labor

3. The Work in Process Inventory account would *not* be increased for
   a. actual factory overhead.
   b. direct labor.
   c. applied factory overhead.
   d. direct materials used.

4. The Manufacturing Overhead account decreases when
   a. recording actual manufacturing overhead costs.
   b. assigning the manufacturing overhead costs to production.
   c. paying for indirect labor.
   d. transferring indirect materials from the Materials Inventory account.

5. A process costing system does *not*
   a. contain several Work in Process Inventory accounts.
   b. accumulate costs by job or batch of products.
   c. base costing on weekly or monthly time periods.
   d. apply to goods produced in a continuous flow.

6. Materials Inventory is reduced when
   a. materials are purchased.
   b. the related manufactured goods are sold.
   c. payment is made for materials.
   d. materials are issued into production.

7. Which of the following managerial uses of cost information is *most* likely to occur in the reviewing stage of the management cycle?
   a. Determining the cost of a product or service
   b. Reporting the cost of goods sold and inventory balances
   c. Computing unit costs based on actual costs incurred and units produced
   d. Evaluating performance by comparing budgeted costs with actual costs

8. Which of the following would *not* be included in the cost of a manufactured product?
   a. Advertising costs
   b. Materials
   c. Direct labor
   d. Factory foreperson's salary

APPLYING YOUR KNOWLEDGE

Exercises

1. Located in Las Cruces, New Mexico, Melvin's Septic Service Company employs 15 people. It uses job order cost cards to track the costs incurred on each of its jobs. Job costs include materials and supplies, labor, and service overhead. Melvin's categorizes these costs as septic design, septic tank installation, and job site cleanup. The company has tracked costs for the Gonzales job, and now that it has finished the job, it needs to complete the cost accounting. The service overhead charge for septic design is 30 percent of design labor cost, and the service overhead charge for septic tank installation is 50 percent of installation labor cost. The cost-plus contract has a 25 percent profit guarantee. The costs for the Gonzales job are as follows:

Beginning balances:

Septic design	$ 5,270
Septic tank installation	28,500
Job site cleanup	150

Costs during October:

Septic design	
Supplies	0
Design labor	500
Septic tank installation	
Materials and supplies	4,300
Direct labor	12,800
Job site cleanup	
Janitorial service	1,050

Complete the job cost card for the Gonzales job.

Job Order Cost Card
Melvin's Septic Service Company

Customer:	Gonzales
Contract Type:	Cost-plus
Type of Service:	Septic Services

Cost Summary:

Costs Charged to Job	Total
Septic design	
Beginning balance	$ 5270
Design labor	500
Service overhead (30% of design labor)	150
Totals	$5920
Septic tank installation	
Beginning balance	$ 28,500
Materials and supplies	4300
Installation labor	12,800
Service overhead (50% of installation labor)	6400
Totals	$52,000
Job site cleanup	
Beginning balance	$ 150
Janitorial service cost	1050
Totals	$1200
Totals	$59,120
Cost of job	$59,120
Markup (25% of cost)	14,780
Amount billed	$73,900

2. Watchung Shoe Company manufactures shoes of unusual lengths and widths on special order. It uses a job order costing system. For each item described below, enter increases or decreases in the T accounts on the next page.

Dec. 23 Purchased (on credit) materials that cost $2,950.

26 Issued materials costing $850 into production. Of this amount, $50 was for indirect materials.

26 Paid the following bills:

Utilities	$350
Rent	700
Telephone	150

27 The week's gross payroll of $1,500 was distributed to production accounts. Of this amount, 80 percent represents direct labor. (Do not prepare the entries when the payroll is *paid*.)

27 The week's overhead costs are applied to production based on direct labor dollars. Estimated overhead for the year is $165,000, and estimated direct labor dollars are $55,000.

29 Goods costing $3,900 were completed.

30 Finished goods costing $2,000 were shipped to a customer. The selling price was 70 percent greater than the cost, and payment for the goods is expected next month.

31 Applied overhead for the year was $132,500, and actual overhead was $130,000. The difference is closed into Cost of Goods Sold.

$$\frac{165,000}{55,000} = 3 \quad 3 \times 1200 = 3600$$

Materials Inventory		Accounts Payable		Work In Process Inventory	
2950	850		2950	800	3900
Bal 2100				1200	

Manufacturing Overhead		Factory Payroll		Cash	
50			1500		350
350					700
700					150
150					1200 Bal
300					
2500					

Finished Goods Inventory		Cost of Goods Sold	
3900	2000	2000	2500
Bal 1900			500 Bal

Sales		Accounts Receivable	
	3400	3400	

CHAPTER 4 COSTING SYSTEMS: PROCESS COSTING

REVIEWING THE CHAPTER

Objective 1: Describe the process costing system, identify the reasons for its use, and discuss its role in the management cycle.

1. A **process costing system** is a product costing system used by companies that produce large amounts of similar products or liquid products or that have a continuous production flow. Companies that produce paint, beverages, bricks, canned foods, milk, and paper are typical users of a process costing system.

2. A process costing system accumulates the costs of direct materials, direct labor, and manufacturing overhead for each process, department, or work cell and assigns those costs to products as they are produced during a particular period.

3. In the planning stage of the management cycle, managers use product cost information to decide what a product should cost and to determine the targeted number of units to be sold. All product-related costs for that targeted number can then be computed and used in the budget. During the executing stage, actual costs are incurred as units are produced, so managers are able to compute actual unit costs. In the reviewing stage, managers evaluate performance by comparing targeted costs with actual costs. If costs have exceeded expectations, they analyze why this has occurred and recommend changes. In the reporting stage, they use actual units produced and costs incurred to value inventory on the balance sheet and cost of goods sold on the income statement.

Objective 2: Relate the patterns of product flows to the cost flow methods in a process costing environment.

4. Before a product is completed, it usually must go through several processes, departments, or work cells. For example, a bookcase might go through the cutting, assembling, and staining departments. A process costing system accumulates costs by process, department, or work cell and passes them along to each subsequent process, department, or work cell as the product is being made. At the end of every accounting period, a process cost report assigns the costs that have accumulated during the period to the units that have transferred out of the process, department, or work cell and to the units that are still work in process.

5. A process cost report may use the FIFO costing method or the average costing method to assign the accumulated costs.
   a. With the **FIFO costing method,** the cost flow follows the logical flow of production; the costs assigned to the first materials processed are the first costs transferred out when the materials flow to the next process, department, or work cell.
   b. The **average costing method** does not attempt to match cost flow with product flow;

instead, it assigns an average cost to all products made during an accounting period.

Objective 3: Explain the role of the Work in Process Inventory accounts in a process costing system.

6. A process costing system maintains a separate Work in Process Inventory account for each process, department, or work cell. As products move from one process, department, or work cell to the next, the costs associated with them flow to the Work in Process Inventory account of that process, department, or work cell. Once the products are completed and ready for sale, their costs are transferred out of the Work in Process Inventory account to the Cost of Goods Sold account.

7. The process cost report prepared at the end of each period assigns the costs that have accumulated in each Work in Process Inventory account to the units transferred out and to the units still in process. The costs from all processes, departments, or work cells are used in computing the product unit cost.

Objective 4: Define *equivalent production* and compute equivalent units.

8. A process costing system assigns the costs incurred in a process, department, or work cell to the units worked on during an accounting period by computing an average cost per unit—that is, by dividing the total manufacturing costs by the total number of units worked on during the period. **Equivalent production** (also called *equivalent units*) is calculated to measure the number of equivalent whole units produced during the period. It expresses partially completed units in terms of completed whole units. The number of equivalent units produced is the sum of (a) total units started and completed during the period and (b) an amount representing the work done on partially completed products in both the beginning and the ending work in process inventories. A percentage of completion factor is applied to partially completed units to calculate the number of equivalent whole units.

9. Equivalent production must be computed separately for direct materials and conversion costs. Direct materials are usually added to the production process at the beginning of the process; therefore, equivalent units for materials typically reflect 100 percent completion. **Conversion costs,** which are the combined total costs of direct labor and manufacturing overhead, are often incurred uniformly throughout the production process. The computation of equivalent production for conversion costs consists of three components: the cost to finish the beginning work in process inventory, the cost to begin and finish the completed units, and the cost to begin work on the units in the ending work in process inventory.

Objective 5: Prepare a process cost report using the FIFO costing method.

10. A **process cost report** helps managers track and analyze costs in a process costing system. In a process cost report that uses the FIFO costing method, the cost flow follows the logical physical flow of production—that is, the costs assigned to the first materials processed are the first costs transferred when those materials flow to the next process, department, or work cell.

11. Preparation of a process cost report involves five steps:
    a. Steps 1 and 2 account for the physical flow of products and compute equivalent production for both direct materials costs and conversion costs.
    b. In Step 3, all direct materials and conversion costs for the current period are added to the costs of beginning inventory to arrive at the total costs to be accounted for.
    c. In Step 4, the cost per equivalent unit for both direct materials and conversion costs is found by dividing those costs by their respective equivalent units. These unit costs are then added to yield the total cost per equivalent unit for the period.
    d. In Step 5, costs are assigned to the units completed and transferred out during the period, as well as to the ending work in process inventory. The information needed to perform this step is provided by the equivalent units computed in Step 2 and the cost per equivalent unit computed in Step 4. When figures for the cost of ending work in process inventory and the cost of goods transferred out of the department are determined, they are totaled and compared with the total costs to be accounted for (computed in Step 3). If the figures do not agree, the difference is due to rounding or to an error in arithmetic.

12. When a company has more than one production process, department, or work cell, it must have a Work in Process Inventory account for each.

Objective 6: Prepare a process cost report using the average costing method.

13. A process cost report that uses the average costing method involves the same five steps as a

process report prepared with the FIFO costing method. However, the procedures for completing some of the steps differ.

   a. Step 1 is the same under both the average and FIFO costing methods: the physical units in beginning inventory are added to the physical units started during the period to arrive at total units to be accounted for.

   b. In Step 2, the number of units completed and transferred out and the number of units in ending inventory are added to arrive at units accounted for, and the equivalent units for direct materials and conversion costs are computed.

   c. In Step 3, all direct materials costs and conversions costs for beginning inventory and the current period are added to arrive at the total costs to be accounted for.

   d. In Step 4, the total of the costs in beginning inventory and the current period are divided by the equivalent units to determine the cost per equivalent unit.

   e. In Step 5, the costs of the units completed and transferred out are assigned by multiplying the equivalent units for direct materials and conversion (computed in Step 2) by their respective cost per equivalent unit (computed in Step 4) and then totaling these assigned values. The costs of the units in ending work in process inventory are assigned in the same way.

Objective 7: Evaluate operating performance using information about product cost.

14. Product costing systems provide information that managers can use to evaluate an organization's operating performance. Such an analysis may include consideration of the cost trends of a product or product line, units produced per time period, materials usage per unit produced, labor cost per unit produced, special needs of customers, and the cost-effectiveness of changing to a more advanced production process.

SELF-TEST

Test your knowledge of the chapter by choosing the best answer for each item below.

1. Which of the following companies is *most* likely to use a process costing system?
   a. Bridge-building company
   b. Oil-refining company
   c. Highway construction company
   d. Made-to-order boat company

2. When a company uses a process costing system, how many Work in Process Inventory accounts does it maintain?
   a. Depends on the number of products produced
   b. One
   c. One for each process, department, or work cell
   d. Three

3. In a recent accounting period, a department that uses a process costing system and the FIFO costing method had 1,400 units in beginning Work in Process Inventory, 40 percent complete; started and completed 4,900 units; and had 1,200 units in ending Work in Process Inventory, 60 percent complete. What is the number of equivalent units for materials costs, assuming materials are added at the beginning of the process?
   a. 6,100
   b. 7,500
   c. 6,300
   d. 4,900

4. Assuming the same facts as in **3,** what is the number of equivalent units for conversion costs if those costs are incurred uniformly throughout the process?
   a. 6,180
   b. 7,120
   c. 6,460
   d. 7,500

5. Hood Corporation uses a process costing system and the FIFO costing method. In its production process, materials are added at the outset, and conversion costs are incurred throughout the process. The following information pertains to Hood's operations in May:

   Beginning work in process inventory: 1,000 units, 50 percent complete; materials costs, $14,700; conversion costs, $13,550

   Units started and completed: 8,000

   Ending work in process inventory: 640 units, 80 percent complete

   Current period costs: materials, $127,872; conversion, $243,324

   Equivalent units: materials costs, 8,640 units; conversion costs, 9,012 units

   Given this information, what was the unit cost for materials in May?
   a. $27.10
   b. $27.00
   c. $14.70
   d. $14.80

6. Assuming the same facts as in **5,** what was the unit cost for conversion costs in May?
   a. $27.10
   b. $27.00
   c. $14.70
   d. $14.80

7. Assuming the same facts as in **5,** what were the total costs transferred to Finished Goods Inventory during May?
   a. $23,296
   b. $41,750
   c. $334,400
   d. $376,150

8. Assuming the same facts as in **5,** what was the ending balance of Work in Process Inventory?
   a. $23,296
   b. $41,750
   c. $334,400
   d. $376,150

9. A process cost report includes all of the following *except* the
   a. unit cost for conversion costs.
   b. equivalent production (units).
   c. schedule of finished goods.
   d. unit cost for direct materials.

10. A process costing system provides information about all of the following *except*
   a. sales revenue.
   b. product cost trends.
   c. material usage per unit.
   d. units produced per period.

TESTING YOUR KNOWLEDGE

Matching*

Match each term with its definition by writing the appropriate letter in the blank.

_____ 1. Process costing system

_____ 2. Step 2: accounting for equivalent units

_____ 3. Step 4: computing cost per equivalent unit

_____ 4. Step 5: assigning costs

_____ 5. Equivalent production

_____ 6. Conversion costs

_____ 7. FIFO costing method

_____ 8. Average costing method

a. A costing method that assumes that beginning work in process was started and completed during the accounting period

b. Combined direct labor and manufacturing overhead costs

c. The step in a process cost report in which costs are distributed to ending Work in Process Inventory and to units transferred out during the period

d. The product costing system used by companies that make large quantities of identical products

e. A costing method in which cost flow follows product flow

f. The step in a process cost report in which a cost per unit is computed

g. A measure that expresses partially completed units in terms of completed whole units

h. The step in a process cost report in which equivalent production is computed

Short Answer

Use the lines provided to answer each item.

1. List the five steps involved in preparing a process cost report in the order in which the steps are performed.

   _____

   _____

   _____

   _____

   _____

2. Using the FIFO costing approach, show the computation for equivalent units.

   _____

   + _____

   + _____

   = _____

3. What two costs are computed in Step 5 of a process cost report?

   _____

   _____

4. Using the FIFO costing approach, show the computation for the cost of goods completed and transferred out of a process, department, or work cell.

   _____

   + _____

   + _____

   = _____

_____

*Note to student: The matching quiz might be completed more efficiently by starting with the definition and searching for the corresponding term.

∟

True-False

Circle T if the statement is true, F if it is false. Provide explanations for the false answers, using the blank lines below. (For all statements, assume a process costing system.)

T F **1.** Because process costing is used when large quantities of identical items are produced, only one Work in Process Inventory account is ever needed.

T F **2.** Manufacturing overhead must be applied to production for the period.

T F **3.** The finished units of one department become, in effect, the materials input of the next department.

T F **4.** Product unit cost is made up of cost elements used in all departments.

T F **5.** Equivalent units produced equal the number of units that were started and completed during the period.

T F **6.** Conversion costs equal direct labor plus manufacturing overhead.

T F **7.** Separate unit cost figures are normally computed for direct labor and manufacturing overhead.

T F **8.** When the average costing method is used to compute equivalent production, beginning inventory is multiplied by the percentage completed as of the beginning of the period.

T F **9.** Cost per equivalent unit must be determined before costs are assigned to units.

T F **10.** Ending Work in Process Inventory is determined by multiplying total units by total cost per unit.

T F **11.** Units completed minus units in beginning inventory equal units started and completed (assuming that all units in beginning inventory have been completed).

T F **12.** Process costing information is used in all stages of the management cycle.

T F **13.** A FIFO costing approach follows the logical product flow.

Multiple Choice

Circle the letter of the best answer.

1. A department started and completed 10,000 units during the period. Beginning inventory of 5,000 units was 60 percent complete for conversion costs, and ending inventory of 7,000 units was 30 percent complete for conversion costs. What is equivalent production for conversion costs for the period under the FIFO costing method?
   a. 4,000 units
   b. 14,100 units
   c. 15,000 units
   d. 17,100 units

2. Assuming the same facts as in **1,** what is equivalent production for conversion costs for the period under the average costing method?
   a. 4,000 units
   b. 14,100 units
   c. 15,000 units
   d. 17,100 units

3. Which of the following is *not* a component of cost of goods manufactured and transferred out?
   a. Costs necessary to complete units in beginning inventory
   b. Costs attached to units in beginning inventory
   c. Costs of units started and completed
   d. Costs necessary to complete units in ending inventory

4. In which step of a process cost report do equivalent units *not* appear?
   a. Step 2
   b. Step 4
   c. Step 5
   d. Step 1

5. A department began the period with 5,000 units that were 80 percent complete, started and completed 12,000 units, and ended with 2,000 units that were 30 percent complete. Under the average costing method, equivalent units produced would equal
   a. 13,600.
   b. 14,400.
   c. 17,600.
   d. 19,000.

6. Conversion costs are the sum of
   a. direct materials and direct labor.
   b. direct labor and manufacturing overhead.
   c. manufacturing overhead and direct materials.
   d. direct materials, direct labor, and manufacturing overhead.

7. The cost of ending work in process inventory is computed in
   a. Step 2 of a process cost report.
   b. Step 5 of a process cost report.
   c. Step 4 of a process cost report.
   d. the income statement.

8. The cost of goods transferred to finished goods inventory is computed in
   a. Step 2 of a process cost report.
   b. Step 5 of a process cost report.
   c. Step 3 of a process cost report.
   d. the balance sheet.

9. In which stage of the management cycle do managers use process costing information to forecast unit costs?
   a. Executing
   b. Planning
   c. Reviewing
   d. Reporting

10. A process costing system would be used by companies that produce all of the following *except*
   a. beverages.
   b. computers.
   c. custom-made suits.
   d. vacuum cleaners.

APPLYING YOUR KNOWLEDGE

Exercises

1. Data for Department 1 of Jaquette Manufacturing Company for the month of May are as follows:

   Beginning Work in Process Inventory
   Units = 2,000
   Direct materials = 100% complete
   Conversion costs = 30% complete
   Direct materials costs = $12,000
   Conversion costs = $3,000

   Ending Work in Process Inventory
   Direct materials = 100% complete
   Conversion costs = 30% complete

   Operations for May
   Units started = 24,000
   Direct materials costs = $114,000
   Conversion costs = $30,750
   Units completed and transferred to the next department
       = 19,000

   Using the FIFO costing approach, complete the process cost report on the next page. Round off unit cost computations to two decimal places.

Jaquette Manufacturing Company
Process Cost Report: FIFO Costing Method
For the Month Ended May 31, 20xx

Crossword Puzzle
for Chapters 3 and 4

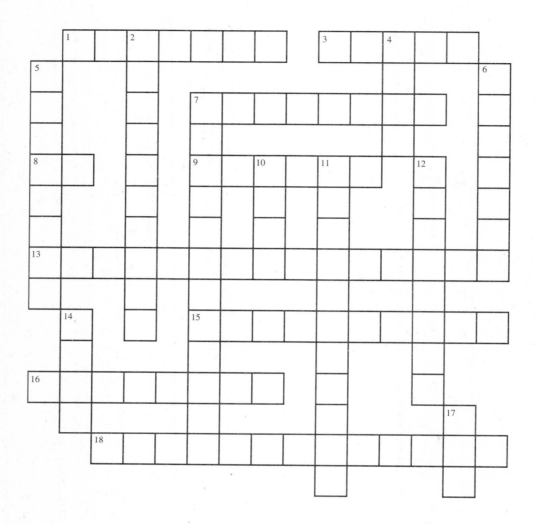

ACROSS

1. _____ Payroll account
3. Management _____ (a process divided into stages)
7. Outlay per manufactured item (2 words)
8. Cost _____ goods sold
9. Cost that can be traced to a specific job or product
13. Productive output of 6-Down (2 words)
15. Manufacturing output
16. First stage of 3-Across
18. With 10-Down, used in applying overhead to jobs

DOWN

2. _____ costs (combined total costs of direct labor and manufacturing overhead)
4. _____-plus contract
5. Costing system for batches of products (2 words)
6. Costing system for mass production
7. Term for actual overhead that exceeds allocated overhead
10. See 18-Across
11. Component of a job order cost card (2 words)
12. Manufacturing task or function
14. Work center
17. For each, as in cost for each unit

CHAPTER 5 ACTIVITY-BASED SYSTEMS: ABM AND JIT

REVIEWING THE CHAPTER

Objective 1: Explain the role of activity-based systems in the management cycle.

1. **Activity-based systems** are information systems that provide quantitative information about an organization's activities. These systems help managers view the organization as a collection of related activities. The cost information they provide enables managers to improve operating processes and make better pricing decisions.

2. In the planning stage of the management cycle, activity-based systems help managers identify value-adding activities, determine the resources required for those activities, and estimate product costs. In the executing and reviewing stages, activity-based systems help managers determine the **full product cost** (which includes not only the costs of direct materials and direct labor, but also the costs of all production and nonproduction activities), identify actions that may reduce product cost, and determine if cost-reduction goals for nonvalue-adding activities were achieved. In the reporting stage, managers report the cost of inventory and determine the degree to which product goals were achieved.

Objective 2: Define *activity-based management (ABM)* and discuss its relationship to the supply chain and the value chain.

3. **Activity-based management (ABM)** is an approach to managing an organization that identifies all major operating activities, determines the re-

sources consumed by each activity and the cause of the resource usage, and categorizes the activities as either adding value to a product or service or not adding value. ABM focuses on reducing or eliminating nonvalue-adding activities. Because it provides financial and performance information at the activity level, ABM is useful both for strategic planning and for making operational decisions about business segments, such as product lines, market segments, and customer groups. It also helps managers eliminate waste and inefficiencies and redirect resources to activities that add value to a product or service.

4. A **value chain** is a sequence of activities, or primary processes, that add value to a company's product or service; the value chain also includes support services, such as management accounting, that facilitate the primary processes. ABM enables managers to see their organization's value chain as part of a larger system that includes the value chains of suppliers and customers. This larger system is the **supply chain** (also called the *supply network*)—the path that leads from the suppliers of the materials from which a product is made to the final customer. Managers who understand the supply chain and how their company's value-adding activities fit into their suppliers' and customers' value chains can see their company's role in the overall process of creating and delivering products or services. Such an understanding can make a company more profitable. When organizations work cooperatively with others in their

supply chain, they can develop new processes that reduce the total costs of their products or services.

Objective 3: Distinguish between value-adding and nonvalue-adding activities, and describe process value analysis.

5. A **value-adding activity** adds value to a product or service as perceived by the customer. Examples include assembling a car, painting it, and installing seats and airbags. A **nonvalue-adding activity** is an activity that adds cost to a product or service but does not increase its market value. ABM focuses on eliminating nonvalue-adding activities that are not essential to an organization and on reducing the costs of those that are essential, such as legal services, materials handling, and building maintenance. It thus enables managers to redirect resources to value-adding activities.

6. **Process value analysis (PVA)** is a technique that managers use to identify and link all the activities involved in the value chain. It analyzes business processes by relating activities to the events that prompt the activities and to the resources that the activities consume. PVA forces managers to look critically at all phases of their operations. It improves cost traceability and results in significantly more accurate product costs, which in turn improves management decisions and increases profitability.

Objective 4: Define *activity-based costing* and explain how a cost hierarchy and a bill of activities are used.

7. **Activity-based costing (ABC)** is a method of assigning costs that calculates a more accurate product cost than traditional methods. It does so by categorizing all indirect costs by activity, tracing the indirect costs to those activities, and assigning those costs to products using a cost driver related to the cause of the cost. Implementing ABC involves five steps: (a) identifying and classifying each activity, (b) estimating the cost of resources for each activity, (c) identifying a cost driver for each activity and estimating the quantity of each cost driver, (d) calculating an activity cost rate for each activity, and (e) assigning costs to cost objects based on the level of activity required to make the product or provide the service.

8. Two tools that help managers implement ABC are a cost hierarchy and a bill of activities. A **cost hierarchy** is a framework for classifying activities according to the level at which their costs are incurred. In a manufacturing company, a cost hierar-

chy typically has four levels. **Unit-level activities** are performed each time a unit is produced. **Batch-level activities** are performed each time a batch of goods is produced. **Product-level activities** are performed to support the diversity of products in a manufacturing plant. **Facility-level activities** are performed to support a facility's general manufacturing process. A cost hierarchy includes both value-adding and nonvalue-adding activities; the frequency of activities varies across levels. Service organizations can also use a cost hierarchy to group activities.

9. After managers have created a cost hierarchy, they prepare a summary in the form of a bill of activities. A **bill of activities** is a list of activities and related costs that is used to compute the costs assigned to activities and the product unit cost. A bill of activities may be used as the primary document or as a supporting schedule for calculating product unit cost in both job order and process costing systems and in both manufacturing and service organizations.

Objective 5: Define the *just-in-time (JIT) operating philosophy* and identify the elements of a JIT operating environment.

10. The **just-in-time (JIT) operating philosophy** is one of the management philosophies that evolved to help companies stay competitive in today's business environment. It requires that all resources—materials, personnel, and facilities—be acquired and used only as needed. Its objectives are to enhance productivity, eliminate waste, reduce costs, and improve product quality. To meet the objectives of this management philosophy, a company must redesign its operating systems, plant layout, and management methods to conform to several basic concepts.

11. The elements in a JIT operating environment that support the concepts of the JIT philosophy are (a) maintaining minimum inventory levels; (b) using **pull-through production,** in which production is triggered by a customer order (as opposed to the traditional **push-through method,** in which products are manufactured in long production runs and stored in anticipation of customers' orders); (c) performing quick, inexpensive machine setups by using a cluster of machinery known as a **work cell,** an autonomous production line that can efficiently and continuously perform all required operations; (d) developing a multiskilled work force; (e) maintaining high levels of product quality; (f) enforcing a system of effective pre-

ventive maintenance; and (g) encouraging continuous improvement of the work environment.

Objective 6: Identify the changes in product costing that result when a firm adopts a JIT operating environment.

12. The traditional operating environment divides the production process into five time frames: (a) **processing time,** the actual time required to work on a product; (b) **inspection time,** the time spent detecting product flaws or reworking defective units; (c) **moving time,** the time needed to transfer a product from one operation or department to another; (d) **queue time,** the time a product waits to be worked on once it reaches the next operation or department; and (e) **storage time,** the time a product spends in materials storage, work in process inventory, or finished goods inventory.

13. In product costing under JIT, costs associated with processing time are categorized as either direct materials costs or conversion costs. **Conversion costs** are the sum of the direct labor costs and manufacturing overhead costs incurred by a production department, JIT work cell, or other work center. According to the JIT philosophy, product costs associated with inspection, moving, queue, and storage time should be reduced or eliminated because they do not add value to the product.

14. The key measure in a JIT operating environment is **throughput time,** the time it takes to move a product through the entire production process. Measures of product movement are used to apply conversion costs to products. With computerized monitoring of the JIT work cells, many costs that are treated as indirect costs in traditional manufacturing settings, such as the costs of utilities and operating supplies, can be traced directly to work cells. The only costs that remain indirect costs of the work cells are those associated with building occupancy, insurance, and property taxes.

Objective 7: Define and apply *backflush costing,* and compare the cost flows in traditional and backflush costing.

15. A JIT environment can reduce waste of resources and time not only in production operations, but in other areas as well, including the accounting process. Because materials arrive just in time to be used in the production process, there is little reason to maintain a separate Materials Inventory account, and because a JIT environment reduces labor costs, the accounting system can add direct labor costs and allocated manufacturing costs into the Work in Process Inventory account. Thus, by simplifying cost flows through the accounting records, a JIT environment makes it possible to reduce the time it takes to record and account for the costs of the manufacturing process.

16. A JIT organization can also streamline its accounting process by using **backflush costing.** When backflush costing is used, all product costs are first accumulated in the Cost of Goods Sold account, and at the end of the accounting period, they are "flushed back," or worked backward, into the appropriate inventory accounts. By having all product costs flow straight to a final destination and working back to determine the proper balances for the inventory accounts at the end of the period, backflush costing saves recording time.

17. When direct materials arrive at a factory in which traditional costing methods are used, their costs flow into the Materials Inventory account. Then, when the direct materials are requisitioned into production, their costs flow into the Work in Process Inventory account. When direct labor is used, its costs are added to the Work in Process Inventory account. Manufacturing overhead is then applied and is added to the other costs in the Work in Process Inventory account. At the end of the manufacturing process, the costs are transferred to the Finished Goods Inventory account, and when the units are sold, their costs are transferred to the Cost of Goods Sold account.

18. In a JIT setting in which backflush costing is used, the direct materials costs and the conversion costs (direct labor and manufacturing overhead) are immediately charged to the Cost of Goods Sold account. At the end of the period, the costs of goods in work in process inventory and in finished goods inventory are determined, and those costs are flushed back to the Work in Process Inventory account and the Finished Goods Inventory account. Once those costs have been flushed back, the Cost of Goods Sold account contains only the costs of units completed and sold during the period.

Objective 8: Compare ABM and JIT as activity-based systems.

19. ABM and JIT are similar in that as activity-based systems, both analyze processes and identify value-adding and nonvalue-adding activities. Both seek to eliminate waste, reduce costs, improve product or service quality, and enhance an

organization's efficiency and productivity. Both also improve the quality of the information managers use in making decisions.

20. ABM and JIT differ in their approaches to the calculation of product cost and cost assignment. Using ABC, ABM calculates product cost by using cost drivers to assign indirect manufacturing overhead costs to cost objects. ABC is used with job order and process costing systems.

21. JIT reorganizes activities so that they are performed within work cells. The costs of those activities become direct costs of the work cell. The total production costs within the work cell can be assigned by using simple cost drivers, such as process hours or direct materials cost. This approach focuses on the output at the end of the production process and simplifies the accounting system.

SELF-TEST

Test your knowledge of the chapter by choosing the best answer for each item below.

1. Which of the following is *not* a basic concept underlying just-in-time operations?
   a. An emphasis on quality and continuous improvement
   b. Producing goods only as they are needed
   c. Maintaining inventory levels to support probable demand
   d. The belief that simple is better

2. A switch to a just-in-time operating environment is facilitated by
   a. creating production work cells that comprise several different types of operations.
   b. enhancing a factory's storage capabilities.
   c. concentrating on areas of possible cost reduction rather than on the reduction of processing time.
   d. increasing inventories so that customers' demands can always be met.

3. Pull-through production means that
   a. the size of production runs is determined by how much can be pulled through the production process.
   b. production processes rely on long production runs to reduce the number of machine setups.
   c. it is very difficult to pull products through the production process.
   d. a customer order triggers the purchase of materials and the scheduling of production for the required products.

4. An activity that adds costs to a product or service but does not increase its market value is a
   a. cost-adding activity.
   b. cost driver.
   c. nonvalue-adding activity.
   d. value-adding activity.

5. In what stage of the management cycle are activity-based systems used?
   a. Executing
   b. Planning
   c. Reviewing
   d. All of the above

6. In a backflush costing system, all product costs are first charged to the
   a. Materials Inventory account.
   b. Finished Goods Inventory account.
   c. Cost of Goods Sold account.
   d. Work in Process Inventory account.

7. Which of the following would most likely be a value-adding cost in the production of a table?
   a. Salary of job foreman
   b. Electric utility cost
   c. The cost of using solid mahogany rather than a veneer
   d. Depreciation of factory building

8. Which of the following is *not* an activity level in a cost hierarchy?
   a. Cost level
   b. Batch level
   c. Unit level
   d. Product level

9. Processing time is the time
   a. spent detecting product flaws.
   b. required to work on a product.
   c. a product waits to be worked on once it reaches the next operation or department.
   d. a product spends in materials storage, work in process inventory, or finished goods inventory.

10. When direct materials arrive at the factory in which a traditional costing system is used, their costs flow first into the
    a. Cost of Goods Sold account.
    b. Finished Goods Inventory account.
    c. Materials Inventory account.
    d. Work in Process Inventory account.

TESTING YOUR KNOWLEDGE

Matching*

Match each term with its definition by writing the appropriate letter in the blank.

_____ 1. Conversion costs

_____ 2. Inspection time

_____ 3. Activity-based system

_____ 4. Just-in-time (JIT) operating philosophy

_____ 5. Value chain

_____ 6. Pull-through production

_____ 7. Supply chain

_____ 8. Nonvalue-adding activity

_____ 9. Work cell

_____ 10. Cost hierarchy

_____ 11. Push-through method

_____ 12. Bill of activities

_____ 13. Unit-level activities

a. The time spent looking for product flaws or reworking defective units

b. A concept of management in which all resources are acquired and used only as needed

c. An activity that adds costs to a product or service but does not increase its market value

d. A sequence of activities that add value to a company's product or service

e. An interdependent web of organizations that supplies materials, products, or services to a customer

f. A system in which a customer order triggers the purchase of materials and the scheduling of production for the required products

g. An information system that provides quantitative information about an organization's activities

h. An autonomous production line that can perform all required operations efficiently and continuously

i. Direct labor and manufacturing overhead costs incurred by a department, work cell, or other work center

j. A framework for classifying activities according to the level at which their costs are incurred

k. A production system in which products are manufactured in long production runs and stored in anticipation of customers' orders

l. Activities performed each time a unit is produced

m. A list of activities and related costs that is used to compute the costs assigned to activities and the product unit cost

---

Note to student: The matching quiz might be completed more efficiently by starting with the definition and searching for the corresponding term.

Short Answer

Use the lines provided to answer each item.

1. Briefly define the just-in-time operating philosophy.

   _____

   _____

   _____

   _____

   _____

   _____

   _____

2. List the five steps involved in implementing an activity-based costing system.

   _____

   _____

   _____

   _____

   _____

3. Define *process value analysis (PVA)* and explain how it can be helpful to managers.

   _____

   _____

   _____

   _____

   _____

   _____

4. Just-in-time is not an inventory system. Explain why.

   _____

   _____

   _____

   _____

   _____

True-False

Circle T if the statement is true, F if it is false. Provide explanations for the false answers, using the blank lines at the end of the section.

T F   **1.** Activity-based management and just-in-time have different primary goals.

T F   **2.** Eliminating waste is a key concept of the just-in-time operating philosophy.

T F   **3.** In a JIT environment, materials and other resources are acquired and used only as needed in order to eliminate waste.

T F   **4.** Pull-through production means that a customer order triggers the purchase of materials and the scheduling of production.

T F   **5.** A primary goal of the JIT operating philosophy is to reduce processing time.

T F   **6.** Product inspections are not performed in a just-in-time operating environment.

T F   **7.** Queue time is the time spent moving a product from one operation or department to another.

T F   **8.** Processing time is the actual time required to work on a product.

T F   **9.** Service organizations can use a cost hierarchy to group activities.

T F **10.** A service organization's cost hierarchy includes only unit-level and batch-level activities.

T F **11.** A bill of activities is used in traditional costing systems.

T F **12.** When an organization uses a backflush costing system, it backs costs out of the Cost of Goods Sold account.

T F **13.** A nonvalue-adding activity adds costs to a product but does not increase its market value.

T F **14.** Installing an airbag in an automobile is an example of a value-adding activity.

T F **15.** Activity-based systems can be used in all stages of the management cycle.

_____

_____

_____

_____

_____

_____

_____

_____

Multiple Choice

Circle the letter of the best answer.

1. Which of the following activities is *not* a batch-level activity?
   a. Production-line setup
   b. Production-line inspection
   c. Installation of a vehicle's engine
   d. Scheduling

2. Which of the following is *not* an element of the just-in-time operating philosophy?
   a. Maintaining minimum inventory levels
   b. Developing a multiskilled labor force
   c. Emphasizing direct labor variance analysis
   d. Encouraging continuous improvement in the work environment

3. Pull-through production means that
   a. automated machinery is used to pull products through the production process.
   b. a customer order triggers the purchase of materials and the scheduling of production.
   c. a customer complaint triggers the scheduling of rework on a defective product.
   d. production and scheduling are not functioning properly and a special device must be used to correct the situation.

4. Maintaining minimum inventory levels is a goal of JIT because
   a. carrying inventory is a waste of resources.
   b. carrying inventory maximizes the use of factory floor space.
   c. customer needs are not a major consideration in the JIT operating philosophy.
   d. doing so increases a company's current ratio.

5. Unit costs in a JIT operating environment are minimized by
   a. using inexpensive materials and supplies.
   b. performing quick, inexpensive machine setups.
   c. sacrificing quality for high-speed processes.
   d. using unskilled labor whenever possible.

6. Which of the following is *not* part of the traditional production process?
   a. Storage time
   b. Processing time
   c. Queue time
   d. Decision time

7. Which of the following would be a nonvalue-adding activity for a pizzeria?
   a. Home delivery
   b. Buying fresh pepperoni
   c. Recording daily cash receipts
   d. Preparing thick pizza dough

8. When backflush costing is used in a JIT environment, which of the following costs would *not* initially flow into the Cost of Goods Sold account?
   a. Sales salaries
   b. Manufacturing overhead
   c. Direct materials
   d. Direct labor

9. In the planning stage of the management cycle, an activity-based system can provide information that helps managers
   a. estimate product costs.
   b. attain production goals.
   c. determine inventory cost on the balance sheet.
   d. do all of the above.

10. Processing time is
   a. the time spent looking for product flaws or reworking defective units.
   b. the actual time spent working on a product.
   c. the time a product waits to be worked on.
   d. none of the above.

APPLYING YOUR KNOWLEDGE

Exercises

1. Puffy Corporation produces ten types of bicycles. The fully suspended titanium model is the most expensive and the most difficult to produce. The rigid-frame steel model is the easiest to produce and is the company's leading seller. Other models range from a fully suspended aluminum frame to a front-suspension steel frame; they become more complex as suspension is added and frame materials change. Bikes Incorporated recently ordered 350 of the front-suspended aluminum bicycles. Paula Jas, Puffy Corporation's controller, has decided to use this order to compare activity-based costing with the traditional costing approach. Costs directly traceable to the order are as follows:

Direct materials	$28,645
Purchased parts	$38,205
Direct labor hours	660
Average direct labor pay rate per hour	$7.00

With the traditional costing approach, Jas applies manufacturing overhead costs at a rate of 160 percent of direct labor dollars.

a. Use a traditional costing approach to compute the total cost and the product unit cost of the Bikes Incorporated order.

b. Use activity-based costing to compute the total cost and the product unit cost of the order.

Activity-based costing approach:

Activity	Activity Cost Rate	Cost Driver Level
Unit level:		
Parts production	$19 per machine hour	190 machine hours
Assembly	$9.50 per direct labor hour	42 direct labor hours
Packaging and shipping	$13 per unit	350 units
Batch level:		
Work cell setup	$45 per setup	8 setups
Product level:		
Product design	$31 per engineering hour	38 engineering hours
Product simulation	$45 per testing hour	14 testing hours
Facility level:		
Building occupancy	125% of direct labor costs	$4,620 direct labor costs

2. Listed below are several costs commonly incurred in a manufacturing environment:

Direct labor	Operating supplies
Depreciation, machinery	Fire insurance, plant
Raw materials	Setup labor
Product design costs	Rework costs
President's salary	Supervisory salaries
Small tools	Utilities costs, machinery

Classify each cost as direct or indirect when it is incurred in (a) a traditional manufacturing setting and (b) a JIT operating environment. Explain why some of these cost classifications differ between settings.

3. Kim Lazar is adapting UCF Manufacturing Company's accounting system to the company's new JIT environment. The Work in Process Inventory account has been installed. The following transactions took place last week:

Dec. 22 Metal brackets for Jobs 213 and 216 were ordered and received, $4,890.

23 Steel castings for the product's body were received, $13,300.

23 Work began on both jobs.

24 Both jobs were completed. Total costs for Job 213 were $14,870; for Job 216, they were $17,880.

26 Job 216 was shipped to customer.

The company uses a 60 percent markup over cost to price its products. Use the T accounts that follow to record the above transactions.

Work in Process Inventory

Finished Goods Inventory

Cost of Goods Sold

Accounts Payable

Accounts Receivable

Sales

CHAPTER 6 COST BEHAVIOR ANALYSIS

REVIEWING THE CHAPTER

Objective 1: Define *cost behavior* **and explain how managers use this concept in the management cycle.**

1. **Cost behavior**—the way costs respond to changes in volume or activity—affects decisions that managers make in all stages of the management cycle. In the planning stage, managers use cost behavior to determine how many units must be sold to generate a targeted amount of profit and how changes in operating, investing, and financing activities will affect operating income. During the executing stage, managers must understand cost behavior to determine the impact of their decisions on operating income. When reviewing operations and preparing reports, managers use cost behavior to analyze how changes in cost and sales affect the profitability of various business segments, as well as to make decisions about whether to eliminate a product line, accept a special order, or outsource certain activities.

Objective 2: Identify variable, fixed, and mixed costs, and separate mixed costs into their variable and fixed components.

2. Total costs that change in direct proportion to changes in productive output (or any other measure of volume) are **variable costs.** Examples include hourly wages and the costs of direct materials and operating supplies.
   a. Because variable costs change in relation to volume or output, it is important to know an organization's **operating capacity**—that is, its upper limit of productive output, given its existing resources. There are three common measures of operating capacity. **Theoretical (ideal) capacity** is the maximum productive output for a given period in which all machinery is operating continuously at optimal speed. **Practical capacity** is theoretical capacity reduced by normal and expected work stoppages. Theoretical capacity and practical capacity are useful when estimating maximum production levels, but they are unrealistic measures when planning operations. In contrast, **normal capacity**—the average annual level of operating capacity needed to meet expected sales demand—is a realistic measure of what an organization is likely to produce, not what it *can* produce.
   b. The traditional definition of variable cost assumes a linear relationship between costs and activity levels. However, many variable costs behave in a nonlinear fashion; for example, an additional hourly rental rate for computer usage may be higher than the previous hour's rental rate. *Linear approximation* is a method of converting nonlinear variable costs into linear variable costs. It relies on the concept of **relevant range,** which is range of volume or activity in which a company's actual operations are likely to occur.

3. **Fixed costs** are total costs that remain constant within a relevant range of volume or activity. Salaries, annual property taxes, and depreciation expense are examples. Fixed costs change only

when volume or activity exceeds the relevant range—for example, when additional supervisory personnel must be hired to accommodate increased activity. Fixed *unit* costs vary inversely with activity or volume. If more units are produced than anticipated, the fixed costs are spread over more units, thus decreasing the fixed cost per unit; if fewer units are produced than anticipated, the fixed costs are spread over fewer units, thus increasing the fixed cost per unit. (Note, however, that fixed costs are usually considered as a total rather than on a per unit basis.)

4. **Mixed costs** have both fixed and variable cost components. For example, monthly electricity charges include both a fixed service charge and a per kilowatt-hour charge. For planning and control purposes, mixed costs must be broken down into their fixed and variable components. The following four methods are commonly used to do this:

   a. The **engineering method** (sometimes called a *time and motion study*) separates costs into their fixed and variable components by performing a step-by-step analysis of the tasks, costs, and processes involved in completing an activity or product.

   b. A **scatter diagram**—a chart of plotted points representing past costs and related measures of volume—helps determine whether a linear relationship exists between a cost item and the related measure. If the diagram suggests a linear relationship, a cost line drawn through the points can provide an approximate representation of the relationship.

   c. The **high-low method** is a three-step approach to separating a mixed cost into its variable and fixed components. It calculates the variable cost per activity base, the total fixed costs, and a formula to estimate the total costs (fixed and variable) within the relevant range.

   d. Statistical methods, such as **regression analysis,** mathematically describe the relationship between costs and activities. Because these methods use all data observations, their results are more representative of cost behavior than that those produced by either the high-low or scatter diagram methods.

Objective 3: Define *cost-volume-profit (C-V-P) analysis* **and discuss how managers use it as a tool for planning and control.**

5. **Cost-volume-profit (C-V-P) analysis** is an examination of the cost behavior patterns that underlie the relationships among cost, volume of output,

and profit. The techniques and problem-solving procedures involved in the analysis express relationships among revenue, sales mix, cost, volume, and profit. Those relationships provide a general model of financial activity that managers use for short-range planning, evaluating performance, and analyzing alternative courses of action. For example, managers use C-V-P analysis to project profit at different activity levels, to develop budgets, to evaluate a department's performance, and to measure the effects of alternative courses of action, such as the effects of changes in variable or fixed costs, selling prices, and sales volume. C-V-P analysis is also useful in making decisions about product pricing, product mix, adding or dropping a product line, and accepting special orders.

6. C-V-P analysis is, however, useful only under certain conditions and only when certain assumptions hold true. If any of the following are absent, C-V-P analysis can be misleading:

   a. The behavior of variable and fixed costs can be measured accurately.

   b. Costs and revenues have a close linear relationship (e.g., when costs rise, revenues rise proportionately).

   c. Efficiency and productivity hold steady within the relevant range of activity.

   d. Cost and price variables also hold steady during the period being planned.

   e. The sales mix does not change during the period being planned.

   f. Production and sales volume are roughly equal.

Objective 4: Define *breakeven point* **and use contribution margin to determine a company's breakeven point for multiple products.**

7. The **breakeven point** is the point at which sales revenues equal the sum of all variable and fixed costs. A company can earn a profit only by surpassing the breakeven point. The breakeven point is useful in assessing the likelihood that a new venture will succeed. If the margin of safety is low, the profitability of the venture is unlikely. The **margin of safety** is the number of sales units or the amount of sales dollars by which actual sales can fall below planned sales without resulting in a loss.

8. Sales (S), variable costs (VC), and fixed costs (FC) are used to compute the breakeven point, as follows:

$$S - VC - FC = 0.$$

A rough estimate of the breakeven point can also be made by using a scatter, or breakeven, graph. Although less exact, this method does yield meaningful data. A breakeven graph has (a) a horizontal axis for units of output, (b) a vertical axis for dollars of revenue, (c) a horizontal fixed-cost line, (d) a sloping line representing total cost that begins where the fixed-cost line crosses the vertical axis, and (e) a sloping line representing total revenue that begins at the origin. At the point at which the total revenue line crosses the total cost line, revenues equal total costs.

9. **Contribution margin** (CM) is the amount that remains after all variable costs have been subtracted from sales:

$$S - VC = CM$$

A product's contribution margin represents its net contribution to paying off fixed costs and earning a profit (P):

$$CM - FC = P$$

Using the contribution margin, the breakeven point (BE) can be expressed as the point at which contribution margin minus total fixed costs equals zero. Stated another way, the BE is at the point at which the contribution margin equals total fixed costs.

10. The breakeven point for multiple products can be computed in three steps:
   a. Compute the weighted-average contribution margin by multiplying the contribution margin for each product by its percentage of the sales mix. The **sales mix** is the proportion of each product's unit sales relative to the company's total unit sales.
   b. Calculate the weighted-average breakeven point by dividing total fixed costs by the weighted-average contribution margin.
   c. Calculate the breakeven point for each product by multiplying the weighted-average breakeven point by each product's percentage of the sales mix.

Objective 5: Use C-V-P analysis to project the profitability of products and services.

11. The primary goal of a business venture is not to break even; it is to generate a profit. A targeted profit can be factored into the C-V-P analysis to estimate a new venture's profitability. This approach is excellent for "what-if" analyses, in which managers select several scenarios and compute the profit that may be anticipated from each.

12. Managers in a manufacturing business can estimate the profitability of a product by using the following equation, in which P is the targeted profit, and solving for the number of unit sales needed to achieve the desired profit:

$$S - VC - FC = P$$

The contribution margin approach is also useful for profit planning. For example, it can be used to project operating income given a change in one or more of the income statement components. In contribution income statements, all variable costs related to production, selling, and administration are subtracted from sales to determine the total contribution margin; all fixed costs related to those functions are subtracted from the total contribution margin to determine operating income.

13. C-V-P analysis can also be used to estimate the profitability of a service. In this case, managers do the following:
   a. Estimate service overhead costs by calculating (1) the variable service overhead cost per service, (2) the total fixed service overhead costs, (3) the total service overhead costs for a period, and (4) the total service overhead costs for that period assuming a certain number services will be performed.
   b. Determine the breakeven point by using the following formula, in which x = number of services (e.g., number of tax returns prepared by an accountant):

$$Sx = VCx + FC$$

   c. Determine the effect of a change in operating costs (i.e., the effect on profitability if fixed or variable costs change).
   d. Compute targeted profit for a given number of services by using the following formula, in which x = targeted sales in units:

$$Sx = VCx + FC + P$$

SELF-TEST

Test your knowledge of the chapter by choosing the best answer for each item below.

1. "The way that costs respond to changes in volume or activity" is the definition of
   a. cost flow.
   b. cost behavior.
   c. period costs.
   d. product costs.

2. An operating unit's ideal capacity reduced by normal and expected work stoppages is called
   a. theoretical capacity.
   b. excess capacity.
   c. practical capacity.
   d. normal capacity.

3. The records of Technology Company reveal the following data about electrical costs:

Month	Activity Level	Cost
April	960 machine hours	$ 8,978
May	940 machine hours	8,842
June	1,120 machine hours	10,066

   If the high-low method is applied to these figures, the variable cost per machine hour for the quarter would be
   a. $6.80.
   b. $8.60.
   c. $7.40.
   d. $4.70.

4. Assuming the same facts as in **3,** the monthly fixed costs would be
   a. $2,230.
   b. $2,450.
   c. $2,540.
   d. $1,890.

5. Product AB has a suggested selling price of $27 per unit and a projected variable cost per unit of $15. Fixed costs are expected to increase by $197,040 per month. The breakeven point in sales units per month is
   a. 16,240.
   b. 11,590.
   c. 11,950.
   d. 16,420.

6. Assuming the same facts as in **5,** the breakeven point in sales dollars per month is
   a. $443,340.
   b. $322,650.
   c. $312,930.
   d. $438,480.

7. Assuming the same facts as in **5,** how many units must be sold each month to earn a profit of $6,000 per month?
   a. 12,450
   b. 16,740
   c. 16,920
   d. 12,090

8. Assuming the same facts as in **5,** how many units must be sold each month to support an additional fixed monthly cost of $15,000 for advertising and earn a profit of $9,000 per month?
   a. 18,240
   b. 18,420
   c. 13,590
   d. 13,950

9. Products A, B, and C have contribution margins of $3, $5, and $4 per unit, respectively. Granada Company intends to manufacture one of the products and expects sales to be $30,000 regardless of which product it manufactures. If the same machinery and workers are used to produce each product, which one will yield the highest profit?
   a. A
   b. B
   c. C
   d. More information is needed.

10. Which of the following statements is *true*?
    a. Fixed costs vary within the relevant range.
    b. Fixed costs vary directly with activity levels.
    c. Fixed unit costs vary inversely with activity.
    d. Fixed unit costs are constant in the relevant range.

TESTING YOUR KNOWLEDGE

*Matching**

Match each term with its definition by writing the appropriate letter in the blank.

_____ 1. Cost behavior

_____ 2. Variable costs

_____ 3. Fixed costs

_____ 4. Relevant range

_____ 5. Mixed costs

_____ 6. Theoretical (ideal) capacity

_____ 7. Practical capacity

_____ 8. Normal capacity

_____ 9. Cost-volume-profit (C-V-P) analysis

_____ 10. Breakeven point

_____ 11. Contribution margin

a. The operating level needed to satisfy expected sales demand
b. The maximum productive output possible over a given period
c. The point at which total revenues equal total costs
d. The way costs respond to changes in volume or activity
e. Sales minus total variable costs
f. A method of determining profit at different levels of volume
g. Costs that vary in direct proportion to volume
h. Costs that remain constant within a relevant range of volume or activity
i. Ideal capacity reduced by normal work stoppages
j. Costs with both fixed and variable components
k. The span of activity in which actual operations are likely to occur

Short Answer

Use the lines provided to answer each item.

1. What is the breakeven formula?

   _____

   _____

2. Define *mixed cost* and give three examples of such a cost.

   _____

   _____

   _____

   _____

3. Briefly explain the purpose of the high-low method.

   _____

   _____

   _____

4. Distinguish between the concepts of sales and contribution margin.

   _____

   _____

   _____

   _____

   _____

5. Show how profit is calculated using the contribution margin format.

   _____

   − _____

   = _____

   − _____

   = _____

Note to student: The matching quiz might be completed more efficiently by starting with the definition and searching for the corresponding term.

6. Briefly describe how managers in a service business use C-V-P analysis to estimate the profitability of a service.

_____

_____

_____

_____

_____

_____

True-False

Circle T if the statement is true, F if it is false. Provide explanations for the false answers, using the blank lines below.

T F **1.** On a per unit basis, variable costs remain constant with changes in volume.

T F **2.** On a breakeven graph, fixed costs are represented by a horizontal line.

T F **3.** A fixed cost may change when it is outside the relevant range.

T F **4.** Factory insurance is an example of a variable cost.

T F **5.** The most realistic measure of plant capacity is practical capacity.

T F **6.** At the breakeven point, sales equal total costs.

T F **7.** A contribution margin cannot occur until the breakeven point has been surpassed.

T F **8.** The breakeven point in dollars can be determined by multiplying breakeven units by the selling price.

T F **9.** Property taxes are a fixed cost.

T F **10.** An assumption of C-V-P analysis is that the sales mix does not change during the period being planned.

T F **11.** A mixed cost has both variable and fixed cost components.

T F **12.** On a breakeven graph, the horizontal axis represents dollars of cost or revenue.

T F **13.** At the breakeven point, the total contribution margin equals fixed costs.

T F **14.** A reduction in sales dollars reduces the contribution margin per unit.

T F **15.** At the point at which the total revenue line crosses the total cost line on a breakeven graph, revenues equal total costs.

T F **16.** C-V-P analysis does not apply to service industries.

_____

_____

_____

_____

_____

_____

_____

_____

_____

_____

Multiple Choice

Circle the letter of the best answer.

1. A taxi fare with a base price plus a mileage charge would be an example of a
   a. fixed cost.
   b. variable cost.
   c. mixed cost.
   d. standard cost.

2. When fixed costs are $10,000, variable cost is $8 per unit, and selling price is $10 per unit, the breakeven point is
   a. 1,000 units.
   b. 1,250 units.
   c. 5,000 units.
   d. 10,000 units.

3. When volume equals zero units,
   a. fixed cost equals $0.
   b. variable cost equals $0.
   c. total cost equals $0.
   d. net income equals $0.

4. At the breakeven point,
   a. total contribution margin equals fixed cost.
   b. sales equal variable cost.
   c. total cost equals contribution margin.
   d. profit equals total cost.

5. In graph form, the breakeven point is at the intersection of the
   a. total-revenue and variable-cost lines.
   b. total-cost line and vertical axis.
   c. variable-cost and fixed-cost lines.
   d. total-cost and total-revenue lines.

6. The operating capacity required to satisfy anticipated sales demand is
   a. normal capacity.
   b. excess capacity.
   c. practical capacity.
   d. theoretical capacity.

7. As volume decreases,
   a. variable cost per unit decreases.
   b. fixed cost in total decreases.
   c. variable cost in total remains the same.
   d. fixed cost per unit increases.

8. When both the selling price and the variable cost per unit are increased by $5,
   a. more units need to be sold to break even.
   b. fewer units need to be sold to break even.
   c. the contribution margin per unit also increases by $5.
   d. the breakeven point remains the same.

9. Product X has a selling price of $50 and a variable cost per unit of 70 percent of the selling price. If fixed costs total $30,000, how many units must be sold to earn a profit of $45,000?
   a. 900
   b. 1,500
   c. 2,143
   d. 5,000

10. Product Y has a variable cost per unit of $10 and requires a fixed investment of $40,000. If sales are anticipated at 10,000 units, what selling price must be established to earn a profit of $26,000?
    a. $16.60
    b. $14.00
    c. $12.60
    d. $6.60

11. When calculating the breakeven point for multiple products, a weighted-average contribution margin is computed by
    a. multiplying variable costs of each product by units of each product.
    b. multiplying the contribution margin for each product by its percentage of the sales mix.
    c. multiplying total number of units of each product by sales price for each product.
    d. adding total fixed costs and total variable costs for each product.

12. Which of the following is a step in calculating the breakeven point for a service business?
    a. Estimating service overhead costs
    b. Computing variable overhead cost per service
    c. Computing total overhead cost, based on an estimated number of services
    d. All of the above

APPLYING YOUR KNOWLEDGE

Exercises

1. Leisure Manufacturing Company is planning to introduce a new line of bowling balls. Annual fixed costs are estimated to be $80,000. Each ball will be sold to retailers for $13 and requires $9 of variable costs.

   a. The breakeven point in units is

   _____.

   b. The breakeven point in dollars is

   _____.

   c. If 12,000 balls are sold per year, the overall profit or loss will be

   _____.

   d. The number of balls that must be sold for an annual profit of $50,000 is

   _____.

2. Using the letters listed below, identify the elements on the breakeven graph that follows. The **a** has already been used to indicate volume.
   a. Volume
   b. Cost or revenue
   c. Breakeven point
   d. Profit area
   e. Loss area
   f. Fixed cost
   g. Total cost
   h. Contribution margin
   i. Sales

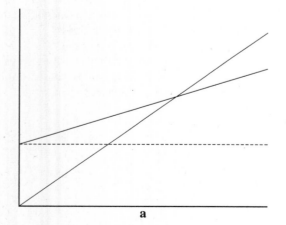

a

3. Chess Cab Company assembled the following figures for repairs to company vehicles during the first four months of 20xx:

Month	Activity Level	Cost
January	10,000 miles	$3,400
February	12,400	3,900
March	11,200	3,550
April	9,600	3,200

   a. Using the high-low method, produce a total cost formula that describes the cost behavior of the company's vehicle repairs.

   b. Based on your answer to **a**, approximately what repair cost should the company expect to have at an activity level of 16,000 miles?

4. Evans Corporation sold 20,000 units of Product Z last year. Each unit sold for $40 and had a variable cost of $26. Annual fixed costs totaled $300,000. This year, management is thinking of reducing the selling price by 15 percent, purchasing less expensive material to save $2 per unit, and spending $50,000 more on advertising. It is expected that with the proposed changes, sales will double.
   a. What was the corporation's profit or loss last year?
   b. What would the corporation's per unit contribution margin be after the proposed changes are made?
   c. If the projections are accurate, what would the corporation's profit be after the changes are made?

Crossword Puzzle
for Chapters 5 and 6

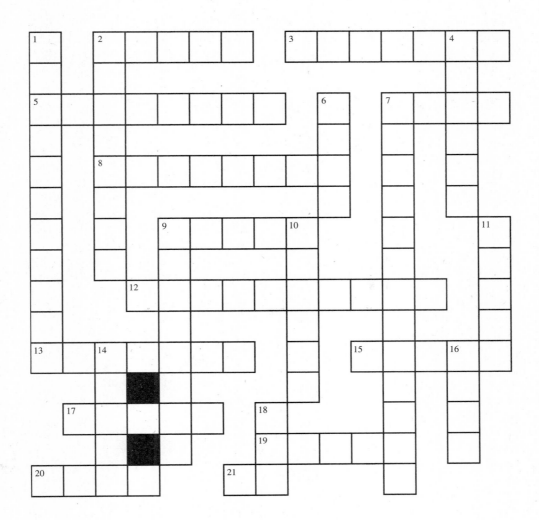

ACROSS

2. See 2-Down

3. _____ value analysis (PVA)

5. Proportion of each product's unit sales relative to total unit sales (2 words)

7. Full product _____

8. Cost affected by volume change

9. Cost not affected by volume change

12. Value-adding and nonvalue-adding _____

13. Method of separating mixed costs (hyphenated)

15. _____ chain

17. Common accounting period

19. _____-level activities (by job)

20. The "J" of JIT

21. S – VC = _____

DOWN

1. Method of long production runs (hyphenated)

2. With 2-Across, expected span of activity

4. Activity-based _____ (such as JIT or ABM)

6. Break _____

7. Framework for classifying activities by level (2 words)

9. _____-level activities (by plant)

10. Cost causer

11. _____ (waiting) time

14. _____ margin

16. _____-level activities (by item)

18. Kin to JIT, for short

CHAPTER 7 THE BUDGETING PROCESS

REVIEWING THE CHAPTER

Objective 1: Define *budgeting* **and explain its role in the management cycle.**

1. **Budgeting** is the process of identifying, gathering, summarizing, and communicating financial and nonfinancial information about an organization's future activities. It is an essential part of the continuous planning all types of organizations must do to accomplish their long-term goals. **Budgets**—plans of action based on forecasted transactions, activities, and events—are synonymous with managing an organization. They are used for a variety of purposes, including communicating information, coordinating activities, and resource usage, motivating employees, and evaluating performance.

2. **Strategic planning** is the process by which management establishes an organization's long-term goals. These goals define the strategic direction an organization will take over a five- to ten-year period and are the basis for making annual operating plans and preparing budgets. Annual operating plans involve every part of an enterprise and are much more detailed than long-term strategic plans. To formulate an annual operating plan, an organization must restate its long-term goals in terms of what it needs to accomplish during the next year. The short-term goals identified in an annual operating plan are the basis of an organization's operating budgets for the year.

3. The key to a successful budget is **participative budgeting.** This is a process in which personnel at all levels of an organization take an active and meaningful part in the creation of the budget.

4. Budgeting is helpful to managers at each stage of the management cycle.
   a. During the planning stage, budgeting helps managers relate long-term strategic goals to short-term activities, distribute resources and workloads, communicate responsibilities, select performance measures, and set standards for bonuses and rewards.
   b. In the executing stage, managers use budget information to communicate expectations, measure performance and motivate employees, coordinate activities, and allot resources.
   c. In the reviewing stage, budgets helps managers evaluate performance, including its timeliness; find variances between planned and actual performance; and create solutions to any significant variances that they detect.
   d. To provide continuous feedback about an organization's financing, investing, and operating activities, managers issue reports based on budget information throughout the year.

Objective 2: Identify the elements of a master budget in different types of organizations and the guidelines for preparing budgets.

5. A **master budget** consists of a set of *operating* budgets and a set of *financial* budgets that detail an organization's financial plans for a specific accounting period, generally a year. **Operating budgets** are plans used in daily operations. They

are also the basis for preparing the **financial budgets,** which are projections of financial results for the accounting period. Financial budgets include a budgeted income statement, a capital expenditures budget, a cash budget, and a budgeted balance sheet. The budgeted income statement and budgeted balance sheet are also called **pro forma statements,** meaning that they show projections rather than actual results.

6. The process of preparing a master budget is similar in manufacturing, retail, and service organizations in that each prepares a set of operating budgets that serve as the basis for preparing the financial budgets. The process differs mainly in the kinds of operating budgets that each type of organization prepares.

    a. Manufacturing organizations prepare operating budgets for sales, production, direct materials purchases, direct labor, manufacturing overhead, selling and administrative expenses, and cost of goods manufactured.

    b. Retail organizations prepare operating budgets for sales, purchases, selling and administrative expenses, and cost of goods sold.

    c. Service organization prepare operating budgets for service revenue, labor, services overhead, and selling and administrative expenses.

    d. The sales budget (or in service organizations, the service revenue budget) is prepared first because it is used to estimate sales volume and revenues. Once managers know the quantity of products or services to be sold and how many sales dollars to expect, they can develop other budgets that will enable them to manage their organization's resources so that they generate profits on those sales.

7. No standard format for budget preparation exists. The only universal requirement is that budgets communicate the appropriate information to the reader in a clear and understandable manner. General guidelines for preparing budgets include identifying the purpose of the budget, the user group and its information needs, and appropriate sources of budget information; establishing a clear format for the budget; using suitable formulas and calculations to derive the quantitative information; and revising the budget until it includes all planning decisions.

Objective 3: Prepare the operating budgets that support the financial budgets.

8. A **sales** (or service revenue) **budget** is a detailed plan, expressed in both units and dollars, that identifies expected product (or service) sales for a future period. The following equation is used to determine budgeted sales:

$$\begin{array}{l} \text{Total} \\ \text{Budgeted} \\ \text{Sales} \end{array} = \begin{array}{l} \text{Estimated} \\ \text{Selling Price} \\ \text{per Unit} \end{array} \times \begin{array}{l} \text{Estimated} \\ \text{Sales in} \\ \text{Units} \end{array}$$

Estimated sales volume is very important because it will affect the level of operating activities and the amount of resources needed for operations. A sales forecast can help in making this estimate. A **sales forecast** is a projection of sales demand (the estimated sales in units) based on an analysis of external and internal factors.

9. Once the sales budget has been established, managers can prepare a production budget. A **production budget** shows how many units a company must produce to meet budgeted sales and inventory needs. The production budget is based on the following formula:

$$\begin{array}{l} \text{Total} \\ \text{Production} \\ \text{Units} \end{array} = \begin{array}{l} \text{Budgeted} \\ \text{Sales in} \\ \text{Units} \end{array} + \begin{array}{l} \text{Desired} \\ \text{Units of} \\ \text{Ending} \\ \text{Finished} \\ \text{Goods} \\ \text{Inventory} \end{array} - \begin{array}{l} \text{Desired} \\ \text{Units of} \\ \text{Beginning} \\ \text{Finished} \\ \text{Goods} \\ \text{Inventory} \end{array}$$

10. After the production budget has been prepared, managers can prepare a **direct materials purchases budget**. This budget is a detailed plan that identifies the quantity of purchases required to meet budgeted production and inventory needs and the costs associated with those purchases. The first step in preparing a direct materials purchases budget is to calculate the total production needs in units of materials. In the second step, the following formula is used to determine the quantity of direct materials to be purchased during each accounting period in the budget:

$$\begin{array}{l} \text{Total} \\ \text{Units of} \\ \text{Direct} \\ \text{Materials} \\ \text{to Be} \\ \text{Purchased} \end{array} = \begin{array}{l} \text{Total} \\ \text{Production} \\ \text{Needs in} \\ \text{Units of} \\ \text{Direct} \\ \text{Materials} \end{array} + \begin{array}{l} \text{Desired} \\ \text{Units of} \\ \text{Ending} \\ \text{Direct} \\ \text{Materials} \\ \text{Inventory} \end{array} - \begin{array}{l} \text{Desired} \\ \text{Units of} \\ \text{Beginning} \\ \text{Direct} \\ \text{Materials} \\ \text{Inventory} \end{array}$$

The third step is to calculate the cost of the direct materials purchases by multiplying the total number of unit purchases by the direct materials cost per unit.

11. A **direct labor budget** is a detailed plan that estimates the direct labor needed in an accounting period and the associated costs. The first step in preparing a direct labor budget is to estimate the total direct labor hours by multiplying the estimated direct labor hours per unit by the antici-

pated units of production. The second step is to calculate the total budgeted direct labor cost by multiplying the estimated total direct labor hours by the estimated direct labor cost per hour. A company's human resources department provides an estimate of the hourly labor wage.

12. A **manufacturing overhead budget** is a detailed plan of anticipated manufacturing costs, other than direct materials and direct labor costs, that must be incurred to meet budgeted production needs. It has two purposes: to integrate the overhead cost budgets of the production department and production-related departments, and to group information for the calculation of manufacturing overhead rates for the forthcoming period.

13. A **selling and administrative expense budget** is a detailed plan of operating expenses, other than those related to production, that are needed to support sales and overall operations in a future accounting period.

14. A **cost of goods manufactured budget** is a detailed plan that summarizes the costs of production in a future period. The sources of information for this budget are the direct materials, direct labor, and manufacturing overhead budgets. (See Exhibit 7 in the text for an example of a cost of goods manufactured budget.)

Objective 4: Prepare a budgeted income statement, a cash budget, and a budgeted balance sheet.

15. After revenues and expenses have been itemized in the operating budgets, the budgeted income statement can be prepared. A **budgeted income statement** projects an organization's net income in an accounting period based on the revenues and expenses estimated for that period. Data related to projected sales and costs come from several of the operating budgets.

16. A **capital expenditures budget** is a detailed plan outlining the anticipated amount and timing of capital outlays for long-term assets in an accounting period. Managers rely on the capital expenditures budget when making decisions about such matters as buying equipment or building a new facility. The information in this budget affects the cash budget and the budgeted balance sheet.

17. A **cash budget** is a projection of the cash an organization will receive and the cash it will pay out in an accounting period. It summarizes all planned cash transactions found in the operating budgets and the budgeted income statement. The information it provides enables managers to plan for short-term loans when the cash balance is low and for short-term investments when the cash balance is high. The components of a cash budget are estimated cash receipts, cash payments, beginning cash balance, and ending cash balance. The ending cash balance is computed as follows:

Estimated Ending Cash Balance	=	Total Estimated Cash Receipts	−	Total Estimated Cash Payments	+	Estimated Beginning Cash Balance

Estimates of cash receipts and cash payments are based on information from several sources, including the operating budgets. For example, the sales budget may be the main source of data for predicting cash receipts.

18. A **budgeted balance sheet** projects an organization's financial position of at the end of an accounting period. It uses the estimated data compiled in the course of preparing a master budget and is the final step in that process. (See Exhibit 12 in the text for a complete list of the data sources.)

Objective 5: Describe management's role in budget implementation.

19. A **budget committee** made up of top management has overall responsibility for budget implementation. The committee oversees each stage in the preparation of the master budget, decides any departmental disputes that may arise in the process, and gives final approval to the budget. After the committee approves the master budget, periodic reports from department managers enable it to monitor the progress the company is making in attaining budget targets. To ensure the cooperation of personnel in implementing the budget, top managers must clearly communicate performance expectations and budget targets. They must also show their support for the budget and encourage its implementation.

SELF-TEST

Test your knowledge of the chapter by choosing the best answer for each item below.

1. Which of the following is *not* a guideline for preparing a budget?
   a. Know the purpose of the budget.
   b. Identify the user group and their information needs.
   c. Provide a clearly stated heading.
   d. All of the above are guidelines.

2. Participative budgeting is the key to a successful budgeting process because
   a. senior executives set goals and expect all employees to implement them.
   b. the budget director prepares the master budget and its supporting budgets.
   c. middle managers prepare the budgets; top managers are involved only with strategic planning.
   d. personnel at all levels of the organization take a meaningful and active part in the creation of the budget.

3. Costabile Enterprises uses three gallons of material 2D, two gallons of material 4R, five gallons of material 6T, and ten gallons of material 8K to make each of the twenty-gallon barrels of plant food that it produces. Expected costs per gallon are as follows: 2D, $2.40; 4R, $1.80; 6T, $10.50; and 8K, $3.30. The production budget indicates that 12,400 barrels will be produced in April; 10,800 barrels, in May; and 9,800 barrels, in June. Materials are purchased one month ahead of production. What is the total dollar value of budgeted materials purchases in April?
   a. $1,040,040
   b. $1,194,120
   c. $549,040
   d. $449,620

4. Which of the following cannot be prepared until after a cash budget has been prepared?
   a. Capital expenditures budget
   b. Sales budget
   c. Budgeted balance sheet
   d. Budgeted income statement

5. Which of the following are needed to prepare a cash budget?
   a. Total estimated cash receipts
   b. Total estimated cash payments
   c. Estimated beginning cash balance
   d. All of the above

6. A retail organization would *not* have which of the following operating budgets?
   a. Direct materials purchases budget
   b. Service revenue budget
   c. Cost of goods sold budget
   d. Selling and administrative expense budget

7. The initial step in developing a master budget is to prepare the
   a. cash budget.
   b. capital expenditures budget.
   c. cost of goods sold budget.
   d. sales budget.

8. Which of the following budgets has inputs from essentially all other budgets?
   a. Sales budget
   b. Direct materials purchases budget
   c. Budgeted balance sheet
   d. Production budget

9. Using budgets to evaluate performance is usually done in which stage of the management cycle?
   a. Reviewing
   b. Planning
   c. Reporting
   d. None of the above

10. Which of the following summarizes the costs of production in a future period?
    a. Direct materials purchases budget
    b. Cost of goods manufactured budget
    c. Budgeted balance sheet
    d. Manufacturing overhead budget

TESTING YOUR KNOWLEDGE

*Matching**

Match each term with its definition by writing the appropriate letter in the blank.

_____ 1. Operating budgets

_____ 2. Master budget

_____ 3. Cash budget

_____ 4. Sales budget

_____ 5. Budget committee

_____ 6. Production budget

_____ 7. Budgeted income statement

_____ 8. Cost of goods manufactured budget

_____ 9. Sales forecast

_____ 10. Direct materials purchases budget

_____ 11. Budgeted balance sheet

a. A statement that projects an organization's financial position at the end of an accounting period

b. A projection of sales demand based on an analysis of internal and external factors

c. A detailed plan that summarizes the costs of production in a future period

d. A projection of net income in an accounting period based on revenues and expenses estimated for that period

e. A detailed plan that identifies the purchases required for budgeted production

f. The basis for all operating budgets

g. A consolidation of operating budgets and financial budgets that establishes a company's financial plans for an accounting period

h. The basis for the direct materials, direct labor, and manufacturing overhead budgets

i. The group with overall responsibility for budget implementation

j. The budget that is prepared after the budgeted income statement

k. Plans used in daily operations

Short Answer

Use the lines provided to answer each item.

1. Briefly define *budgeting*.

_____
_____
_____
_____

2. Define the two categories of budgets that constitute a master budget.

_____
_____
_____
_____

3. How is a cash budget useful to managers?

_____
_____
_____
_____

4. What are the three steps in preparing a direct materials purchases budget?

_____
_____
_____
_____

_____

Note to student: The matching quiz might be completed more efficiently by starting with the definition and searching for the corresponding term.

True-False

Circle T if the statement is true, F if it is false. Provide explanations for the false answers, using the blank lines below.

T F **1.** A master budget covers a period of five to ten years.

T F **2.** A master budget applies to just one business segment.

T F **3.** A projection of sales must be made before a production budget can be prepared.

T F **4.** A service organization does not have a direct materials budget.

T F **5.** Depreciation expense is listed as a cash payment in the cash budget.

T F **6.** An annual operating plan identifies a company's short-term goals.

T F **7.** A capital expenditures budget estimates capital outlays for long-term assets.

T F **8.** Total sales for an accounting period are included in that period's cash budget as part of cash receipts.

T F **9.** Preparation of a selling and administrative expense budget relies on information from the cash budget.

T F **10.** The first step in preparing a direct labor budget is to calculate the estimated total direct labor hours for the period.

T F **11.** External factors have no influence on a sales forecast.

T F **12.** A sales budget must be prepared before a production budget can be prepared.

T F **13.** The first step in developing a master budget is to prepare a budgeted balance sheet.

_____

_____

_____

_____

_____

_____

_____

Multiple Choice

Circle the letter of the best answer.

1. The first step in developing a master budget is to prepare
   a. a budgeted income statement.
   b. pro forma statements.
   c. a budgeted balance sheet.
   d. detailed operating budgets.

2. Which of the following components of a master budget must be prepared before the others?
   a. Direct labor budget
   b. Manufacturing overhead budget
   c. Production budget
   d. Direct materials purchases budget

3. The cash budget is prepared
   a. before all operating budgets are prepared.
   b. after the budgeted income statement but before the budgeted balance sheet.
   c. as the last step in preparing the master budget.
   d. only if a company has doubts about its debt-paying ability.

4. Which of the following data would *not* be found in a direct labor budget?
a. Direct labor hours per unit
b. Total budgeted direct labor cost
c. Estimated total direct labor hours
d. Forecasted sales in dollars

5. Which of the following would *not* be a source of data for estimates of cash payments in the cash budget?
a. Sales budget
b. Capital expenditures budget
c. Selling and administrative expense budget
d. Direct labor budget

6. The cash budget consists of
a. projected cash receipts.
b. the ending cash balance.
c. projected cash payments.
d. all of the above.

7. Woodley Company has the following budget information for the first three quarters of its fiscal year:

Quarter	1	2	3
Units produced	23,000	24,000	21,000

Each finished unit requires three pounds of material. The inventory of material at the end of each quarter should equal 10 percent of the following quarter's production needs. How many pounds of material should be purchased for the second quarter?
a. 71,100 pounds
b. 72,000 pounds
c. 74,400 pounds
d. 75,000 pounds

8. A service organization would prepare all of the following budgets *except* the
a. direct labor budget.
b. services overhead budget.
c. cash budget.
d. direct materials budget.

9. Timbo Company typically pays 40 percent of its purchases on account in the month of purchase and 60 percent in the month following purchase. Given the following projections of expenditures for direct materials, what would Timbo's expected cash payments be in March 20xx?

	Purchases on Account	Cash Purchases
February 20xx	$10,000	$ 5,000
March 20xx	15,000	20,000
April 20xx	4,000	8,000

a. $35,000
b. $30,000
c. $32,000
d. $20,000

10. To determine total budgeted direct labor costs, estimated direct labor cost per hour must be multiplied by the
a. predetermined manufacturing overhead rate.
b. unit sales projection.
c. total estimated units of production.
d. estimated total direct labor hours.

APPLYING YOUR KNOWLEDGE

Exercises

1. Donlevy Company produces and sells a single product. Expected sales for the next four months are as follows:

Month	Units
April	10,000
May	12,000
June	15,000
July	9,000

   The company needs a production budget for the second quarter. Experience indicates that end-of-month finished goods inventory must equal 10 percent of the following month's sales in units. At the end of March, 1,000 units were on hand. Compute production needs for the second quarter by preparing a production budget.

Donlevy Company
Production Budget
For the Quarter Ended June 30, 20xx

---

2. Monahan Enterprises needs a cash budget for the month of June. The following data are available:

   a. The cash balance on June 1 is $7,000.
   b. Sales for May and June are $80,000 and $60,000, respectively. Cash collections on sales are 30 percent in the month of the sale, 65 percent in the following month, and 5 percent uncollectible.
   c. General and administrative expenses are budgeted at $24,000 for June. Depreciation represents $2,000 of this amount.
   d. Inventory purchases totaled $40,000 in May and will total $30,000 in June. Half of inventory purchases are always paid for in the month of the purchase. The remainder are paid for in the following month.
   e. Office furniture costing $3,000 will be purchased for cash in June, and selling expenses (exclusive of $2,000 in depreciation) are budgeted at $14,000.
   f. The company must maintain a minimum ending cash balance of $4,000 and can borrow from the bank in multiples of $100. All loans are repaid after 60 days.

In the space provided below, prepare a cash budget for Monahan Enterprises for the month of June.

Monahan Enterprises
Cash Budget
For the Month Ended June 30, 20xx

3. Jeppo Titanium Company manufactures three products in a single plant with two departments: Bending and Welding. The company has estimated costs for products X and Y and is currently analyzing direct labor hour requirements for the budget year 20xx. The departmental data are as follows:

	Estimated Hours per Unit	
	Bending	Welding
Product X	1	2
Product Y	.6	3
Hourly labor rate	$10	$15

Budgeted unit production in 20xx of Product X is 10,000 and of Product Y, 20,000. Prepare a direct labor budget for 20xx that shows the budgeted direct labor costs for each department and for the company as a whole.

Jeppo Titanium Company
Direct Labor Budget
For the Year Ended December 31, 20xx

4. Explain the role of budgeting in each stage of the management cycle.

_____   _____

_____   _____

_____   _____

_____   _____

_____   _____

_____   _____

_____   _____

_____   _____

_____   _____

_____   _____

_____   _____

CHAPTER 8 STANDARD COSTING AND VARIANCE ANALYSIS

REVIEWING THE CHAPTER

Objective 1: Define *standard costs* **and describe how managers use standard costs in the management cycle.**

1. **Standard costs** are realistic estimates of costs based on analyses of both past and projected costs and operating conditions. They provide a standard, or predetermined, performance level for use in **standard costing,** a method of cost control that also includes a measure of actual performance and a measure of the difference, or **variance,** between standard and actual performance. This method of measuring and controlling costs differs from the actual and normal costing methods in that it uses estimated costs only to compute all three elements of product cost—direct materials, direct labor, and manufacturing overhead.

2. In the planning stage of the management cycle, managers use standard costs to develop budgets for direct materials, direct labor, and variable manufacturing overhead. These estimated costs not only serve as targets for product costing; they are also useful in making decisions about product distribution and pricing. During the executing stage, managers use standard costs to measure expenditures and to control costs as they occur. At the end of an accounting period, they compare actual costs with standard costs and compute the variances. The variances provide measures of performance that can be used to control costs. Managers also use standard costs to report on operations and managerial performance. A variance report tailored to a manager's responsibilities provides useful information about how well operations are proceeding and how well the manager is controlling them.

Objective 2: Explain how standard costs are developed and compute a standard unit cost.

3. A fully integrated standard costing system uses standard costs for all the elements of product cost. Inventory accounts for materials, work in process, and finished goods, as well as the Cost of Goods Sold account, are maintained and reported in terms of standard costs, and standard unit costs are used to compute account balances. Actual costs are recorded separately so that managers can compare what should have been spent (the standard costs) with the actual costs incurred.

4. A standard unit cost for a manufactured product has six elements: (a) a direct materials price standard, (b) a direct materials quantity standard, (c) a direct labor rate standard, (d) a direct labor time standard, (e) a standard variable overhead rate, and (f) a standard fixed overhead rate. (A standard unit cost for a service includes only the elements that relate to labor and overhead.)

5. To compute a standard cost per unit of output, the following amounts must be identified:
   a. **Standard Direct Materials Cost** = Direct Materials Price Standard × Direct Materials Quantity Standard
      (1) The **direct materials price standard** is the estimated cost of a specific direct material to be used in the next accounting period.

(2) The **direct materials quantity standard** is the estimated amount of direct materials to be used in the period.

b. **Standard Direct Labor Cost** = Direct Labor Rate Standard × Direct Labor Time Standard
   (1) The **direct labor rate standard** is the hourly direct labor cost expected to prevail during the next accounting period for each function or job classification.
   (2) The **direct labor time standard** is the expected time required for each department, machine, or process to complete the production of one unit or one batch of output.

c. **Standard Manufacturing Overhead Cost** = Standard Variable Overhead Rate + Standard Fixed Overhead Rate
   (1) The **standard variable overhead rate** is the total budgeted variable overhead costs divided by an appropriate application base, such as standard machine hours or standard direct labor hours.
   (2) The **standard fixed overhead rate** is the total budgeted fixed overhead costs divided by an expression of capacity, usually normal capacity in terms of standard hours or units.

6. A product's standard unit cost is determined by adding the standard direct materials cost, the standard direct labor cost, and the standard manufacturing overhead cost.

Objective 3: Prepare a flexible budget and describe how variance analysis is used to control costs.

7. **Variance analysis** is the process of computing the differences between standard (or budgeted) costs and actual costs and identifying the causes of those differences.

8. The accuracy of variance analysis depends to a large extent on the type of budget managers use when comparing variances. A **flexible budget** (also called a *variable budget*) is a summary of expected costs for a range of activity levels. Unlike a static budget, which forecasts revenues and expenses for just one level of sales and just one level of output, a flexible budget provides forecasted data that can be adjusted for changes in the level of output. It presents budgeted fixed and variable costs and their totals, as well as the budgeted variable cost per unit. The variable cost per unit and total fixed costs are components of the **flexible budget formula,** an equation that can be used to determine the expected, or budgeted, cost

for any level of output. The formula is as follows: (Variable Cost per Unit × Number of Units Produced) + Budgeted Fixed Costs = Total budgeted Costs. The total budgeted costs can be compared with actual costs to measure the performance of individuals and departments.

9. A flexible budget improves the accuracy of variance analysis, which is a four-step approach to controlling costs. First, managers compute the amount of the variance. If the amount is insignificant, no corrective action is needed. If the amount is significant, managers analyze the variance to identify its cause. In identifying the cause, they are usually able to pinpoint the activities that need to be monitored. They then select performance measures that will enable them to track those activities, analyze the results, and determine the action needed to correct the problem. Their final step is to take the appropriate corrective action.

Objective 4: Compute and analyze direct materials variances.

10. The **total direct materials cost variance** is the difference between the standard cost and actual cost of direct materials. When standard costs exceed actual costs, the variance is favorable (F). When the reverse is true, the variance is unfavorable (U). The total direct materials cost variance is broken down into the direct materials price variance and direct materials quantity variance.
    a. **Direct Materials Price Variance** = (Standard Price – Actual Price) × Actual Quantity
    b. **Direct materials quantity variance** = Standard Price × (Standard Quantity Allowed – Actual Quantity)

Objective 5: Compute and analyze direct labor variances.

11. The **total direct labor cost variance** is the sum of the direct labor rate variance and the direct labor efficiency variance.
    a. **Direct Labor Rate Variance** = (Standard Rate – Actual Rate) × Actual Hours
    b. **Direct Labor Efficiency Variance** = Standard Rate × (Standard Hours Allowed – Actual Hours)

Objective 6: Compute and analyze manufacturing overhead variances.

12. **Total manufacturing overhead variance** is the difference between actual overhead costs and standard overhead costs. The latter costs are ap-

plied to production by using a standard overhead rate. A standard overhead rate has two parts: a variable rate and a fixed rate. The standard fixed rate is calculated by dividing total budgeted fixed overhead by normal capacity. The total manufacturing overhead variance can be broken down into variable overhead variances and fixed overhead variances.

    a. The **total variable overhead variance** is the difference between the variable overhead spending variance and the variable overhead efficiency variance. The **variable overhead spending variance** is computed by multiplying the actual hours worked by the difference between actual variable overhead costs and the standard variable overhead rate. The **variable overhead efficiency variance** is the difference between the standard direct labor hours allowed for good units produced and the actual hours worked multiplied by the standard variable overhead rate per hour.

    b. The **total fixed overhead variance** is the difference between actual fixed overhead costs and the standard fixed overhead costs that are applied to good units produced using the standard fixed overhead rate. For effective performance evaluation, managers break down the total fixed overhead cost variance into two additional variances: the fixed overhead budget variance and the fixed overhead volume variance. The **fixed overhead budget variance** is the difference between budgeted and actual fixed overhead costs. The **fixed overhead volume variance** is the difference between budgeted fixed overhead costs and the overhead costs that are applied to production using the standard fixed overhead rate. Because the fixed overhead volume variance gauges the use of existing facilities and capacity, a volume variance will occur if more or less than normal capacity is used.

    c. The total manufacturing overhead variance is also the amount of over- or underapplied overhead, which must be computed and reconciled at the end of each accounting period. By breaking down the total manufacturing overhead variance into variable and fixed variances, managers can more accurately control costs and reconcile their causes. An analysis of these two overhead variances will help explain why the amount of manufacturing overhead applied to units produced differs from the actual manufacturing overhead costs incurred.

Objective 7: Explain how variances are used to evaluate managers' performance.

13. To ensure that performance evaluation is effective and fair, a company's evaluation policies should be based on input from managers and employees and should be specific about the procedures managers are to follow. The evaluation process becomes more accurate when managerial performance reports include variances from standard costs. A managerial performance report based on standard costs and related variances should identify the causes of each significant variance, as well as the personnel involved, and the corrective actions taken. It should be tailored to the manager's specific areas of responsibility. Managers should be held accountable only for the cost areas under their control.

Test your knowledge of the chapter by choosing the best answer for each item below.

1. In which of the following stages of the management cycle do managers use standard costs?
   a. Planning
   b. Reviewing
   c. Executing
   d. All of the above

2. The direct labor efficiency variance is the difference between standard direct labor hours allowed for the good units produced and the
   a. standard hours allowed and standard rate per hour.
   b. actual direct labor hours worked, multiplied by the standard direct labor rate.
   c. direct labor rate per hour.
   d. none of the above.

3. An unfavorable fixed overhead volume variance exists when
   a. budgeted fixed overhead for the level of production is less than fixed overhead applied.
   b. total fixed overhead is less than the predetermined overhead rate.
   c. budgeted fixed overhead for the level of production is greater than standard fixed overhead applied.
   d. none of the above obtain.

4. Which of the following is the correct formula for determining the direct materials price variance?
   a. (Standard Price ÷ Actual Price) × Actual Quantity
   b. (Standard Price − Actual Price) × Standard Quantity
   c. (Standard Price − Actual Price) × Actual Quantity
   d. (Standard Quantity − Actual Quantity) × Actual Price

5. Which of the following is *not* an element of a standard unit cost?
   a. Direct materials price standard
   b. Actual direct labor costs
   c. Direct labor rate standard
   d. All of the above are included in a standard unit cost.

6. Product engineering specifications, the quality of direct materials, and the age and productivity of machinery influence the direct
   a. materials quantity standard.
   b. labor rate standard.
   c. materials price standard.
   d. labor time standard.

7. To compute the standard fixed overhead rate, total budgeted fixed overhead costs are divided by the
   a. flexible budget formula.
   b. actual hours worked.
   c. standard hours allowed.
   d. normal capacity.

8. The Sahlen Company uses a standard costing system in its glass division. The standard cost of making one glass windshield is as follows:

Direct materials (60 lb @ $1/lb)	$ 60.00
Direct labor (3 hr @ $10/hr)	30.00
Manufacturing overhead (3 hr @ $8/hr)	24.00
Total standard unit cost	$114.00

The current variable overhead rate is $3 per labor hour, and the budgeted fixed overhead is $27,000. During January, the division produced 1,650 windshields; normal capacity is 1,800 windshields. The actual cost per windshield was as follows:

Direct materials (58 lb @ $1.10/lb)	$ 63.80
Direct labor (3.1 hr @ $10/hr)	31.00
Manufacturing overhead ($39,930/1,650 products)	24.20
Total actual unit cost	$119.00

The total direct materials quantity variance for January is
   a. $9,570 (U).
   b. $9,570 (F).
   c. $3,300 (F).
   d. $3,300 (U).

9. Assuming the same facts as in 8, the direct labor rate variance for January is
   a. 0.
   b. $1,650 (U).
   c. $1,920 (F).
   d. $1,650 (F).

10. In the flexible budget formula, the variable cost per unit is multiplied by the
   a. standard hours worked.
   b. number of units produced.
   c. standard hours allowed.
   d. number of units planned.

TESTING YOUR KNOWLEDGE

Matching*

Match each term with its definition by writing the appropriate letter in the blank.

_____ **1.** Fixed overhead budget variance

_____ **2.** Variance

_____ **3.** Direct materials price standard

_____ **4.** Variance analysis

_____ **5.** Standard costs

_____ **6.** Favorable variance

_____ **7.** Unfavorable variance

_____ **8.** Direct materials price variance

_____ **9.** Direct materials quantity variance

_____ **10.** Direct labor rate variance

_____ **11.** Direct labor efficiency variance

_____ **12.** Performance report

_____ **13.** Flexible budget

a. The difference between the standard direct labor rate and the actual direct labor rate, times actual direct labor hours worked

b. A variance in which actual costs exceed standard costs

c. A summary of expected costs for various levels of production

d. The difference between standard price and actual price, times actual quantity of material purchased

e. A written comparison between actual costs and budgeted costs for a business segment

f. The difference between standard quantity and quantity of material used, times standard price

g. A variance in which standard costs exceed actual costs

h. The difference between standard direct labor hours allowed and actual direct labor hours worked, times standard direct labor rate

i. Predetermined costs that are expressed as a cost per unit of finished product

j. The difference between actual fixed overhead incurred and the fixed overhead budgeted

k. The difference between a standard cost and an actual cost

l. A standard based on a careful estimate of the cost of a specific direct material in the next accounting period

m. The process of computing the difference between standard costs and actual costs and identifying the causes of those differences

---

Note to student: The matching quiz might be completed more efficiently by starting with the definition and searching for the corresponding term.

Short Answer

Use the lines provided to answer each item.

1. Briefly describe how managers use standard costs in each stage of the management cycle.

_____

_____

_____

_____

_____

2. When does a favorable fixed overhead volume variance exist?

_____

_____

_____

_____

_____

3. List the six standards used to compute total standard unit cost.

_____

_____

_____

_____

_____

_____

4. When does a favorable direct materials quantity variance exist?

_____

_____

5. When does an unfavorable direct labor rate variance exist?

_____

_____

_____

True-False

Circle T if the statement is true, F if it is false. Provide explanations for the false answers, using the blank lines at the end of the section.

T F **1.** Time and motion studies of workers are used in establishing direct labor rate standards.

T F **2.** In a standard costing system, all costs that flow through the inventory accounts are standard costs.

T F **3.** Computing variances is an essential part of the managerial planning function.

T F **4.** When direct materials price and quantity variances are unfavorable, it is impossible to have a favorable total direct materials cost variance.

T F **5.** The flexible budget includes both budgeted fixed costs and budgeted variable costs for each level of anticipated activity.

T F **6.** The total direct labor cost variance is the sum of the direct labor rate variance and the direct labor efficiency variance.

T F **7.** The standard overhead rate consists of the standard variable rate only.

T F **8.** Computing the total direct labor cost variance is more important than computing the direct labor rate and direct labor efficiency variances.

T F **9.** A managerial performance report should contain only cost items controllable by the manager who is being evaluated.

T F **10.** A flexible budget is also known as a *fixed budget.*

T F **11.** It is possible to have both an unfavorable fixed overhead volume variance and a favorable total manufacturing overhead variance.

T F **12.** Once an unfavorable variance has been calculated, it is unnecessary to determine its cause.

T F **13.** The flexible budget formula is an equation that determines the budgeted cost for any level of output.

_____

_____

_____

_____

_____

_____

_____

_____

_____

_____

_____

_____

_____

_____

_____

_____

_____

_____

_____

_____

_____

_____

_____

_____

Multiple Choice

Circle the letter of the best answer.

1. Workers' wages paid during a period are all that is needed to compute the
   a. actual direct labor cost.
   b. direct labor rate standard.
   c. standard direct labor cost.
   d. direct labor cost variance.

2. Which of the following would *not* be a cause of a direct materials price variance?
   a. Increases or decreases in vendors' prices
   b. Inaccurate direct materials price standards
   c. Differences between expected quantity discounts and the actual discounts received
   d. Each of the above could be a cause.

3. If an organization is not using a flexible budget that adjusts with changes in activity, it is probably using a
   a. master budget.
   b. production budget.
   c. cash disbursements budget.
   d. static budget.

4. When a company's actual manufacturing overhead is $140,000 and the standard overhead applied to good units produced is $100,000, the company has a(n)
   a. unfavorable variance of $40,000.
   b. favorable variance of $40,000.
   c. error in calculation.
   d. none of the above.

5. Given the following information, what would be the total budgeted costs at 10,000 units of output?

   Variable costs:
Direct materials	$4.00 per unit
Direct labor	$1.00 per unit
Variable manufacturing overhead	$3.00 per unit
Fixed manufacturing overhead	$20,000

   a. $80,000
   b. $100,000
   c. $40,000
   d. Undeterminable without more data

6. Assuming the same facts as in 5, what would be the total budgeted costs at a production level of 20,000 units?
   a. $180,000
   b. $160,000
   c. $20,000
   d. Undeterminable without more data

7. Which of the following variances could be used to evaluate a purchasing manager's performance?
   a. Direct materials price variance
   b. Direct labor rate variance
   c. Direct labor efficiency variance
   d. Direct materials quantity variance

8. If employees take more time to achieve a given level of production than the standard allows, there will be a(n)
   a. favorable direct labor rate variance.
   b. unfavorable direct labor rate variance.
   c. favorable direct labor efficiency variance.
   d. unfavorable direct labor efficiency variance.

9. In a flexible budget, which total costs would *not* change, given different levels of production?
   a. Fixed manufacturing overhead
   b. Variable manufacturing overhead
   c. Direct labor costs
   d. Direct materials costs

10. Managers can use standard costing for
    a. evaluating performance.
    b. identifying inefficiencies.
    c. product pricing.
    d. all of the above.

APPLYING YOUR KNOWLEDGE

Exercises

1. Goethe Company employs a standard costing system in the manufacture of hand-painted dishes. The standards for the current year are as follows:

Direct materials price standards

Porcelain	$.80/pound
Red paint	$1.00/tube
Blue paint	$1.00/tube

Direct materials quantity standards

Porcelain	½ pound/dish
Red paint	1 tube/20 dishes
Blue paint	1 tube/50 dishes

Direct labor time standards

Molding department	.03 hour/dish
Painting department	.05 hour/dish

Direct labor rate standards

Molding department	$4.00/hour
Painting department	$6.00/hour

Standard manufacturing overhead rates

Standard variable overhead rate	$3.00/direct labor hour
Standard fixed overhead rate	$2.00/direct labor hour

Compute the standard cost per dish.

Porcelain	$_____
Red paint	_____
Blue paint	_____
Molding department wages	_____
Painting department wages	_____
Variable overhead	_____
Fixed overhead	_____
Standard cost of one dish	$_____

2. Sturchio Company expects fixed overhead for 20xx to total $50,000. Variable costs per unit are expected to be as follows: direct labor, $4.50; direct materials, $1.25; and variable overhead, $2.75. Using these data, prepare a flexible budget for volumes of 10,000 units, 15,000 units, and 20,000 units. In addition, determine the flexible budget formula.

Sturchio Company
Flexible Budget
For the Year Ended December 31, 20xx

3. Mississippi Sporting Goods Company uses a standard costing system in its manufacture of 10-pound steel dumbbells. The standard cost for steel is $.60 per pound, and each dumbbell should require .3 standard direct labor hours. The standard direct labor rate is $4.50 per hour. During March, the company produced 65,000 dumbbells, and it purchased and used 657,000 pounds of steel; the steel cost $381,060. Direct labor hours totaled 22,100; direct labor cost was $100,555. Using these data, compute the following variances for March; indicate whether each variance is favorable or unfavorable by putting an *F* or a *U* in the parentheses after each amount:

a. Direct materials price variance =

   $ _____ ( )

b. Direct materials quantity variance =

   $ _____ ( )

c. Direct labor rate variance =

   $ _____ ( )

d. Direct labor efficiency variance =

   $ _____ ( )

Crossword Puzzle
for Chapters 7 and 8

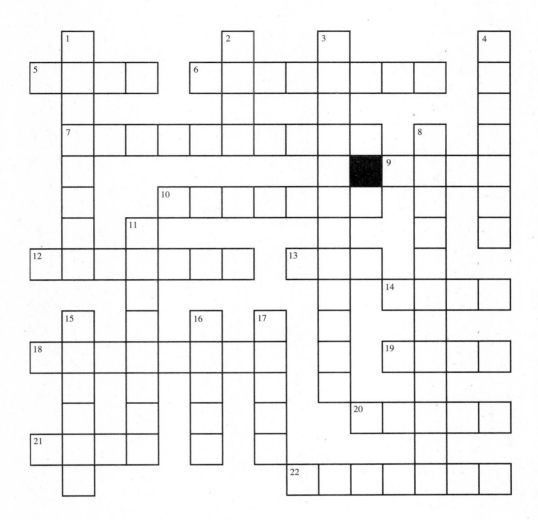

ACROSS

5. Type of budget disclosing receipts and payments
6. Direct materials _____ variance
7. Purchase made with idle cash
9. Item in 5-Across
10. _____ expenditures budget
12. _____ and administrative expense budget
13. Opposite of "less" in a budget
14. Short-term _____ (a budget objective)
18. Operating, investing, or financing _____
19. Cash movement
20. Type of budget expressed in hours and dollars
21. Direct labor _____ standard
22. Business plans based on forecasted transactions, activities, or events

DOWN

1. Difference between standard performance and actual performance
2. Part of "JIT"
3. Estimated amount to be paid for materials, labor, or overhead (2 words)
4. Budgeted _____ sheet
8. Capable of being contained, as a cost
11. Type of budget covering a range of volumes
15. _____ Costs (column head in a performance report)
16. Static, like some budgets
17. Management _____ (a four-stage process)

CHAPTER 9 PERFORMANCE MANAGEMENT AND EVALUATION

REVIEWING THE CHAPTER

Objective 1: Describe how the balanced scorecard aligns performance with organizational goals, and explain the role of the balanced scorecard in the management cycle.

1. The **balanced scorecard** is a framework that links the perspectives of an organization's four basic stakeholder groups with the organization's mission and vision, performance measures, strategic plan, and resources. The four groups are investors, employees, internal business processes, and customers. To add value for these groups, an organization determines each group's objectives and translates them into performance measures that have specific, quantifiable targets.

2. During the planning stage of the management cycle, managers use the balanced scorecard to translate their organization's vision and strategy into operational objectives that will benefit all stakeholder groups. Once they have established these objectives, they set performance targets and select performance measures. In the executing stage, managers use the organization's operational objectives as the basis for decision making within their individual areas of responsibility. In the reviewing stage, they evaluate their strategies in meeting the performance targets set during the planning stage and compare planned performance with actual results. The reports prepared during the reporting stage enable managers to monitor and evaluate performance measures that add value for the stakeholder groups.

Objective 2: Discuss performance measurement, and state the issues that affect management's ability to measure performance.

3. A **performance management and evaluation system** is a set of procedures that account for and report on both financial and nonfinancial performance. Such a system enables a company to identify how well it is doing, the direction it is taking, and what improvements will make it more profitable.

4. **Performance measurement** is the use of quantitative tools to gauge an organization's performance in relation to a specific goal or an expected outcome. Each organization must develop a unique set of performance measures appropriate to its specific situation that will help managers distinguish between what is being measured and the actual measures used to monitor performance.

Objective 3: Define _responsibility accounting_, and describe the role responsibility centers play in performance management and evaluation.

5. **Responsibility accounting** is an information system that classifies data according to areas of responsibility and reports each area's activities by including only the revenue, cost, and resource categories that the assigned manager can control.

6. A **responsibility center** is an organizational unit whose manager has been assigned the responsibility of managing a portion of the organization's

resources. The five types of responsibility centers are as follows:

   a. A **cost center** is a responsibility center whose manager is accountable only for controllable costs that have well-defined relationships between the center's resources and products or services.

   b. A **discretionary cost center** is a responsibility center whose manager is accountable only for costs in which the relationship between resources and products or services produced is not well defined. These centers, like cost centers, have approved budgets that set spending limits.

   c. A **revenue center** is a responsibility center whose manager is accountable primarily for revenue and whose success is based on its ability to generate revenue.

   d. A **profit center** is a responsibility center whose manager is accountable for both revenue and costs and for the resulting operating income.

   e. An **investment center** is a responsibility center whose manager is accountable for profit generation; the manager can also make significant decisions about the resources the center uses. The manager can control revenues, costs, and the investments of assets to achieve the organization's goals.

7. An **organization chart** is a visual representation of an organization's hierarchy of responsibility for the purposes of management control. A responsibility accounting system establishes a communications network within an organization that is ideal for gathering and reporting information about the operations of each these areas of responsibility. The system is used to prepare budgets by responsibility area and to report on the actual performance of each responsibility center. The performance report for a responsibility center should contain only **controllable costs and revenues**—that is, the costs, revenues, and resources that the manager of the center can control.

Objective 4: Prepare performance reports for cost centers using flexible budgets and for profit centers using variable costing.

8. Performance reports allow comparisons between actual performance and budget expectations. Such comparisons enable management to evaluate an individual's performance with respect to responsibility center objectives and companywide objectives and to recommend changes. The con-

tent and format of a performance report depend on the nature of the responsibility center.

9. The performance of a cost center can be evaluated by comparing its actual costs with the corresponding amounts in the flexible and master budgets. A flexible budget is a cost control tool used to evaluate performance and is derived by multiplying actual unit output by standard unit costs for each cost item in the report. Variances between actual costs and the flexible budget can be examined further by using standard costing to compute specific variances for direct materials, direct labor, and manufacturing overhead.

10. A profit center's performance is usually evaluated by comparing its actual income statement with its budgeted income statement. When **variable costing** is used, the profit center manager's controllable costs are classified as variable or fixed. The variable cost of goods sold and the variable selling and administrative expenses are subtracted from sales to arrive at the center's contribution margin; all controllable fixed costs are subtracted from the contribution margin to determine operating income. The variable costing income statement takes the form of a contribution income statement rather than a traditional income statement. A traditional income statement (also called a *full costing* or *absorption costing income statement*) assigns all manufacturing costs to cost of goods sold. A variable costing income statement uses only direct materials, direct labor, and variable manufacturing overhead to compute variable cost of goods sold. Fixed manufacturing overhead is considered a cost of the current accounting period and is listed with fixed selling expenses.

Objective 5: Prepare performance reports for investment centers using traditional measures of return on investment and residual income and the newer measure of economic value added.

11. **Return on investment (ROI)** is a performance measure that takes into account both operating income and the assets invested to earn that income. It is computed as follows:

$$\text{Return on Investment (ROI)} = \frac{\text{Operating Income}}{\text{Assets Invested}}$$

In this formula, assets invested are the average of the beginning and ending asset balances for the period. Return on investment can also be examined in terms of profit margin and asset turnover.

Profit margin is the ratio of operating income to sales; it represents the percentage of each sales dollar that results in profit. **Asset turnover** is the ratio of sales to average assets invested; it indicates the productivity of assets, or the number of sales dollars generated by each dollar invested in assets. Return on investment is equal to profit margin multiplied by asset turnover:

$$\text{ROI} = \text{Profit Margin} \times \text{Asset Turnover}$$

or

$$\text{ROI} = \frac{\text{Operating Income}}{\text{Sales}} \times \frac{\text{Sales}}{\text{Assets Invested}} = \frac{\text{Operating Income}}{\text{Assets Invested}}$$

12. **Residual income (RI)** is the operating income that an investment center earns above a minimum desired return on invested assets. The formula for computing residual income is

$$\text{Residual Income} = \text{Operating Income} - (\text{Desired ROI} \times \text{Assets Invested})$$

13. **Economic value added (EVA)** is an indicator of performance that measures the shareholder wealth created by an investment center. A manager can improve the economic value of an investment center by increasing sales, decreasing costs, decreasing assets, or lowering the cost of capital. The **cost of capital** is the minimum desired rate of return on an investment. The formula for computing economic value added is as follows:

$$\text{Economic Value Added} = \text{After-Tax Operating Income} - \text{Cost of Capital in Dollars}$$

or

$$\text{Economic Value Added} = \text{After-Tax Operating Income} - [\text{Cost of Capital} \times (\text{Total Assets} - \text{Current Liabilities})]$$

Objective 6: Explain how properly linked performance incentives and measures add value for all stakeholders in performance management and evaluation.

14. The effectiveness of a performance management and evaluation system depends on how well it coordinates the goals of responsibility centers, managers, and the entire company. Performance can be optimized by linking goals to measurable objectives and targets and by tying appropriate compensation incentives to the achievement of those targets through **performance-based pay.** Cash bonuses, awards, profit-sharing plans, and stock option programs are common types of incentive compensation. Each organization's unique circumstances will determine its correct mix of performance measures and compensation incentives. If management values the perspectives of all stakeholder groups, its performance management and evaluation system will balance and benefit all interests.

SELF-TEST

Test your knowledge of the chapter by choosing the best answer for each item below.

1. During the planning stage of the management cycle, the balanced scorecard provides
   a. reports that enable managers to monitor performance measures.
   b. performance measures for evaluating managers' strategies.
   c. a framework that enables managers to translate their organization's vision and strategy into operational objectives.
   d. objectives that managers use as a basis for decision making within their individual areas of responsibility.

2. A responsibility center whose manager is accountable for both revenues and costs and for the resulting operating income is a(n)
   a. investment center.
   b. profit center.
   c. cost center.
   d. discretionary cost center.

3. The difference between a variable costing income statement and a traditional income statement is that in a variable statement, cost of goods sold includes
   a. all expenses.
   b. only fixed costs.
   c. all variable costs.
   d. fixed overhead but not fixed selling costs.

4. Operating income divided by assets invested is the formula for which of the following performance measures?
   a. Return on investment
   b. Residual income
   c. Economic value added
   d. Cost of capital

5. An accounting, personnel, or legal department is a(n)
   a. discretionary cost center.
   b. cost center.
   c. profit center.
   d. investment center.

6. The standard cost for producing a bottle of mustard is as follows:

Direct materials	$.35
Direct labor	$.10
Variable overhead	$.05
Total fixed overhead	$3,000

   The company estimated that it would produce 10,000 bottles during April. The actual number of bottles produced was 11,000. The amount in the flexible budget will equal
   a. $5,000.
   b. $3,000.
   c. $8,000.
   d. $8,500.

7. Which of the following would *not* be included as a variable cost in a candy manufacturer's flexible budget?
   a. Sugar
   b. Depreciation expense
   c. Candy wrappers
   d. Sales commissions

8. The minimum desired rate of return on an investment is called
   a. cost of capital.
   b. return on investment.
   c. operating income.
   d. profit margin.

9. The objective of performance-based pay is to
   a. give all employees an annual bonus.
   b. guarantee that all employees get a pay raise each year.
   c. link compensation to an employee's measurable performance targets.
   d. link an employee's overtime with the production for a given period.

TESTING YOUR KNOWLEDGE

Matching*

Match each term with its definition by writing the appropriate letter in the blank.

_____ 1. Profit center

_____ 2. Organization chart

_____ 3. Residual income

_____ 4. Cost center

_____ 5. Balanced scorecard

_____ 6. Cost of capital

_____ 7. Profit margin

_____ 8. Asset turnover

_____ 9. Performance-based pay

_____ 10. Economic value added

a. Minimum desired rate of return on an investment
b. A framework that links the perspectives of an organization's four basic stakeholder groups with the organization's mission and vision, performance measures, strategic plan, and resources
c. The ratio of operating income to sales
d. An indicator of performance that measures the shareholder wealth created by an investment center
e. A responsibility center whose manager is accountable only for controllable costs that have well-defined relationships between the center's resources and products or services
f. The operating income that an investment center earns above a minimum desired return on invested assets
g. A responsibility center whose manager is accountable for both revenue and costs and for the resulting operating income
h. A visual representation of an organization's hierarchy of responsibility for the purposes of management control
i. The ratio of sales to average assets invested
j. Compensation based on the achievement of measurable performance targets

Short Answer

Use the lines provided to answer each item.

1. What is the formula for economic value added?

   _____

   _____

   _____

2. What are the five types of responsibility centers?

   _____

   _____

   _____

   _____

   _____

3. Explain the difference between a variable costing income statement and a traditional income statement.

   _____

   _____

   _____

   _____

4. What is the purpose of a balanced scorecard?

   _____

   _____

   _____

_____

*Note to student: The matching quiz might be completed more efficiently by starting with the definition and searching for the corresponding term.

Circle T if the statement is true, F if it is false. Provide explanations for the false answers, using the blank lines below.

T F   1. Responsibility accounting is an information system that classifies data according to areas of responsibility.

T F   2. The manager of a discretionary cost center is accountable for costs in which the relationship between resources and products or services is well defined.

T F   3. Return on investment is equal to profit margin divided by asset turnover.

T F   4. Performance reports should contain all costs, revenues, and resources, regardless of whether managers can control them.

T F   5. The traditional income statement, the variable income statement, and the contribution income statement produce the same net income.

T F   6. An organization's four basic stakeholder groups are investors, customers, employees, and creditors.

T F   7. Asset turnover is the ratio of sales to current assets.

T F   8. The manager of an investment center is accountable for profit generation and can make significant decisions about the resources the center uses.

T F   9. The reports prepared during the reporting stage of the management cycle should be designed to give managers a standard format for comparing performance among departments.

_____

_____

_____

_____

_____

_____

_____

_____

_____

_____

_____

_____

_____

_____

_____

_____

Multiple Choice

Circle the letter of the best answer.

1. In a flexible budget, which total costs would *not* change for different levels of production?
   a. Fixed manufacturing overhead
   b. Variable manufacturing overhead
   c. Direct labor costs
   d. Direct materials costs

2. Given the following information, what would the total dollar amount in a flexible budget be at 20,000 units of output?

   Variable costs:

Direct materials	$4 per unit
Direct labor	1 per unit
Variable overhead	3 per unit
Fixed overhead	$20,000

   a. $160,000
   b. $20,000
   c. $180,000
   d. $80,000

3. The four basic stakeholder groups are
   a. investors, employees, internal business processes, and customers.
   b. employees, lenders, customers, and managers.
   c. investors, employees, creditors, and customers.
   d. investors, government tax agencies, employees, and customers.

4. Which of the following equations is used to compute return on investment?
   a. Operating Income ÷ Assets Invested
   b. Operating Income – (Desired ROI × Assets Invested)
   c. Operating Income × Assets Invested
   d. Operating Income + (Desired ROI × Assets Invested)

5. Which of the following represents the percentage of each sales dollar that results in profit?
   a. Cost of capital
   b. Profit margin
   c. Net sales
   d. Net income after taxes

6. A responsibility center that is accountable primarily for revenue and whose success is judged on its ability to generate revenue is a(n)
   a. profit center.
   b. investment center.
   c. revenue center.
   d. discretionary cost center.

7. In a variable income statement, which of the following costs are included in the cost of goods sold?
   a. Direct materials, direct labor, and all manufacturing overhead
   b. Direct materials, direct labor, and fixed manufacturing overhead
   c. Direct materials, direct labor, and variable manufacturing overhead
   d. Manufacturing overhead only

8. All of the following are responsibility centers *except*
   a. cost centers.
   b. operating centers.
   c. profit centers.
   d. investment centers.

9. Managers use the asset turnover ratio to determine the
   a. productivity of assets, or the number of sales dollars generated by each dollar invested in assets.
   b. productivity of liabilities, or the number of sales dollars generated by each dollar owed.
   c. productivity of sales by the number of asset dollars generated by each dollar of sales.
   d. None of the above.

APPLYING YOUR KNOWLEDGE

Exercises

1. Corwin Company manufactures scented candles. For the year ended December 31, 20xx, it expects its fixed manufacturing overhead to be $135,000. Variable costs are expected to be as follows: direct materials, $1.80; direct labor, $.35; and variable manufacturing overhead, $.60. Using these data and assuming the production of 350,000 candles, prepare a flexible budget for Corwin.

Corwin Company
Flexible Budget
For the Year Ended December 31, 20xx

---

2. The following report compares Cazuelas Company's budgeted costs and actual costs for 20xx and presents the variances:

Cazuelas Company
Budgeted Versus Actual Costs
For the Year Ended December 31, 20xx

	Budgeted	Actual	Variance
Sales	$120,000	$125,000	$5,000
Cost of goods sold	70,000	79,000	(9,000)
Gross margin	50,000	46,000	(4,000)
Operating expenses	30,000	28,000	2,000
Net income	20,000	18,000	(2,000)

Cazuelas sells each unit for $100. The standard cost per unit is $62.50. What is the amount of variance that each of the following responsibility centers would be accountable for?

a. Revenue center

b. Profit center

c. Cost center (Production Department)

CHAPTER 10 SHORT-RUN DECISION ANALYSIS

REVIEWING THE CHAPTER

Objective 1: Explain how managers make short-run decisions during the management cycle.

1. **Short-run decision analysis** is the systematic examination of any decision whose effects will be felt over the course of the next year. To perform this type of analysis, managers need both historical and estimated quantitative and qualitative information. The information should be relevant, timely, and presented in a format that is easy to use in decision making.

2. Short-run decision analysis is an important component of the management cycle.
   a. Analyzing short-run decisions in the planning stage involves discovering a problem or need, identifying alternative courses of action to solve the problem or meet the need, analyzing the effects of each alternative on business operations, and selecting the best alternative. Short-run decisions should support the company's strategic plan and objectives and take into consideration not only quantitative factors, such as projected costs and revenues, but also qualitative factors, such as the competition, economic conditions, social issues, product or service quality, and timeliness.
   b. In the executing stage, managers make and implement many decisions that affect their organization's profitability and liquidity in the short run. For example, they may decide to outsource a product or service, accept a special order, or change the sales mix. All these decisions affect operations in the current period.

c. In the reviewing stage, managers analyze each decision to determine if it produced the desired results, and, if necessary, they identify and prescribe corrective action.
d. Managers prepare reports related to short-run decisions throughout the management cycle. In addition to developing budgets and compiling analyses of data that support their decisions, they issue reports that measure the effects their decisions had on the organization.

Objective 2: Define *incremental analysis* and describe how it applies to short-run decision analysis.

3. **Incremental analysis** (also called *differential analysis*) is a technique that helps managers compare alternative courses of action by focusing on differences in the projected revenues and costs. Only data that differ among the alternatives are included in the analysis. A cost that differs among alternatives is called a **differential** (or *incremental*) **cost**.

4. The first step in incremental analysis is to eliminate irrelevant revenues and costs—that is, those do not differ among the alternatives. Also eliminated are sunk costs. A **sunk cost** is a cost that was incurred because of a previous decision and cannot be recovered through the current decision. Once all irrelevant revenues and costs have been identified, the incremental analysis can be prepared using only projected revenues and expenses that differ for each alternative. The alternative that results in the highest increase in net income or

cost savings is the one that managers generally choose.

5. Incremental analysis simplifies the evaluation of a decision and reduces the time needed to choose the best course of action. However, it is only one input to the final decision. Managers also need to consider other issues, such as **opportunity costs,** which are the benefits forfeited or lost when one alternative is chosen over another.

Objective 3: Perform incremental analysis for outsourcing decisions.

6. **Outsourcing** is the use of suppliers outside the organization to perform services or produce goods that could be performed or produced internally. **Make-or-buy decisions** are decisions about whether to make a part internally or to buy it from an external supplier. Such decisions may also be concerned with the outsourcing of operating activities.

7. To focus their resources on their core competencies (i.e., the activities they perform best), many companies outsource nonvalue-adding activities, especially those that involve relatively low levels of skill (such as payroll processing or storage and distribution) or highly specialized knowledge (such as information management).

8. Incremental analysis of the costs and revenues of outsourcing a product or service as opposed to producing or performing it internally helps managers identify the best alternative.

Objective 4: Perform incremental analysis for special order decisions.

9. **Special order decisions** are decisions about whether to accept or reject special orders at prices below the normal market prices. A special order should be accepted only if it maximizes operating income. Like all short-run decisions, a special order decision should support the organization's strategic plan and objectives and be based on the relevant costs and revenues, as well as qualitative factors.

10. One approach to analyzing a special order decision is to compare its price with the costs of producing, packaging, and shipping the order to see if a profit can be generated. Another approach is to prepare a bid price by calculating the minimum selling price for the special order; the bid price equals the relevant costs plus an estimated profit.

11. Qualitative factors that can influence a special order decision are the special order's impact on

sales to regular customers, its potential to lead the company into new sales areas, and the customer's ability to maintain an ongoing relationship with the company that includes good ordering and paying practices.

Objective 5: Perform incremental analysis for segment profitability decisions.

12. The objective of analyzing a decision about segment profitability is to identify segments that have a negative segment margin. A **segment margin** is a segment's sales revenue minus its direct costs (direct variable costs and direct fixed costs traceable to the segment). These direct costs are **avoidable costs** because if management decides to drop the segment, they will be eliminated; because they vary among segments, they are relevant to the decision. If a segment has a positive segment margin (i.e., if the segment's revenue is greater than its direct costs), the segment should be kept. If a segment has a negative segment margin (i.e., if its revenue is less than its direct costs), it should be dropped. Certain costs will occur regardless of the decision; because these costs are unavoidable and are common to all alternatives, they are excluded from the calculation of the segment margin.

13. An analysis of segment profitability includes the preparation of a segmented income statement using variable costing to identify variable and fixed costs.

Objective 6: Perform incremental analysis for sales mix decisions involving constrained resources.

14. **Sales mix decisions** arise when limited resources, such as machine time or labor, restrict the types or quantities of products that a company can manufacture or the services it can deliver. The objective of a sales mix decision is to select the alternative that maximizes the contribution margin per constrained resource, as well as operating income.

15. Incremental analysis of a sales mix decision involves two steps:
    a. Calculate the contribution margin per unit for each product or service line affected by the constrained resource. The contribution margin per unit equals the selling price per unit less the variable costs per unit.
    b. Calculate the contribution margin per unit of the constrained resource. The contribution margin per unit of the constrained resource equals the contribution margin per unit divided

by the quantity of the constrained resource required per unit.

Objective 7: Perform incremental analysis for sell or process-further decisions.

16. A **sell or process-further decision** is a decision about whether to sell a joint product or service at the split-off point or to sell it after further processing. **Joint products** are two or more products or services composed of a common material or process that cannot be identified as separate during some or all of the production process. Only at a specific point, called the **split-off point,** do joint products or services become separate and identifiable. At that point, a company may decide to sell the product or service as is, or it may decide to process it into another form for sale to a different market. The objective of a sell or process-further decision is to select the alternative that maximizes operating income.

SELF-TEST

Test your knowledge of the chapter by choosing the best answer for each item below.

1. In which stage of the management cycle do managers estimate cost and revenue information that can be used to make short-run decisions during the coming year?
   a. Reviewing stage
   b. Executing stage
   c. Reporting stage
   d. Planning stage

2. An approach to decision analysis that considers only revenue and cost items that differ among alternatives is known as
   a. contribution margin analysis.
   b. incremental analysis.
   c. outsourcing decision analysis.
   d. special order decision analysis.

3. Which of the following costs are considered when using incremental analysis?
   a. Sunk costs
   b. Relevant costs
   c. Opportunity costs
   d. Irrelevant costs

4. Likely candidates for outsourcing include all of the following *except*
   a. information management.
   b. storage and distribution.
   c. payroll processing.
   d. a company's core competencies.

5. A management decision to accept or reject a sizable but unusual order at a price below the market price is
   a. an outsourcing decision.
   b. a special order decision.
   c. a sell or process-further decision.
   d. a segment profitability decision.

6. Products A and B can be sold at the split-off point for $27.50 and $32.50, respectively. Each unit of Product A can be sold for $45.00 if the company spends an additional $15.20 per unit on the product. Product B can be sold for $50.25 per unit if an additional $18.00 is spent processing each unit. Joint product costs are $12.40 per unit of Product A and $14.40 per unit of Product B. The company should
   a. process only Product A further.
   b. process only Product B further.
   c. process both products further.
   d. sell both products at the split-off point.

7. Short-run decision making requires
   a. information about relevant variable costs.
   b. relevant estimated nonfinancial information.
   c. relevant estimated financial information.
   d. all of the above.

8. A service organization may use short-term decision analysis for all of the following decisions *except* whether to
   a. outsource a service.
   b. accept or bid on a special order.
   c. allow more floor space for a product.
   d. drop an unprofitable service.

9. Costs incurred because of previous decisions that *cannot* be recovered through the current decision are called
   a. relevant costs.
   b. fixed costs.
   c. variable costs.
   d. sunk costs.

TESTING YOUR KNOWLEDGE

Matching*

Match each term with its definition by writing the appropriate letter in the blank.

_____ 1. Sunk costs

_____ 2. Incremental analysis

_____ 3. Sales mix decision

_____ 4. Avoidable costs

_____ 5. Irrelevant costs

_____ 6. Contribution margin

_____ 7. Special order decision

_____ 8. Sell or process-further decision

_____ 9. Opportunity costs

_____ 10. Outsourcing

a. The benefits forfeited or lost when one alternative is chosen over another

b. Relevant costs in short-run decisions

c. Sunk costs and costs that do not differ among alternatives

d. Costs incurred because of a previous decision that cannot be recovered through the current decision

e. The use of suppliers outside the organization to perform services or produce goods that could be performed or produced internally

f. A method of comparing alternative courses of action by focusing on differences in their projected revenues and costs

g. A decision to sell a joint product or service at split-off or to subject it to additional processing

h. A decision concerning the most profitable combination of product or service sales

i. Sales revenue minus all variable costs

j. A decision to accept or reject a large, one-time order at a price below the normal market price

Short Answer

Use the lines provided to complete each item.

1. List the four steps involved in analyzing short-run decisions in the planning stage of the management cycle.

   _____

   _____

   _____

   _____

2. Distinguish between relevant and irrelevant decision information.

   _____

   _____

   _____

3. List three possible benefits of outsourcing.

   _____

   _____

   _____

4. Identify five types of short-run decisions.

   _____

   _____

   _____

   _____

   _____

Note to student: The matching quiz might be completed more efficiently by starting with the definition and searching for the corresponding term.

True-False

Circle T if the statement is true, F if it is false. Provide explanations for the false answers, using the blank lines below.

T F **1.** Irrelevant costs are costs that do not differ among alternatives.

T F **2.** When applying incremental analysis to a special order decision, a service company considers only sunk costs.

T F **3.** Managers use cost information in each stage of the management cycle.

T F **4.** The main concern in incremental analysis is to project the operating income that each alternative will produce.

T F **5.** Incremental analysis is very useful for outsourcing decisions.

T F **6.** In a special order decision, the only relevant costs are those that vary because of the decision.

T F **7.** Management decisions require that a course of action be selected from a defined set of alternatives.

T F **8.** A segment that has a positive contribution margin and a negative segment margin should not be eliminated.

T F **9.** When decision alternatives involve both costs and revenues, the typical objective is to maximize annual operating income.

T F **10.** Joint products are two or more products or services that cannot be identified as separate during some or all of the production process.

T F **11.** Avoidable costs are sunk costs.

T F **12.** A special order decision requires a determination of the most profitable combination of product or service sales.

T F **13.** Only quantitative factors should be considered in special order decisions.

_____

_____

_____

_____

_____

_____

_____

_____

_____

_____

Circle the letter of the best answer.

1. When a service business is deciding on a sales mix involving constrained resources, the approach that it uses focuses on
   a. fixed costs.
   b. contribution margin.
   c. sunk costs.
   d. full costs.

2. The best method to use in deciding whether to outsource a product is
   a. variable costing.
   b. equivalent unit analysis.
   c. incremental analysis.
   d. opportunity costing.

3. The Machining Department of Onufer Company has a total capacity of 2,400 machine hours per month. The company makes three different products. Data for the products are as follows:

	Machine Hours Required per Unit	Contribution Margin per Unit	Current Unit Sales Demand
Superior	2	$6.00	1,000
Deluxe	1	4.00	1,500
Standard	½	2.50	2,000

   To produce the highest operating income, the sales mix should be as follows:
   a. Produce 1,000 units of Superior, 800 units of Standard, and 0 units of Deluxe.
   b. Produce 500 units of Superior, 750 units of Deluxe, and 1,300 units of Standard.
   c. Produce 1,500 units of Deluxe, 450 units of Superior, and 0 units of Standard.
   d. Produce 2,000 units of Standard, 1,400 units of Deluxe, and 0 units of Superior.

4. Which of the following would *not* be a valid reason to outsource a product?
   a. To improve cash flows
   b. To capitalize on the fact that manufacturing the product requires only unskilled labor
   c. To increase operating income
   d. To share critical information with competitors

5. A make-or-buy decision would be classified as
   a. an outsourcing decision.
   b. a sales mix decision.
   c. a segment profitability decision.
   d. a special order decision.

6. Estimated costs that differ among alternative courses of action are called
   a. relevant costs.
   b. opportunity costs.
   c. irrelevant costs.
   d. sunk costs.

7. For several years, a company has produced a joint product that is processed after split-off. The product is salable at the split-off point. To justify the additional processing, a decision analysis should demonstrate that
   a. ultimate revenues exceed all joint and separable costs.
   b. additional processing increases the revenue potential.
   c. the costs of further processing are less than incremental revenues.
   d. unit production costs are lower after additional processing.

8. The point in the production process at which a joint product or service becomes separate and identifiable is the
   a. breakeven point.
   b. split-off point.
   c. point of indifference.
   d. point of inflection.

9. Costs that can be eliminated if a segment is discontinued are called
   a. avoidable costs.
   b. fixed costs.
   c. historical costs.
   d. unnecessary costs.

10. In a sell or process-further decision,
    a. the method chosen to allocate joint costs is a critical factor.
    b. the assignment of joint costs can be influenced by the final decision.
    c. joint costs are irrelevant to the decision and should be ignored.
    d. joint costs must be minimized.

APPLYING YOUR KNOWLEDGE

Exercises

1. A company must decide whether to purchase machine A for $10,000 or machine B for $17,000. Both machines are expected to have a life of only one year. Machine A would require the use of two operators, each of whom earns $8,000 per year, and maintenance of $300 per year. However, it would cost $50 per year less for electricity than the machine currently in use. Machine B would require only one part-time operator at $8,000 per year. It would require maintenance of $500 per year, but it would cost $80 per year more for electricity than the machine currently in use. Each machine would generate the same amount of revenue. Prepare an incremental analysis to determine which machine the company should purchase.

2. On June 30, 20xx, Time, LLP, had 100,000 unsold 20xx calendars. The director of marketing thinks these calendars can no longer be sold to the company's regular customers at the normal selling price. Direct materials cost is $3 per calendar, direct labor cost is $2 per calendar, variable overhead is $.50 per calendar, and fixed overhead (based on a production volume of 300,000 calendars) is $1 per calendar. The cost of shipping and packaging (paid by the company) is $1.75 per calendar. The normal selling price is $12 per calendar. What is the *minimum* special price that the company could set for the unsold calendars?

3. Houses for the Needy, a not-for-profit organization, has offered Matt Printing Company $600 to prepare a custom brochure to be used in soliciting funds. The brochure is to be multicolored and contain a number of graphic designs. Matt estimates that it would take ten hours of design labor at $40 per hour and four printing hours at $15 per hour to produce the brochures. Fixed costs are already covered by regular business. Prepare an incremental analysis of costs to determine whether Matt should accept the order. In addition, briefly discuss other factors that may influence the decision to accept or reject the special order.

Crossword Puzzle
for Chapters 9 and 10

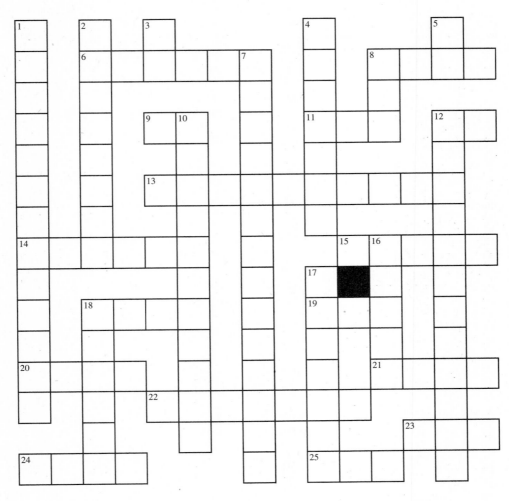

ACROSS

6. Investment or profit _____
8. Measures of short-_____ success
9. 14-Across, for short
11. Sales _____ decision
12. Cost _____ goods sold
13. See 7-Down
14. Residual _____
15. _____ products (products made from the same material)
18. _____-or-buy decision
19. Cause-_____-effect relationships
20. Example of a fixed cost
21. Minimum desired _____ of return
22. Cost of _____ (see 21-Across)
23. 3-Down, for short
24. Discovering a _____ (first step in short-run decision analysis)
25. 2-Down, for short

DOWN

1. Type of cost center
2. _____ value added
3. Return _____ investment
4. _____ margin (sales minus direct costs)
5. Sell _____ process further decision
7. With 13-Across, information system emphasizing assignment of control
8. After-_____ operating income
10. Type of analysis emphasizing cost and revenue differences
12. _____ chart (visual representation of a company's hierarchy)
16. Special _____ decision
17. _____ (residual or scrap) value
18. Supervise

CHAPTER 11 PRICING DECISIONS, INCLUDING TARGET COSTING AND TRANSFER PRICING

REVIEWING THE CHAPTER

Objective 1: Identify the objectives and rules used to establish prices of goods and services, and relate pricing issues to the management cycle.

1. A company's long-term objectives should include a pricing policy. Possible pricing objectives include (a) identifying and adhering to short-run and long-run pricing strategies; (b) maximizing profits; (c) maintaining or gaining market share; (d) setting socially responsible prices; (e) maintaining a minimum rate of return on investment; and (f) being customer focused.

2. Pricing strategies depend on many factors and conditions. Identifying the market being served and meeting the needs of that market are of primary importance. Companies that make standard products for a competitive market have different pricing strategies from firms that make products to customers' specifications.

3. For a company to stay in business, the selling price of its product or service must (a) be equal to or lower than the competition's price, (b) be acceptable to the customer, (c) recover all costs incurred in bringing the product or service to market, and (d) return a profit. If a manager deviates from any of these four selling rules, there must be a specific short-run objective that accounts for the change. Breaking these pricing rules for a long period will force a company into bankruptcy.

4. Pricing issues are addressed at each stage of the management cycle. During the planning stage, managers must decide how much to charge for each product or service. During the executing stage, the product or service is sold at the specified price or on the auction market. During the reviewing stage, managers evaluate sales to determine which pricing strategies were successful and which failed. During the reporting stage, analyses of actual and targeted prices and profits are prepared for use inside the organization.

5. When making and evaluating pricing decisions, managers must consider many factors, some relating to the market and others to internal constraints. Factors related to the market include the demand for the product, customer needs, competition, and the quantity and quality of competing products or services. Internal constraints include the cost of the product or service, the desired return on investment, the quality and quantity of materials and labor, and the allocation of scarce resources.

Objective 2: Describe economic pricing concepts including the auction-based pricing method used on the Internet.

6. Economic pricing concepts are based on microeconomic theory. A product's total revenue and total costs are plotted against units produced. Initially, because of fixed costs, the cost line is above the revenue line, illustrating a loss. When enough products are produced and sold to cover both variable and fixed costs, the lines cross, illustrating a profit. However, the lines are destined to

cross again. Price competition will eventually bend the revenue line down; as more units are sold at a lower price, total revenue will decrease. The cost line will eventually bend upward as production exceeds capacity, causing an increase in fixed costs. Another way of stating this is that the **marginal revenue** (the change in total revenue caused by a one-unit change in output) is decreasing as more units are produced, while the **marginal cost** (the change in total cost caused by a one-unit change in output) is increasing.

7. The point at which the total revenue line and the total cost line are farthest apart (maximum profit) is also the point at which marginal revenue equals marginal cost. Graphs of marginal revenue and marginal cost would cross at this point. Projecting this point onto the product's demand curve indicates the optimal price the market will bring at that level of output and the optimal number of units to produce. However, implementation is difficult and uncertain. An analysis of this type is useful but should not be the only approach relied on when establishing a price.

8. Because of the increasing amount of business conducted over the Internet by both companies and individuals, auction-based pricing has become an important pricing mechanism. The Internet allows sellers and buyers to solicit bids and transact exchanges in an open market environment. A willing buyer and seller set an auction-based price in a sales transaction.

Objective 3: Use cost-based pricing methods to develop prices.

9. Managers may use any of several pricing methods to establish a selling price. Two methods based on the cost of producing a product or service are gross margin pricing and return on asset pricing.

10. **Gross margin pricing** is a cost-based pricing method that establishes a selling price at a percentage above an item's total production costs. The following formulas are used:

$$\text{Markup Percentage} = \frac{\text{Desired Profit + Total Selling, General, and Administrative Expenses}}{\text{Total Production Costs}}$$

$$\begin{aligned}\text{Gross Margin–Based Price} =\ &\text{Total Production Costs per Unit +} \\ &\text{(Markup Percentage} \times \text{Total Production Costs per Unit)}\end{aligned}$$

11. Whereas gross margin pricing is based on a percentage above total costs, **return on assets pricing** is based on a specific rate of return on assets

employed in the generation of a product or service. Assuming that a company has a specified minimum rate of return, the following formula is used to calculate the selling price:

$$\begin{aligned}\text{Return on Assets–Based Price} =\ &\text{Total Costs and Expenses per Unit +} \\ &\text{[Desired Rate of Return} \times \text{(Total Costs of Assets Employed} \div \text{Anticipated Units to Be Produced)]}\end{aligned}$$

12. **Time and materials pricing** is common practice in service businesses. The two primary types of costs used in this method are the cost of actual materials and parts and the cost of actual direct labor. An overhead rate, which includes a profit factor, is computed for each of these cost categories. When preparing a billing, the two overhead percentages are added to the two major cost categories.

13. Although managers may depend on traditional, objective, formula-driven pricing methods to set prices, they must at times deviate from those approaches and rely on their own experience.

Objective 4: Describe target costing and use that concept to analyze pricing decisions and evaluate a new product opportunity.

14. **Target costing** is a pricing method that (a) uses market research to identify the price at which a new product will be competitive in the marketplace, (b) defines the desired profit to be made on the product, and (c) computes the target cost for the product by subtracting the desired profit from the competitive market price. The following formula is used to determine the target cost:

$$\text{Target Price – Desired Profit = Target Cost}$$

The company's engineers use the target cost as the maximum amount to be incurred in designing and manufacturing the product. If this cost goal cannot be met, the product is not manufactured.

15. Target costing gives managers the ability to control the costs of a new product in the planning stage of the product's life cycle. The pricing decision is made as soon as market research has revealed the potential demand for the product and the maximum price that customers would be willing to pay for it. In contrast, when traditional cost-based pricing methods are used, the pricing decision must wait until production has taken place and costs have been incurred and analyzed. At that point, a profit factor is added to the product's cost, and the product is ready to be offered to customers. Because target costing enables managers to analyze a product's potential before

they commit resources to its production, it enhances a company's ability to compete, especially in new or emerging markets. The philosophy underlying target costing is that a product should be designed and built so that it produces a profit as soon as it is introduced to the marketplace.

16. Two types of cost patterns are involved as a new product moves through its life cycle. **Committed costs** are design, development, engineering, testing, and production costs that are engineered into a product or service at the design stage of development; these costs should be incurred if all design specifications are followed. **Incurred costs** are the actual costs of making the product. When cost-based pricing is used, controlling the costs of a new product from the planning phase through the production phase is very difficult; management has a hard time setting realistic targets because the product is being produced for the first time. Because customers are expected to pay whatever amount cost-based pricing identifies, the focus is on sales rather than on design and manufacture, and efforts at cost control focus on costs incurred after the product has been introduced to the marketplace. With target costing, committed costs are minimized because the product has been designed and built to a specific cost goal. Target costing allows profitability to be built into the selling price from the outset.

17. A company's engineers sometimes determine that a product cannot be manufactured at or below its target cost. In this case, the company should try to adjust the product's design and the approach to production. If those attempts fail, it should either invest in new equipment and procedures or abandon its plans to market the product.

Objective 5: Describe how transfer pricing is used for transferring goods and services and evaluating performance within a division or segment.

18. A **decentralized organization** has several divisions or operating segments. These divisions or segments sell their goods and services both inside and outside the organization. The price a division or segment charges for exchanging goods and services with another division or segment is called a **transfer price**. This internal pricing mechanism enables an organization to assess both the internal and external profitability of its products or services. There are three basic kinds of transfer prices:

a. A **cost-plus transfer price** is the sum of costs incurred by the producing division plus an agreed-on profit percentage. The weakness of cost-plus pricing is that it guarantees that the selling division will recover its costs. Guaranteed cost recovery does not take into account any inefficiencies in a division's operations or the incurrence of excessive costs.

b. A **market transfer price** is based on the price a product could command on the open market. The danger in using market prices as transfer prices is that a decision to sell to outside customers at the market price may cause an internal shortage of critical materials; the selling division may realize a profit, but the overall profitability of the company will suffer. Market prices are therefore usually used only as a basis for negotiation.

c. A **negotiated transfer price** is reached through bargaining between the managers of the buying and selling divisions. This approach allows the selling division to recover its costs and still earn a profit. To develop a negotiated transfer price, the managers should compute the unit cost of the item being transferred and an appropriate profit markup. If the item has an external market or if the buying division can purchase the same item from an outside source, the market price should be included in the negotiations. The transfer price on which the managers ultimately agree should be beneficial to the company as a whole.

19. Because transfer prices include an estimated amount of profit, they can be used as a basis for measuring performance. Even divisions that sell their products only within the company can be evaluated as profit centers by using transfer prices to simulate revenues.

Test your knowledge of the chapter by choosing the best answer for each item below.

1. Setting socially responsible prices means
   a. the customer should have the final word on price setting.
   b. the price should not be so high that people with average incomes cannot afford the product or service.
   c. a company's pricing policy takes into consideration social concerns, such as environmental factors, legal constraints, and ethical issues.
   d. the buyer no longer has to beware.

2. A company is still increasing its profit margin when
   a. marginal revenue equals marginal cost.
   b. marginal cost is greater than marginal revenue.
   c. marginal revenue is less than marginal cost.
   d. marginal revenue is greater than marginal cost.

3. Which of the following is *not* an external factor affecting a pricing decision?
   a. The company's profit markup percentage
   b. Demand for the product or service
   c. Prices of competing products or services
   d. Seasonal demand or continual demand

4. Desired profit plus total selling, general, and administrative expenses divided by total production costs is the formula for the markup percentage used in
   a. gross margin pricing.
   b. total cost pricing.
   c. target costing.
   d. return on asset pricing.

5. Time and materials pricing would most likely be used by a
   a. manufacturing company.
   b. jewelry store.
   c. plumbing company.
   d. government agency.

6. Which of the following is *not* true about target costing?
   a. Target costing identifies the price at which a product will be competitive in the marketplace.
   b. Target costing defines the minimum desired profit for a product.
   c. Target costing allows managers to assess a product's potential for success before committing resources to its production.
   d. Target costing is a cost-based method used to make pricing decisions.

7. Transfer prices are normally used by
   a. major league ballparks.
   b. city bus companies.
   c. decentralized companies whose divisions use internally produced products.
   d. companies that have divisions in several different countries.

8. A transfer price is
   a. an artificial price used only within a firm.
   b. a fee charged every time a product is transferred between departments.
   c. a price derived through time and materials pricing.
   d. a fee that bus companies charge for transfers among bus lines.

9. A transfer price is negotiated by the
   a. purchasing agent and store clerk.
   b. managers of the buying and selling divisions.
   c. management accountant and the buying department's manager.
   d. selling department's manager and the production superintendent.

TESTING YOUR KNOWLEDGE

*Matching**

Match each term with its definition by writing the appropriate letter in the blank.

_____ **1.** Marginal revenue

_____ **2.** Target costing

_____ **3.** Committed costs

_____ **4.** Gross margin–based price

_____ **5.** Return on assets–based price

_____ **6.** Time and materials pricing

_____ **7.** Transfer price

_____ **8.** Cost-plus transfer price

_____ **9.** Negotiated transfer price

_____ **10.** Marginal cost

a. A pricing approach often used by service firms

b. Total production costs per unit plus the markup percentage times total production costs per unit

c. A price reached through bargaining between the managers of the buying and selling divisions

d. A pricing method that determines a maximum production cost by subtracting the desired profit from the competitive market price

e. The change in total revenue caused by a one-unit change in output

f. Total costs and expenses per unit plus the desired rate of return times total costs of assets employed divided by anticipated units to be made

g. The costs of design, development, engineering, testing, and production that are engineered into a product at the design stage of development

h. The change in total cost caused by a one-unit change in output

i. The sum of costs incurred by the producing division plus an agreed-on profit percentage

j. The price at which goods are exchanged between a company's divisions

Short Answer

Use the lines provided to answer each item.

1. Explain the economic approach to determining a price.

_____

_____

_____

_____

2. List four external factors that can influence a pricing decision.

_____

_____

_____

_____

3. List four internal factors that can influence a pricing decision.

_____

_____

_____

_____

4. Explain the time and materials pricing calculation.

_____

_____

_____

_____

Note to student: The matching quiz might be completed more efficiently by starting with the definition and searching for the corresponding term.

5. List and explain the three basic kinds of transfer prices.

_____

_____

_____

_____

_____

_____

_____

_____

_____

_____

True-False

Circle T if the statement is true, F if it is false. Provide explanations for the false answers, using the blank lines below.

T F   **1.** Because pricing decisions are short-run decisions, a pricing policy does not need to be included in a company's long-term objectives.

T F   **2.** The process of establishing a correct price is more of a science than an art.

T F   **3.** Total revenue is defined as the change in revenue caused by a one-unit change in output.

T F   **4.** Demand for a product or service is an external factor that affects a pricing decision.

T F   **5.** Maintaining or gaining market share is an internal factor that influences a pricing decision.

T F   **6.** One of the benefits of target costing is that a product is not produced if it cannot be designed to be profitable.

T F   **7.** The markup percentage for gross margin pricing is applied to total production costs per unit.

T F   **8.** Service companies often use the return on assets pricing method.

T F   **9.** Managers of the buying and selling divisions bargain for a cost-plus transfer price.

T F **10.** Market transfer prices are usually used only as a basis for negotiations between managers.

T F **11.** When intracompany transfers are priced in excess of cost to the selling division, the total profits of the company increase.

_____

_____

_____

_____

_____

_____

_____

_____

_____

_____

_____

_____

_____

_____

Multiple Choice

Circle the letter of the best answer.

1. Which of the following is *not* an objective of a pricing policy?
   a. Maintaining or gaining market share
   b. Setting socially responsible prices
   c. Being customer focused
   d. Charging unrealistically low prices to eliminate competition

2. Establishing a price for a product or service is more of an art than a science because
   a. the pricing process must be properly displayed.
   b. it takes a creative person with experience in pricing to arrive at a just and fair price.
   c. prices developed without supporting analysis are as good as those backed up by cost studies.
   d. prices are developed on an easel.

3. In the economic pricing concept, a product's sales show more than one breakeven point because
   a. start-up costs double.
   b. after the first breakeven point, marginal costs equal marginal revenues.
   c. after the initial breakeven point, increased competition and volume tend to increase costs and decrease selling prices.
   d. total revenue always equals marginal cost.

4. Which of the following is *not* an external factor influencing a pricing decision?
   a. Return on investment
   b. Total demand for product or service
   c. Prices of competing products or services
   d. Seasonal demand or continual demand

5. Which of the following is *not* true about target costing?
   a. The price of a product is determined before the product is produced.
   b. Committed costs are minimized because the product is designed and built to a specific cost goal.
   c. The product is expected to produce a profit as soon as it is marketed.
   d. After the product is marketed, the production procedure is analyzed to determine a way to reduce costs so the product can be made at a profitable "target" cost.

6. Total production costs per unit plus the markup percentage times total production costs per unit is the formula used in
   a. target costing.
   b. gross margin pricing.
   c. time and materials pricing.
   d. return on assets pricing.

7. Service businesses commonly use
   a. target costing.
   b. gross margin pricing.
   c. time and materials pricing.
   d. transfer pricing.

8. An internal price bargained for by managers of the buying and selling divisions is called a
   a. normal transfer price.
   b. cost-plus transfer price.
   c. market transfer price.
   d. negotiated transfer price.

9. Transfer prices allow a decentralized company to
   a. evaluate individual departments' contributions to the company's profitability.
   b. increase overall profits.
   c. decrease prices to outside customers.
   d. increase company morale.

10. In pricing decisions,
    a. external prices are easier to develop than transfer prices.
    b. the objectives of external pricing and transfer pricing are much the same.
    c. transfer pricing policies are taken more seriously than external pricing policies.
    d. the gross margin and profit margin pricing methods are used to develop both external prices and transfer prices.

APPLYING YOUR KNOWLEDGE

Exercises

1. Gomez Corporation is in the process of developing a price for a new product called Bioderm. Anticipated production data revealed the following cost information:

Direct materials costs	$680,000
Direct labor costs	552,500
Variable manufacturing overhead costs	204,000
Fixed manufacturing overhead costs	263,500
Selling expenses	238,000
General and administrative expenses	510,000
Minimum desired profit	382,500

Management predicts that 850,000 bottles of Bioderm will be produced and sold during the coming year. From the data presented, compute the selling price per bottle using the gross margin pricing method.

2. Zeriscape Landscaping Company has just completed a major job. Costs were $46,500 for materials and $32,800 for labor. Overhead and profit percentages developed at the beginning of the year were 40 percent for materials and supplies and 60 percent for labor. Prepare the billing for the customer using the time and materials pricing method. Show the breakdown of all costs involved.

3. Steel Components Company is considering the development of a new all-steel workbench. After conferring with the design engineers, the accountant's staff put together the information that appears below, which is directly linked to the decision to produce this product.

a. Compute the product's target cost.
b. Compute the product's projected cost based on the design engineer's estimates.
c. What decision should the company make about producing the all-steel workbench? Explain your answer.

Targeted selling price	$575	per unit
Desired profit percentage	25%	of total unit cost
Anticipated unit demand	25,000	units
Per unit data for the workbench		
Raw materials cost	$120	
Purchased parts cost	$80	
Manufacturing labor		
Hours	2	hours
Hourly labor rate	$14	
Assembly labor		
Hours	4	hours
Hourly labor rate	$15	
Machine hours	8	hours
Activity-based cost rates		
Materials and parts handling activity	5%	of raw materials and purchased parts cost
Engineering activity	$20	per workbench unit
Production and assembly activity	$15	per machine hour
Packaging and delivery activity	$33	per workbench unit
Sales and marketing activity	$14	per workbench unit

4. Electra Division and Ohms Division belong to the same company. For several years, Electra Division has produced an electronic component that it sells to Ohms Division at the prevailing market price of $20. Electra manufactures the component only for Ohms Division and has not previously sold this product to outside customers. The product is available from outside suppliers, who would charge Ohms Division $20 per unit. Electra currently produces and sells 20,000 of these components each year and also manufactures several other products. The following annual cost information was compiled for the electronic component after the close of 20xx operations, during which time Electra operated at full capacity.

Electra Division—20xx

Cost Category	Unit Cost
Direct materials	$ 6.50
Direct labor (hourly basis)	8.60
Variable manufacturing overhead	4.50
General fixed overhead of plant	5.20
Traceable fixed overhead	
($60,000 ÷ 20,000)	3.00
Variable shipping expenses	.25
	$28.05

General fixed overhead represents allocated joint fixed costs, such as building depreciation, property taxes, and salaries of production executives. If production of the components were discontinued, $50,000 of the annual traceable fixed overhead costs could be eliminated. The balance of traceable fixed overhead is equipment depreciation on machinery that could be used elsewhere in the plant.

a. Compute the cost per unit of the electronic component made by Electra Division.
b. The division manager contends that producing the component to accommodate other divisions is a sound company policy as long as variable costs are recovered by the sales. Should Electra Division continue to produce the component for Ohms Division?

CHAPTER 12 CAPITAL INVESTMENT ANALYSIS

REVIEWING THE CHAPTER

Objective 1: Define *capital investment analysis* and describe its relation to the management cycle.

1. **Capital investment decisions** are decisions about when and how much to spend on capital facilities and other long-term projects. They are among the most significant decisions that management must make. They involve such matters as installing new equipment, replacing old equipment, expanding a production area by renovating or adding to a building, buying or building a new factory or office building, and acquiring another company.

2. **Capital investment analysis** (also called *capital budgeting*) is the process of identifying the need for a capital investment, analyzing courses of action to meet that need, preparing reports for managers, choosing the best alternative, and allocating funds among competing needs. Personnel from all parts of an organization participate in this decision-making process.

3. Managers pay close attention to capital investments throughout the management cycle.

   a. Decisions about capital investments are vitally important because they involve a large amount of money and may commit a company to a course of action for many years. Most of the analysis of these investments takes place in the planning stage of the management cycle. The analysis involves six steps: (1) identification of capital investment needs; (2) formal requests for capital investments, (3) preliminary screening, (4) establishment of an acceptance-

rejection standard, (5) evaluation of proposals, and (6) final decisions on the proposals.

   b. Capital investment decisions are implemented during the executing stage of the management cycle. This involves scheduling projects and overseeing their development, construction, or purchase.

   c. During the reviewing stage, each project undergoes a postcompletion audit to determine if it is meeting the goals and targets set forth in the planning stage.

   d. In the reporting stage, reports on the results of capital investment decisions are prepared and distributed within the company. They include comparisons of budgeted expenditures with actual expenditures, as well as comparisons of projected net cash flows or cost savings with actual results.

Objective 2: State the purpose of the minimum rate of return and identify the methods used to arrive at that rate.

4. In most companies, management sets a minimum rate of return on investments, and any capital expenditure proposal that predicts a rate of return below that minimum is automatically refused. The most commonly used measures of rate of return are cost of capital, corporate return on investment, industry average return on investment, and bank interest rates.

5. The **cost of capital** is the weighted-average rate of return a company must pay its long-term creditors

and shareholders for the use of their funds. The components of cost of capital are the cost of debt, the cost of preferred stock, the cost of common stock, and the cost of retained earnings.

Objective 3: Identify the types of projected costs and revenues used to evaluate alternatives for capital investment.

6. Managers use a variety of measures to estimate the benefits to be derived from a proposed capital investment.

   a. *Net income and net cash inflows:* Estimating the net income that a capital investment will produce is one way of measuring its benefits. A more widely used measure is projected cash flow. **Net cash inflows** are the balance of increases in projected cash receipts over increases in projected cash payments. They are used when the analysis involves cash receipts. When the analysis involves only cash outlays, **cost savings** are used as the measure.

   b. *Equal versus unequal cash flows:* Projected cash flows may be the same for each year of an asset's life, or they may vary from year to year. Unequal cash flows are common and must be analyzed for each year of the asset's life.

   c. *Carrying value of assets:* **Carrying value** is the undepreciated portion of the original cost of a fixed asset. When analyzing a decision to replace an old asset, carrying value is irrelevant because it is a past, or historical, cost. However, net proceeds from the asset's sale or disposal are relevant.

   d. *Depreciation expense and income taxes:* Depreciation is a noncash expense requiring no cash outlay during the period. However, because depreciation expense is deductible when determining income taxes, it can result in significant savings. Thus, depreciation expense is relevant to evaluations based on after-tax cash flows.

   e. *Disposal or residual values:* Proceeds from the sale of an old asset are current cash inflows and are relevant to evaluating a proposed capital investment. Projected disposal or residual values of replacement equipment are also relevant because they represent future cash inflows and usually differ among alternatives.

Objective 4: Apply the concept of the time value of money.

7. A key question in capital investment analysis is how to measure the return on a fixed asset. When the asset has a long useful life, managers usually analyze the cash flows that it will generate in terms of the time value of money. The **time value of money** is the concept that cash flows of equal dollar amounts separated by an interval of time have different present values because of the effect of compound interest. The notions of interest, present value, future value, and ordinary annuity are all related to the time value of money.

8. **Interest** is the cost associated with the use of money for a specific period. **Simple interest** is the interest cost for one or more periods when the amount on which the interest is computed stays the same from period to period. **Compound interest** is the interest cost for two or more periods when the amount on which interest is computed changes in each period to include all interest paid in previous periods.

9. **Future value** is the amount an investment will be worth at a future date if invested today at compound interest. **Present value** is the amount that must be invested today at a given rate of compound interest to produce a given future value.

10. An **ordinary annuity** is a series of equal payments or receipts that will begin one time period from the current date. The present value of an ordinary annuity is equal to the present value of equal amounts equally spaced over time.

Objective 5: Analyze capital investment proposals using the net present value method.

11. The **net present value method** evaluates a capital investment by discounting its future cash flows to their present values and subtracting the amount of the initial investment from their sum. The advantage of this method is that it incorporates the time value of money into the analysis of proposed capital investments by discounting future cash inflows and outflows by the company's minimum rate of return. If the net present value is positive, the rate of return on the investment will exceed the company's minimum rate of return, and the project can be accepted.

Objective 6: Analyze capital investment proposals using the the payback period method and the accounting rate-of-return method.

12. The **payback period method** of evaluating a capital investment focuses on the minimum length of time needed to recover the initial investment. When two or more investment alternatives are being considered, the one with the shortest payback period should be selected. The payback period is computed as follows:

$$\text{Payback Period} = \frac{\text{Cost of Investment}}{\text{Annual Net Cash Inflows}}$$

The projected annual net cash inflows are found by determining the increase in cash revenue resulting from the investment and subtracting the cash expenses. The advantage of the payback period method is that it is easy to understand and apply. Its disadvantages are that it does not measure profitability; it ignores the time value of money; and by disregarding cash flows after the payback period is reached, it fails to consider long-term returns on the investment.

13. The **accounting rate-of-return method** uses a net income approach. Two variables—estimated annual net income from the investment and the average cost of the investment—are used to measure performance. The basic equation is as follows:

$$\text{Accounting Rate of Return} = \frac{\text{Project's Average Annual Net Income}}{\text{Average Investment Cost}}$$

Average investment in a proposed capital investment is calculated as follows:

$$\text{Average Investment Cost} = \left(\frac{\text{Total Investment} - \text{Residual Value}}{2} \right) + \text{Residual Value}$$

If the rate of return is higher than the desired minimum rate, management may decide to make the investment. Like the payback period method, the accounting rate-of-return method is easy to apply and understand. Its disadvantages are that it averages net income over the life of the investment, it is unreliable if estimated annual income differs from year to year, it ignores cash flows, and it does not consider the time value of money.

Test your knowledge of the chapter by choosing the best answer for each item below.

1. The process of identifying the need for a capital investment, analyzing different courses of action to meet that need, preparing reports for managers, choosing the best alternative, and allocating funds among competing needs is the definition of
   a. special order budgeting.
   b. capital investment analysis.
   c. capital budgeting.
   d. flexible budgeting.

2. Future value is
   a. the amount an investment will be worth at a future date if invested today at compound interest.
   b. the amount an investment will be worth at a future date if invested today at simple interest.
   c. the amount an investment will be worth in today's dollars if invested now at compound interest.
   d. a series of equal payments or receipts that will begin one time period at a future date.

3. Which of the following is *not* relevant when evaluating a capital investment proposal?
   a. Residual value of the new capital asset
   b. Carrying value of the capital asset that is being replaced
   c. Net cash flows from the proposal
   d. Cost savings from the proposal

4. Annual net cash inflows are
   a. annual cash inflows minus annual cash outflows.
   b. annual cash inflows minus the amount of capital investment.
   c. annual revenues minus expenses.
   d. annual cash inflows minus annual cash outflows minus total depreciation expense.

5. Which of the following is *not* a method used in capital investment analysis?
   a. Make-or-buy method
   b. Payback period method
   c. Accounting rate-of-return method
   d. Net present value method

6. JLT Enterprises is contemplating a major investment in a new flexible manufacturing system. The company's minimum desired rate of return is 16 percent. The total investment is $2,500,000. The system is expected to have an eight-year useful life and a 10 percent residual value at the end of that time. The company uses straight-line depreciation. The system should produce $1,400,000 of revenue annually. Annual cash operating costs are expected to be $776,375. Using the accounting rate-of-return method, what is the expected rate of return from the proposed investment?
   a. 37.7 percent
   b. 26.6 percent
   c. 24.9 percent
   d. 19.2 percent

7. Assuming the same facts as in **6** and using the net present value method, what is the expected net present value of the proposed investment?
   a. Positive net present value of $1,051,450
   b. Negative net present value of $12,455
   c. Positive net present value of $285,277
   d. Negative net present value of $62,235

8. Assuming the same facts as in **6** and using the payback period method, what is the expected payback period for the proposed investment?
   a. 4.009 years
   b. 3.954 years
   c. 3.125 years
   d. 3.625 years

9. The accounting rate-of-return is calculated as
   a. average investment cost divided by average annual net income from investment.
   b. average cash flows from investment divided by average investment cost.
   c. average annual net income from investment divided by average investment cost.
   d. average investment cost minus average annual net income from investment.

10. That cash flows of equal dollar amounts separated by an interval of time have different values is the concept of the
    a. money value of time.
    b. time value of money.
    c. cost of capital.
    d. residual value.

TESTING YOUR KNOWLEDGE

Matching*

Match each term with its definition by writing the appropriate letter in the blank.

_____ **1.** Capital investment analysis

_____ **2.** Cost of capital

_____ **3.** Accounting rate-of-return method

_____ **4.** Payback period method

_____ **5.** Net present value method

_____ **6.** Capital investment decision

_____ **7.** Compound interest

_____ **8.** Time value of money

_____ **9.** Carrying value

_____ **10.** Present value

a. The amount that must be invested today at a given rate of compound interest to produce a given future value

b. The concept that cash flows of equal dollar amounts separated by an interval of time have different current values

c. A determination of when and how much to spend on capital facilities

d. The process of identifying the need for a capital investment, analyzing different courses of action, preparing reports, choosing the best alternative, and allocating funds among competing needs

e. A method of evaluating capital investments that determines the minimum length of time it would take to recover an asset's initial cost in net cash inflows

f. A method of evaluating capital investments that divides a proposed project's net income by the average investment cost

g. The weighted-average rate of return a company must pay its long-term creditors and shareholders for the use of their funds

h. The undepreciated portion of the original cost of a fixed asset

i. The interest cost for two or more periods when the amount on which interest is computed changes in each period to include all interest paid in previous periods

j. A method of evaluating capital investments that discounts all net cash inflows back to the present

---

Note to student: The matching quiz might be completed more efficiently by starting with the definition and searching for the corresponding term.

Short Answer

Use the lines provided to complete each item.

1. List the six steps involved in analyzing a capital investment in the planning stage of the management cycle.

   _____

   _____

   _____

   _____

   _____

   _____

2. Identify the four components used to compute cost of capital.

   _____

   _____

   _____

   _____

3. List three methods frequently used to evaluate capital expenditure proposals.

   _____

   _____

   _____

True-False

Circle T if the statement is true, F if it is false. Provide explanations for the false answers, using the blank lines at the end of the section.

T F 1. Capital investment analysis involves obtaining cash for business operations.

T F 2. The simplest method to apply in evaluating a capital investment proposal is the net present value method.

T F 3. Both the accounting rate-of-return and payback period methods ignore the time value of money.

T F 4. The payback period is the maximum length of time it should take to recover in cash the cost of an investment.

T F 5. The payback period equals the cost of the capital investment divided by the annual net cash inflows.

T F 6. A minimum rate of return is not a factor when the net present value method is used.

T F 7. When the net present value method shows that a proposed project has a negative net present value, the project should probably be rejected.

T F 8. Carrying values of existing assets are relevant considerations when analyzing capital expenditure proposals to replace facilities.

T F 9. Managers screen, evaluate, and select capital investment proposals during the executing stage of the management cycle.

T F 10. Disposal or residual values are not relevant to capital investment decisions.

_____   _____
_____   _____
_____   _____
_____   _____
_____   _____
_____   _____
_____   _____
_____   _____
_____   _____
_____   _____
_____   _____

Multiple Choice

Circle the letter of the best answer.

1. Under the accounting rate-of-return method, which of the following is irrelevant?
   a. Residual value of the asset
   b. Net cash inflows
   c. Cost of the asset
   d. Project's average annual net income

2. The average cost of capital is
   a. the cost of each source of available capital.
   b. the Federal Reserve's current lending rate.
   c. an average of the cost of debt, equity, and retained earnings multiplied by the prime rate.
   d. the sum of the products of each financing source's percentage multiplied by its cost rate.

3. The method of capital investment evaluation that brings the time value of money into the analysis is
   a. the net present value method.
   b. the accounting rate of return on initial investment method.
   c. the payback period method.
   d. the accounting rate of return on average investment method.

4. The time value of money is considered in long-range investment decisions by
   a. investing only in short-term projects.
   b. assigning greater value to more immediate cash flows.
   c. using subjective probabilities to weight cash flows.
   d. assuming equal annual cash-flow patterns.

5. The payback period method measures
   a. the time needed to recover investment dollars.
   b. the cash flows from an investment.
   c. the economic life of an investment.
   d. the probability of an investment's success.

6. In which stage of the management cycle does a postcompletion audit determine if a capital investment project is meeting the goals and targets set for it?
   a. Planning stage
   b. Reviewing stage
   c. Executing stage
   d. Reporting stage

7. The net present value method of evaluating proposed capital investments
   a. measures an investment's time-adjusted rate of return.
   b. ignores cash flows beyond the payback period.
   c. applies only to mutually exclusive proposals.
   d. discounts cash flows at a company's minimum rate of return.

8. Cost analysis for capital investment decisions is best accomplished by techniques that
   a. accrue, defer, and allocate costs to short time periods.
   b. emphasize the liquidity of invested costs.
   c. measure total cash flows over a project's life.
   d. clearly distinguish between different equivalent unit computations.

9. Pine Industries is considering a $500,000 capital investment project that has the following projected cash flows:

Year	Net Cash Inflows
1	$160,000
2	140,000
3	120,000
4	80,000
5	60,000
6	30,000

The payback period is

a. 3.2 years.

b. 3.0 years.

c. 4.0 years.

d. 6.0 years.

APPLYING YOUR KNOWLEDGE

Exercises

1. A company is considering the purchase of a machine to produce the plastic chin protectors used in ice hockey. The machine costs $70,000 and will have a five-year life (no residual value). It is expected to produce $8,000 per year in net income (after depreciation). The company's desired rate of return is 25 percent, and the minimum payback period is three years. The company uses straight-line depreciation.

   a. Determine the accounting rate of return.

   b. Using the payback period method, determine whether the company should invest in the machine. Show all your work.

2. A machine that costs $20,000 (no residual value) will produce net cash inflows of $8,000 in the first year of operations and $6,000 in the remaining four years of use. The company's desired rate of return is 16 percent. Present value information for the 16 percent rate of return is as follows:

   Present value of $1 due in 1 year   = .862
   Present value of $1 due in 2 years = .743
   Present value of $1 due in 3 years = .641
   Present value of $1 due in 4 years = .552
   Present value of $1 due in 5 years = .476

   Using the net present value method, determine whether the company should purchase the machine.

3. Quality Donut Company is considering the acquisition of a new automatic donut dropper machine that will cost $400,000. The machine will have a life of five years and produce a cash savings from operations of $160,000 per year. The asset is to be depreciated using the straight-line method and will have a residual value of $40,000 at the end of its useful life. The company's management expects a 20 percent minimum rate of return on all investments and a maximum payback period of three years.

   a. What is the amount of depreciation per year?

   b. What is the accounting rate of return on the machine?

   c. What will the payback period on this machine be?

   d. What is the present value of future net cash inflows?

   e. Should the company invest in this machine?

Crossword Puzzle
for Chapters 11 and 12

ACROSS

2. Type of cost engineered into a product at the design stage

7. _____ value (undepreciated balance)

8. Return on _____ pricing

11. Change caused by a one-unit change in output (2 words)

12. Amount of an investment at a later date (2 words)

14. _____ cost (competitive market price minus desired profit)

16. With 5-Down, benefits, such as reduced costs

18. Equity or _____ financing

19. Having several operating segments

DOWN

1. Weighted-average rate of return paid for use of funds (3 words)

3. Amount charged when goods or services are exchanged between a company's divisions(2 words)

4. _____-run pricing strategy

5. See 16-Across

6. Accounting rate-of-_____ method

9. _____ value of money

10. Cost of using money

13. Supervisor, e.g. (abbreviation)

15. _____ and materials pricing method

17. Present value _____ a single sum

CHAPTER 13 QUALITY MANAGEMENT AND MEASUREMENT

REVIEWING THE CHAPTER

Objective 1: Describe a management information system and explain how it enhances the management cycle.

1. A **management information system (MIS)** is a reporting system that identifies, monitors, and maintains continuous, detailed analyses of a company's activities and provides managers with timely measures of operating results. An MIS captures both financial and nonfinancial information. It is designed to support total quality management, the just-in-time operating philosophy, activity-based costing and activity-based management, and other management philosophies. The primary focus of an MIS is on activities, not costs. By focusing on activities, it provides managers with improved knowledge of the processes under their control. The MIS pinpoints resource usage for each activity and fosters management decisions that lead to continuous improvement throughout the organization.

2. A management information system can be designed as a customized, informally linked series of systems for specific purposes, such as financial reporting, product costing, and process measurement, or as a fully integrated database system known as an **enterprise resource planning (ERP) system.** An ERP system manages all major business functions through one easy-to-access centralized data warehouse.

3. A management information system supplies managers with relevant, reliable information through-

out the management cycle. During the planning stage, managers use the MIS database to obtain the information they need for for formulating strategic plans, making forecasts, and preparing budgets. During the executing stage, managers use the financial and nonfinancial information in the MIS database to implement decisions about personnel, resources, and activities that will minimize waste and improve quality. As managers evaluate all major business functions during the reviewing stage, they use the system to track financial and nonfinancial measures of performance. During the reporting stage, an MIS helps managers generate customized reports that evaluate performance and provide useful information for decision making.

Objective 2: Define *total quality management (TQM)* and identify financial and nonfinancial measures of quality.

4. **Total quality management (TQM)** is an organizational environment in which all business functions work together to build quality into a firm's products or services. The first step in creating a total quality environment is to identify and manage the financial measures of quality, or the costs of quality. The second step is to analyze operating performance using nonfinancial measures and to require that all business processes and products or services be improved continuously.

5. **Quality** is the result of an operating environment in which a company's product or service meets a

customer's specifications the first time it is produced or delivered. **Costs of quality** are costs associated with the achievement or nonachievement of product or service quality. The costs of quality have two components: the costs of conformance and the costs of nonconformance.

    a. **Costs of conformance** are the costs incurred to produce a quality product or service. They include **prevention costs** (the costs of preventing failures) and **appraisal costs** (the costs of measuring quality).

    b. **Costs of nonconformance** are the costs incurred to correct the defects of a product or service. They include **internal failure costs** (costs resulting from defects discovered before shipment) and **external failure costs** (costs resulting from defects discovered after shipment).

    c. There is an inverse relationship between the cost of conformance and the cost of nonconformance; if the cost of one is low, the cost of the other is likely to be high. An organization's overall goal is to avoid the costs of nonconformance because these costs affect customer satisfaction. High initial costs of conformance can be justified if they minimize the total costs of quality over a product's or service's life cycle.

6. Measuring the costs of quality helps a company track how much it has spent in its efforts to improve product or service quality. Nonfinancial measures of quality are used to supplement the cost-based measures. By monitoring and controlling nonfinancial measures, managers can maximize the financial return from operations. Nonfinancial measures of quality include measures of product design, vendor performance, production performance, delivery cycle time, and customer satisfaction.

    a. To improve the quality of product design, many businesses use **computer-aided design (CAD).** CAD is a computer-based engineering system that can detect flaws in product design before production begins.

    b. To ensure that high-quality materials are available when needed, managers monitor the performance of vendors by using measures of quality (such as defect-free materials as a percentage of total deliveries) and measures of delivery (such as on-time deliveries as a percentage of total deliveries).

    c. To improve production performance by reducing waste caused by defective products, scrapped parts, machine maintenance, and downtime, many companies use **computer integrated manufacturing (CIM) systems.** In these systems, production and its support activities are coordinated by computers. Most direct labor hours are replaced by machine hours.

    d. To evaluate their responsiveness to customers, companies measure **delivery cycle time**—the time between acceptance of an order and final delivery of the product or service. The delivery cycle time consists of the **purchase order lead** time (the time it takes for materials to be ordered and received so that production can begin), **production cycle time** (the time it takes to make a product), and **delivery time** (the time between the product's completion and the customer's receipt of the product).

    e. Measures of customer satisfaction include the number and types of customer complaints, the number and causes of warranty claims, and the percentage of shipments returned as a percentage of total shipments.

7. Many measures of the costs of quality and several of the nonfinancial measures of quality apply directly to services and can be used by any type of service organization. For example, a service business can measure customer satisfaction by tracking the number of services accepted or rejected, the number of customer complaints, and the number of returning customers.

Objective 3: Use measures of quality to evaluate operating performance.

8. In analyzing the costs of quality, managers examine the costs of conformance to customer standards, including prevention costs and appraisal costs, and the costs of nonconformance to customer standards, including internal failure costs and external failure costs. By analyzing the costs of quality, as well as nonfinancial measures of quality, managers help a firm meet its goal of continuously improving the production process and product or service quality.

Objective 4: Discuss the evolving concept of quality.

9. Over the years, to meet customers' needs and the demands of a changing business environment, the concept of quality has been constantly evolving. Among the concepts that preceded TQM was re-**turn on quality (ROQ). ROQ** is the trade-off between the costs and benefits of improving quality; the high costs of consistent quality are weighed

against the expected higher returns. In the 1980s, companies emphasized **kaizen,** the continual improvement of quality and processes and the reduction of costs. By the end of the 1980s, companies that applied these concepts had achieved high levels of product reliability.

10. Among the techniques that evolved to help managers understand and measure quality improvements are benchmarking and process mapping. **Benchmarking** is the measurement of the gap between the quality of a company's process and the quality of a parallel process at the best-in-class company. **Process mapping** is a method of diagramming process inputs, outputs, constraints, and flows to help managers identify unnecessary efforts and inefficiencies in a business process.

Objective 5: Recognize the awards and organizations that promote quality.

11. Many awards have been established to recognize and promote the importance of quality. In 1951, the Japanese Union of Scientists and Engineers created the Deming Prize to honor individuals or groups who contribute to the development and dissemination of total quality control. This organization also created the **Deming Application Prize,** which honors companies that achieve distinctive results by carrying out total quality control. In 1987, the U.S. Congress established the **Malcolm Baldrige Quality Award** to recognize U.S. organizations for their achievements in quality and business performance and to raise awareness about the importance of these factors.

12. The International Organization for Standardization (ISO) promotes standardization with a view to facilitating the international exchange of goods and services. To standardize quality management and quality assurance, the ISO developed **ISO 9000,** a set of guidelines covering the design, development, production, final inspection and testing, installation, and servicing of products, processes, and services. To become ISO-certified, an organization must pass a rigorous audit of its manufacturing and service processes.

SELF-TEST

Test your knowledge of the chapter by choosing the best answer for each item below.

1. A management information system
   a. identifies nonvalue-adding activities.
   b. supports just-in-time and activity-based management philosophies.
   c. relies on the concept of continuous improvement to reduce costs and increase quality.
   d. does all of the above.

2. A management information system focuses primarily on
   a. costs.
   b. activities.
   c. net income.
   d. departments.

3. The costs of quality are the total costs of
   a. prevention and appraisal.
   b. internal and external failures.
   c. conformance and nonconformance.
   d. conformance and appraisal.

4. The commitment to quality that underlies TQM operations would justify
   a. prevention costs in excess of internal failure costs.
   b. costs of nonconformance in excess of the costs of conformance.
   c. internal failure costs in excess of appraisal costs.
   d. prevention and appraisal costs in excess of the costs of conformance.

5. The rate of defects per million units produced is a nonfinancial measure of
   a. raw materials input.
   b. product design.
   c. customer acceptance.
   d. production quality.

6. Which of the following costs of quality is a cost of nonconformance?
   a. Cost of inspecting materials
   b. Cost of technical support for vendors
   c. Cost of inspecting rework
   d. Cost of design review

7. Which of the following are prevention costs?
   a. Cost of quality training for employees
   b. Cost of developing an integrated system
   c. Cost of technical support for vendors
   d. All of the above

8. Which of the following is *not* a nonfinancial measure of product quality?
   a. Inventory turnover rate
   b. Number of warranty claims
   c. Data on vendor deliveries
   d. Trend in number of customer complaints

9. The time between acceptance of an order and final delivery of the product or service is called
   a. delivery time.
   b. purchase order lead time.
   c. production cycle time.
   d. delivery cycle time.

10. Which of the following is a set of standards for quality management and quality assurance?
    a. Malcolm Baldrige Quality Award
    b. Deming Application Prize
    c. ISO 9000
    d. None of the above

TESTING YOUR KNOWLEDGE

Matching*

Match each term with its definition by writing the appropriate letter in the blank.

_____ 1. Computer-aided design (CAD)

_____ 2. Total quality management (TQM)

_____ 3. Costs of conformance

_____ 4. Appraisal costs

_____ 5. Internal failure costs

_____ 6. Management information system (MIS)

_____ 7. Prevention costs

_____ 8. External failure costs

_____ 9. Delivery cycle time

_____ 10. Benchmarking

a. The costs of activities that measure, evaluate, or audit products, processes, or services to ensure conformance to quality standards and performance requirements

b. A computer-based engineering system that can detect design flaws

c. A reporting system that identifies, monitors, and maintains continuous, detailed analyses of a company's activities and provides managers with timely measures of operating results

d. The costs incurred to produce a quality product or service

e. The costs incurred when defects are discovered after a product or service has been delivered to a customer

f. The measurement of the gap between the quality of a company's process and the quality of a parallel process at the best-in-class company

g. The costs incurred when defects are discovered before a product or service is delivered to a customer

h. Time between acceptance of an order and final delivery of the product or service to the customer

i. The costs associated with the prevention of defects and failures in products and services

j. An organizational environment in which all business functions work together to build quality into a firm's products or services

---

*Note to student: The matching quiz might be completed more efficiently by starting with the definition and searching for the corresponding term.

Short Answer

Use the lines provided to answer each item.

1. Briefly explain how a management information system enhances the management cycle.

　_____

　_____

　_____

　_____

2. Identify the costs of conformance and the costs of nonconformance, and give two examples of each of these cost categories.

　_____

　_____

　_____

　_____

　_____

　_____

3. Identify the nonfinancial measures of quality, and explain why they are important in maximizing profits.

　_____

　_____

　_____

　_____

　_____

　_____

True-False

Circle T if the statement is true, F if it is false. Provide explanations for the false answers, using the blank lines at the end of the section.

T F 1. CAD is the acronym for commonly adjusted defects.

T F 2. The only valid measurements of quality are financial in nature.

T F 3. The costs of quality are the costs associated with the achievement or nonachievement of product or service quality.

T F 4. As the costs of conformance increase, the costs of nonconformance generally also increase.

T F 5. Benchmarking is a method of diagramming process inputs, outputs, constraints, and flows to help managers identify unnecessary efforts and inefficiencies in a business process.

T F 6. Over the long run, the costs of conformance are less expensive than the costs of nonconformance.

T F 7. Without an effective system of performance measurement, a company is unable to identify the improvements needed to increase profitability.

T F 8. Reductions in delivery cycle time have a negative impact on income.

T F 9. Prevention costs and appraisal costs are components of the costs of conformance.

T F 10. The Malcolm Baldrige Quality Award honors U.S. organizations for achieving high net profits.

_____   _____
_____   _____
_____   _____
_____   _____
_____   _____
_____   _____
_____   _____
_____   _____

Multiple Choice

Circle the letter of the best answer.

1. Which of the following is *not* characteristic of a management information system?
   a. Fosters continuous improvement
   b. Provides only historical cost information
   c. Supports total quality management
   d. Focuses on managing activities

2. Which of the following would *not* be considered a cost of conformance?
   a. Cost of inspecting rework
   b. Cost of vendor audits and sample testing
   c. Cost of product simulation and development
   d. Cost of design review

3. The overall objective of controlling the costs of quality is to eliminate
   a. appraisal costs.
   b. costs of nonconformance.
   c. costs of quality.
   d. costs of conformance.

4. SafeWorld Corporation produces custom-designed safety gear for police vehicles. During April 20xx, the company had the following costs of quality:

Product testing costs	$11,200
Product warranty claims	13,000
Scrap and rework costs	10,500
Product design costs	18,900
Employee training costs	10,100
Product simulation costs	16,400

Total costs of conformance for the month were
   a. $80,100.
   b. $56,600.
   c. $40,200.
   d. $42,400.

5. Assuming the same facts as in **4**, total costs of nonconformance for the month were
   a. $42,400.
   b. $40,200.
   c. $23,500.
   d. $13,000.

6. Nonfinancial measures of quality are important to TQM operations because
   a. cost drivers are identified.
   b. reporting nonfinancial measures encourages continuous improvement of production processes, which results in products of higher quality.
   c. to ensure high-quality products or services, managers need both nonfinancial and financial information
   d. All of the above

7. Production cycle time is the time
   a. between a product's completion and the customer's receipt of the product.
   b. it takes to make a product.
   c. it takes for materials to be ordered and received so that production can begin.
   d. between receipt of a customer's order and shipment to the customer.

8. What are the two components of the costs of quality?
   a. Conformance and nonconformance costs
   b. Appraisal and prevention costs
   c. Prevention and conformance costs
   d. Internal and external costs

9. Delivery cycle time consists of
   a. production cycle time and delivery time.
   b. delivery time and purchase order lead time.
   c. purchase order lead time, production cycle time, and delivery time.
   d. none of the above.

10. Company A and Company B generate the same amount of annual revenues and incurred the following costs of quality during the past year:

    Company A:

Conformance costs	$1,750,000
Nonconformance costs	1,650,000
Total	$3,400,000

    Company B:

Conformance costs	$1,000,000
Nonconformance costs	200,000
Total	$1,200,000

    Based on this information, which company is likely to have a higher level of product quality?

    a. Company A, because it spends more on the costs of quality
    b. Company B, because it spends less on the costs of quality
    c. Company A, because its costs of conformance exceed those of Company B
    d. Company B, because its costs of conformance far exceed its costs of nonconformance

APPLYING YOUR KNOWLEDGE

Exercises

1. At the beginning of the year, Cline Industries initiated a quality improvement program. The program was successful in reducing scrap and rework costs. To help assess the impact of the quality improvement program, the following data were collected for the past two years:

	20x4	20x5
Sales	$1,200,000	$1,500,000
Scrap	20,000	15,000
Rework	50,000	35,000
Prototype design	38,000	42,000
Product simulation	6,000	9,000
Quality training	20,000	30,000
Materials testing	4,000	6,000
Product warranty	40,000	25,000

a. What were the total costs of conformance for the two years?

b. What were the total costs of nonconformance for the two years?

c. Was the quality improvement program successful? Defend your answer.

2. The lab department of Shamrock Hospital is in the process of evaluating its costs of quality. Identify each of the following items as related to the costs of conformance (CC) or the costs of nonconformance (CN):

_____ a. Preventive maintenance on equipment

_____ b. Patient complaints

_____ c. Training of lab technicians

_____ d. Redoing of lab tests

_____ e. Inspection of processes and machines

_____ f. Machine downtime

_____ g. Monitoring of the quality of lab supplies received from vendors

CHAPTER 14 ALLOCATION OF INTERNAL SERVICE COSTS AND JOINT PRODUCT COSTS

REVIEWING THE CHAPTER

Objective 1: Discuss the allocation of internal service costs.

1. All companies have departments or centers that provide services internally to support the activities of the business. To ensure long-term profitability, the cost of these services must be included in the full cost of the company's products or services. The **full cost** includes not only the costs of direct materials and direct labor, but also the costs of all production and nonproduction activities required to satisfy the customer.

2. **Common costs** are the mutually beneficial indirect costs of providing internal services. The process of assigning indirect costs to specific cost objects is called **cost allocation**. The allocation process shifts costs from the centers that provide internal services, which do not bill parties outside the company, to the centers that benefit from those services and that do bill external parties for products or services sold. The company is then able to calculate the full cost of its products or services and set prices accordingly.

3. How a company assigns the costs of internal services has a significant effect on its other costs and its profitability. Managers address this concern at each stage of the management cycle.
   a. In the planning stage, managers select a method of assigning the costs of the service providers to the centers that benefit from the services. They also select an allocation base for measuring the usage of each service.
   b. In the executing stage, managers control the costs of their centers. They use the allocation method and base specified in the planning stage to assign the service centers' costs. An overhead rate is applied to determine the total cost and unit cost of a product or service.
   c. During the reviewing stage, managers evaluate customer profitability and product or service performance. They also evaluate the appropriateness of the allocation base and method and make any necessary adjustments.
   d. In the reporting stage, managers use cost allocation reports to monitor costs and the methods and bases of assigning costs.

Objective 2: Define the two kinds of responsibility centers used in the allocation of service costs.

4. A **responsibility center** is an organizational unit whose manager is responsible for managing a portion of the company's resources. For the purpose of allocating internal service costs, a responsibility center is classified as a revenue center or a service center.
   a. A **revenue center** (also called a *producing center* or *operating center*) is directly responsible for producing products or services sold to external buyers. Revenue centers not only incur their own traceable costs; they are also assigned the costs of the other responsibility centers from which they benefit.
   b. A **service center** (also known as a *support center* or *discretionary cost center*) is a responsibility center that provides benefits to

other responsibility centers. Traceable costs of a service center are collected and controlled by that center and are then assigned to other centers using an appropriate cost driver as an allocation base.

   c. A **cost driver** is an activity that causes another center's use of a service center. The table at the bottom of the page lists some examples of service centers and their cost drivers.

Objective 3: Use the direct method to assign service costs.

5. The **direct method** assigns the cost of service centers to revenue centers only; it ignores the fact that service centers provide support to other service centers. The three steps of the direct method are as follows:

   a. *Step 1.* Calculate allocation fractions. An allocation fraction is a revenue center's specific cost driver amount divided by the sum of all revenue centers' cost driver amounts.

   b. *Step 2.* Determine the dollar amount to assign to each revenue center by multiplying each service center's total costs by the corresponding revenue center's allocation fraction calculated in Step 1.

   c. *Step 3.* Total the costs for each revenue center. This amount includes the assigned service costs and the other costs incurred in the revenue center.

Objective 4: Use the step method to assign service costs.

6. Like the direct method, the **step method** is an activity-based method of allocating costs. However, this method recognizes that service centers provide support not only to revenue centers, but also to other service centers. The step method assigns service center costs to both service and revenue centers based on descending order of use. The costs of the service center used most by other centers are assigned first; the costs of the service center used least by other service centers are as-

signed last. Once the costs of a service center have been assigned, that center cannot be assigned costs from any other service center. Because the steps taken in the step method resemble steps in a staircase, this method is also known as the *step-down method.* The sequence of steps is as follows:.

   a. *Step 1.* Calculate the allocation fraction by dividing a center's specific cost driver amount by the sum of all the other open centers' cost driver amounts. Only the cost driver amounts for the open service centers and revenue centers are used in determining the allocation fraction.

   b. *Step 2.* Determine the dollar amount to assign to each open service center and each revenue center by multiplying each service center's total costs by the corresponding service or revenue center's allocation fraction calculated in Step 1.

   c. *Step 3.* Total the costs for each revenue center.

Objective 5: Describe other methods of service cost allocation, including the two-step method, the simultaneous equation method, the ability to pay method, and the physical measures method.

7. Under the **two-step method,** the step method is performed twice: first, to apportion all service costs among the service centers, with no service center closed to accepting costs; second, to assign all service centers' costs to the revenue centers.

8. Under the **simultaneous equation method** (also called the *reciprocal method*), a cost formula is set up for each service and revenue center; the formula expresses a center's full usage of all other centers' services. All formulas are then solved to determine the full cost of each revenue center.

9. Under the **ability to pay method,** the revenue centers with the greatest ability to pay absorb most of the service centers' costs. If sales dollars are used as the cost driver, the revenue centers

Service Centers	*Possible Cost Drivers*
Housekeeping Service	Square footage occupied by the departments serviced
Truck Maintenance	Number of work orders, minutes spent, number of deliveries
Utilities	Kilowatt hours, square feet, number of departments
Distribution	Number of sorted and repacked items, dollar amount of sorted and repacked items
Shipping Dock	Number of truckloads, number of items in shipment, weight of shipment

with the highest dollar sales are assigned more of the service centers' costs than their less successful counterparts.

10. The **physical measures method** is based on the number of centers rather than on an activity of the centers. A service center's costs are divided by the number of centers that use its services and are assigned in equal portions.

Objective 6: Explain how service cost allocation relates to overhead rates.

11. Once the costs of service centers have been assigned to revenue centers, they are combined with each revenue center's overhead (i.e., the center's traceable indirect costs). A single departmental overhead rate or several activity-based overhead rates are then computed for each revenue center. The rates are used to apply indirect costs to products and services.

12. A **departmental overhead rate** is a single rate that includes all of a department's overhead costs. It is used to determine the full cost of a product or service. The formula is as follows:

$$\frac{\text{Revenue Center Overhead} + \text{Assigned Service Center Costs}}{\text{Cost Driver}} = \text{Overhead Rate}$$

13. Activity-based costing rates are multiple overhead rates based on a revenue center's activities. They are used to assign the costs of the activities to a product or service to determine its full cost.

Objective 7: Apply allocation methods to the costs associated with joint products.

14. **Joint products** are two or more products produced simultaneously from a common material. Some joint products are called **by-products** because their sales value is minor in comparison with the value of the other products with which they are produced.

15. **Joint costs** are the processing costs and materials costs incurred in making joint products. The **split-off point** is the point in the production process at which products first become identifiable as separate products or by-products. Costs incurred after the split-off point that are traceable to the individual products are called **separable costs.**

16. Three methods are commonly used to allocate joint costs to products. The **physical units method** assigns joint costs to products based on physical quantities, such as weight, volume, or units. The **relative sales value method** assigns joint costs to products based on the products' sales value at the split-off point. The **net realizable method** assigns joint costs to products based on their eventual sales value less any separable costs needed to make them salable.

SELF-TEST

Test your knowledge of the chapter by choosing the best answer for each item below.

1. The full cost of a product includes
   a. only costs of direct materials and direct labor.
   b. only costs of direct labor.
   c. costs of direct materials, direct labor, and all production and nonproduction activities.
   d. only costs of all production and nonproduction activities.

2. Which of the following is *not* an activity that managers perform in the reviewing stage of the management cycle?
   a. Evaluating customer profitability
   b. Analyzing the performance of products and services
   c. Evaluating allocation methods
   d. Determining cost allocation methods and allocation bases

3. A revenue center is a
   a. responsibility center that is directly responsible for producing products or services sold to external buyers.
   b. responsibility center that is directly responsible for providing services to internal departments.
   c. center that never accepts costs from other departments.
   d. center that is controlled by all of the service centers that assign costs to the center.

4. Which of the following can be used as a cost driver?
   a. Number of purchase orders
   b. Utilities
   c. Department manager
   d. Housekeeping service

5. The method of allocating service costs that is also called the *reciprocal method* is the
   a. full recognition method.
   b. simultaneous equation method.
   c. step method.
   d. direct method.

6. Using the direct method to assign costs involves
   a. calculating allocation fractions.
   b. totaling the costs for each revenue center.
   c. determining the dollar amount to assign to each revenue center.
   d. doing all of the above.

7. The physical measures method allocates internal service costs by the number of _____ that use the services.
   a. customers
   b. employees
   c. centers
   d. service centers

8. A responsibility center is
   a. a center that supports the activities of other centers.
   b. a center that is directly responsible for producing products or services sold to external buyers.
   c. an organizational unit whose manager is responsible for managing a portion of the company's resources.
   d. none of the above.

9. The step method assigns costs
   a. based on ascending order of use.
   b. based on descending order of use.
   c. from the revenue center that uses the cost center the most.
   d. from the revenue center that uses the cost center the least.

10. Managers use service cost allocation to
    a. determine the full cost of a service or product.
    b. control costs for individual centers.
    c. determine a selling price.
    d. do all of the above.

TESTING YOUR KNOWLEDGE

Matching*

Match each term with its definition by writing the appropriate letter in the blank.

_____ **1.** Cost driver

_____ **2.** Departmental overhead rate

_____ **3.** Common costs

_____ **4.** Simultaneous equation method

_____ **5.** Two-step method

_____ **6.** Responsibility center

_____ **7.** Direct method

_____ **8.** Physical measures method

_____ **9.** Revenue center

_____ **10.** Ability to pay method

a. Mutually beneficial indirect costs of providing internal services

b. An activity that causes another center's use of a service center

c. An activity-based cost allocation method that assigns the costs of service centers to revenue centers only

d. A responsibility center that is directly responsible for producing products or services sold to external buyers

e. A cost allocation method based on the number of centers

f. A method of cost allocation in which the revenue centers with the highest dollar sales absorb most of the service centers' costs

g. A single rate that includes all of a department's overhead costs and that is used to determine the full cost of a product or service

h. An activity-based cost allocation method in which a cost formula expressing a center's full usage of all other centers' services is set up for each service and revenue center

i. An activity-based method of cost allocation in which the step method is performed twice: first, to apportion all service costs among the service centers, with no service center closed to accepting costs, and then to assign all service centers' costs to revenue centers

j. An organizational unit whose manager is responsible for managing a portion of the company's resources

---

*Note to student: The matching quiz might be completed more efficiently by starting with the definition and searching for the corresponding term.

Short Answer

Use the lines provided to answer each item.

1. List the three steps involved in using the step method.

_____

_____

_____

_____

_____

2. List the three steps involved in using the direct method.

_____

_____

_____

_____

_____

3. How do managers use cost allocation reports in the reporting stage of the management cycle?

_____

_____

_____

4. Classify each of the following as either (1) a service center that assigns its costs internally or (2) a revenue center that directly charges external parties.

_____ Branch store

_____ Distribution center

_____ Customer service center

_____ Technology support center

_____ Receptionist

_____ Auto repair service

_____ Physician services

5. List at least four cost drivers that an accounting department could use.

_____

_____

_____

_____

True-False

Circle T if the statement is true, F if it is false. Provide explanations for the false answers, using the blank lines at the end of the section.

T F 1. In the executing stage of the management cycle, managers control the costs of their centers.

T F 2. The number of patient days, number of beds, and number of patient visits could be used as cost drivers for assigning the costs of an inpatient care center.

T F 3. The direct method assigns the costs of service and revenue centers only to service centers.

T F 4. The simultaneous equation method determines the full cost of each revenue center because each center is assigned costs based on its full usage of all other centers' services.

T F 5. A center's full cost is composed of direct materials and direct labor.

T F 6. The amount billed to a customer should include both traceable and assigned costs.

T F 7. A company's total costs will change depending on the method of cost allocation used.

T F 8. Activity centers of a distribution center may include shipping, receiving, repackaging, fuel, and utilities.

T F 9. The ability to pay method encourages revenue centers to increase their sales because the more they sell, the lower their assigned costs will be.

T F 10. A departmental overhead rate is a single rate that includes all of a department's overhead costs.

T F 11. A responsibility center is an organizational unit whose manager is responsible for managing a portion of the company's resources.

T F 12. Activity-based overhead rates help managers manage and control different types of overhead costs.

_____

_____

_____

_____

_____

_____

_____

_____

_____

_____

_____

_____

_____

_____

_____

_____

_____

_____

_____

_____

_____

_____

_____

_____

_____

_____

Multiple Choice

Circle the letter of the best answer.

1. This year, the activity centers of Salas Export Company incurred the following costs: Distribution Center, $15,000; Administrative Center, $20,000; Documentation Center, $40,000; U.S. Revenue Center, $50,000; Mexican Revenue Center, $60,000. What will the company's total costs be after assigning the costs of the service centers to the revenue centers?
   a. $110,000
   b. $75,000
   c. $185,000
   d. $35,000

2. Based on the information in 1, what are the full costs to the Mexican Revenue Center if the company uses the physical measures method to allocate internal service costs?
   a. $60,000
   b. $75,000
   c. $97,500
   d. None of the above

3. The U.S. Revenue Center's total sales were $250,000; the Mexican Revenue Center's total sales were $500,000. Based on the information in **1,** what are the full costs to the U.S. Revenue Center if the company uses the ability to pay method to allocate internal service costs?
   a. $75,000
   b. $60,000
   c. $35,000
   d. $110,000

4. Which of the following methods is also known as the *reciprocal method*?
   a. Ability to pay method
   b. Step method
   c. Simultaneous equation method
   d. Full-cost method

5. A departmental overhead rate is best defined as
   a. a single rate that includes all overhead costs of a department.
   b. an activity cost driver.
   c. an allocation fraction.
   d. a profitability rate.

6. A revenue center's specific cost driver amount divided by the sum of all revenue centers' cost driver amounts is
   a. an activity cost driver.
   b. the departmental overhead rate.
   c. a physical measure.
   d. an allocation fraction.

7. During the planning stage of the management cycle, managers
   a. control the costs of individual centers.
   b. determine the cost allocation method and allocation base to be used.
   c. use cost allocation reports to monitor costs.
   d. assign the costs of service centers to revenue centers.

8. Which of the following cost drivers would be *most* appropriate for allocating the costs of a collection department?
   a. Number of square feet
   b. Number of customer accounts
   c. Total sales of a revenue center
   d. Number of employees

9. For which of the following service centers would number of employees be a suitable cost driver?
   a. Distribution and purchasing centers
   b. Payroll and purchasing centers
   c. Payroll and human resources centers
   d. Human resources and hazardous waste centers

10. The advantages of service cost allocation include
    a. improved information for decision making.
    b. full knowledge of all costs of products and services.
    c. evaluation of customer profitability.
    d. all of the above.

11. A service center is a
    a. responsibility center that provides benefits to other responsibility centers.
    b. responsibility center that provides benefits only to revenue centers.
    c. revenue center that provides benefits to its customers.
    d. revenue center that provides benefits to other service centers.

12. In which stage of the management cycle do managers evaluate customer profitability and product or service performance?
    a. Reviewing
    b. Reporting
    c. Executing
    d. Planning

13. Which of the following is a major disadvantage of using the ability to pay method for cost allocation?
    a. All centers pay the same amount regardless of their actual use.
    b. With this method, it is very difficult to allocate costs.
    c. Managers will increase expenses in order to decrease the allocation of costs to their center.
    d. Because revenue centers with the greatest ability to pay absorb most of the service centers' costs, the manager of a revenue center with increased sales may feel penalized rather than rewarded.

14. Common costs are
    a. direct materials, direct labor, and overhead costs that are traceable to the service of a revenue center.
    b. direct materials and direct labor costs that are traceable to the service of a revenue center.
    c. mutually beneficial indirect costs of a service center that benefits and supports many products and services.
    d. indirect costs of a service center that benefits and supports only one product or service.

APPLYING YOUR KNOWLEDGE

Exercises

1. Sound Bits Company manufactures and sells MP3 players. It specializes in two product lines: car stereos and portable players. The company has several service centers that provide support to the two revenue centers. The costs and cost drivers are as follows:

Center	Total Cost	Cost Driver
Accounting	$ 50,000	Number of employees
Purchasing	80,000	Number of purchase orders
MIS	30,000	Number of reports
Utilities	35,000	Square footage
Advertising	75,000	Number of newspaper ads
Car Stereos	200,000	
Portable Players	350,000	

The following chart shows the usage of the activity centers:

Activity Center	Number of Employees	Number of Purchase Orders	Number of Reports	Square Footage	Number of Newspaper Ads
Accounting	20	200	2,000	10,000	0
Purchasing	15	100	1,000	12,000	0
MIS	8	75	200	5,000	0
Utilities	2	25	50	1,000	0
Advertising	5	100	150	2,000	0
Car Stereos	200	2,000	1,500	100,000	300
Portable Players	650	2,500	1,100	150,000	700
Total	900	5,000	6,000	280,000	1,000

Use the space on the next page to calculate the total costs for each revenue center using (a) the direct method and (b) the step method.

a. Direct method

b. Step method (Assign costs by the highest dollar
amount of the service centers.)

2. Match the following service centers with the *best* possible cost driver:

Service Center	Possible Cost Driver
_____ Utilities	a. Number of work orders, number of hours spent
_____ Purchasing	b. Number of reports, number of processing nanoseconds
_____ Human Resources	
_____ Maintenance	c. Minutes spent, number of pages
_____ MIS	d. Number of purchase orders
_____ Secretarial Pool	e. Number of items sorted
_____ Mailroom	f. Kilowatt hours, square feet
	g. Number of employees

3. All Store Company assigns the costs of its Payroll Department to three revenue centers. The centers and their gross sales are as follows:

Revenue Center	Gross Sales
Cosmetics	$350,000
Housewares	500,000
Tools	650,000

a. If the Payroll Department incurs costs of $12,500, how much will be assigned to each revenue center if the company uses the ability to pay method?

b. If the Payroll Department incurs costs of $15,000, how much will be assigned to each revenue center if the company uses the physical measures method?

c. The Cosmetics, Housewares, and Tools centers have 100, 500, and 250 employees, respectively. How much will be assigned to each of these revenue centers if the Payroll Department incurs costs of $25,500 and the company uses the direct method?

CHAPTER 15 FINANCIAL PERFORMANCE EVALUATION

REVIEWING THE CHAPTER

Objective 1: Describe and discuss financial performance evaluation by internal and external users.

1. **Financial performance evaluation,** or *financial statement analysis,* comprises all the techniques users of financial statements employ to show important relationships in an organization's financial statements and to relate them to important financial objectives. Internal users of financial statements include top managers, who set and strive to achieve financial performance objectives; middle-level managers of business processes; and employee stockholders. External users are creditors and investors who want to assess how well management has accomplished its financial objectives, as well as customers who have cooperative agreements with the company.

2. During the planning phase of the management cycle, managers set financial performance objectives that will achieve the company's strategic goals. In the executing phase, they carry out plans designed to achieve those objectives. In the reviewing phase, they monitor financial performance measures to determine causes for deviations in the measures and propose corrective actions. In the reporting phase, they develop reports that compare actual performance with planned performance in achieving key business objectives.

3. Most creditors and investors put their funds into a **portfolio** to average the returns and risks of making loans and investments. However, they must still make decisions about which loans or stocks to put in their portfolios. In doing so, they use financial performance evaluation to judge a company's past performance and current financial position, as well as its future potential and the risk associated with that potential.

    a. In judging a company's past performance and current status, investors and creditors look at trends in past sales, expenses, net income, cash flows, and return on investment. They also look at a company's assets and liabilities, its debt in relation to equity, and its levels of inventories and receivables.

    b. Information about a company's past and present enables creditors and investors to make more accurate projections about its future—and the more accurate their projections are, the lower their risk of realizing a loss will be. In return for assuming a higher risk, creditors may charge higher interest rates or demand security on their loans; stock investors look for a higher return in the form of dividends or an increase in market price.

4. To bolster investor confidence in the financial reporting systems of public companies, the U.S. Congress passed broad legislation known as the **Sarbanes-Oxley Act**. In addition to establishing a Public Oversight Board for the accounting profession, the act requires top executives to attest to the accuracy of financial statements filed with the SEC and imposes criminal penalties for fraudulent financial reporting. It also specifies the composition and qualifications of audit committee members and requires the audit committee to appoint an auditor who does not consult for the company.

Objective 2: Describe and discuss the standards for financial performance evaluation.

5. When analyzing financial statements, decision makers commonly use three standards of comparison: rule-of-thumb measures, past performance of the company, and industry norms.

   a. Rule-of-thumb measures for key financial ratios are helpful but should not be the only basis for making a decision. For example, a company may report high earnings per share but lack the assets needed to pay current debts.

   b. Analysis of a company's past performance is helpful in showing current trends and may also indicate future trends. However, trends reverse at times, so projections based on past performance should be made with care.

   c. Using industry norms to compare a company's performance with the performance of other companies in the same industry has advantages, but it also has three limitations. First, the operations of two companies in the same industry may be so different that the companies cannot be compared. Second, **diversified companies,** or *conglomerates,* operate in many unrelated industries, which makes it difficult if not impossible to use industry norms as standards. (The FASB requirement that financial information be reported by segments has provided a partial solution to this problem.) Third, companies may use different acceptable accounting procedures for recording similar items.

Objective 3: Identify the sources of information for financial performance evaluation.

6. The major sources of information about publicly held corporations are reports published by the company, SEC reports, business periodicals, and credit and investment advisory services.

   a. A corporation's annual report provides much useful financial information. Its main sections are management's analysis of the past year's operations; the financial statements; the notes to the financial statements, which include a summary of significant accounting policies; the auditors' report; and financial highlights for a five- or ten-year period. Most public companies also publish **interim financial statements** each quarter. These reports present limited financial information in the form of condensed financial statements and may indicate significant trends in a company's earnings.

   b. Publicly held corporations must file an annual report with the SEC on Form 10-K, a quarterly report on Form 10-Q, and a current report of significant events on Form 8-K. These reports are available to the public and are a valuable source of financial information.

   c. Financial analysts obtain information from such sources as *The Wall Street Journal, Forbes, Barron's, Fortune,* the *Financial Times,* Moody's, Standard & Poor's, and Dun & Bradstreet.

Objective 4: Apply horizontal analysis, trend analysis, vertical analysis, and ratio analysis to financial statements.

7. The most widely used tools of financial analysis are horizontal analysis, trend analysis, vertical analysis, and ratio analysis.

   a. **Horizontal analysis** is commonly used to study comparative financial statements, which present data for the current year and previous year side by side. Horizontal analysis computes both dollar and percentage changes in specific items from one year to the next. The first year is called the **base year,** and the percentage change is computed by dividing the amount of the change by the base year amount.

   b. **Trend analysis** is like horizontal analysis, except that it calculates percentage changes for several consecutive years. To show changes in related items over time, trend analysis uses an **index number**, which is calculated by setting the base year equal to 100 percent.

   c. **Vertical analysis** uses percentages to show the relationship of individual items on a statement to a total within the statement (e.g., cost of goods sold as a percentage of net sales). The result is a **common-size statement.** On a common-size balance sheet, total assets are set at 100 percent, as are total liabilities and stockholders' equity; on a common-size income statement, net sales or net revenues are set at 100 percent. Comparative common-size statements enable analysts to identify changes both within a period and between periods They also make it easier to compare companies.

   d. **Ratio analysis** identifies meaningful relationships between the components of the financial statements. The primary purpose of ratios is to identify areas needing further investigation.

Objective 5: Apply ratio analysis to financial statements in a comprehensive evaluation of a company's financial performance.

8. The ratios used in ratio analysis provide information about a company's liquidity, profitability, long-term solvency, cash flow adequacy, and market strength. The most common ratios are shown in the table that follows.

Ratio	Components	Use
Liquidity Ratios		
Current ratio	$$\frac{\text{Current Assets}}{\text{Current Liabilities}}$$	Measure of short-term debt-paying ability
Quick ratio	$$\frac{\text{Cash + Marketable Securities + Receivables}}{\text{Current Liabilities}}$$	Measure of short-term debt-paying ability
Receivable turnover	$$\frac{\text{Net Sales}}{\text{Average Accounts Receivable}}$$	Measure of relative size of accounts receivable and effectiveness of credit policies
Average days' sales uncollected	$$\frac{\text{Days in Year}}{\text{Receivable Turnover}}$$	Measure of average days taken to collect receivables
Inventory turnover	$$\frac{\text{Cost of Goods Sold}}{\text{Average Inventory}}$$	Measure of relative size of inventory
Average days' inventory on hand	$$\frac{\text{Days in Year}}{\text{Inventory Turnover}}$$	Measure of average days taken to sell inventory
Payables turnover	$$\frac{\text{Cost of Goods Sold +/- Change in Inventory}}{\text{Average Accounts Payable}}$$	Measure of relative size of accounts payable
Average days' payable	$$\frac{\text{Days in Year}}{\text{Payables Turnover}}$$	Measure of average days taken to pay accounts payable

(**Note:** The **operating cycle** is the time taken to sell and collect for products sold. It equals average days' inventory on hand plus average days' sales uncollected.)

Ratio	Components	Use
Profitability Ratios		
Profit margin	$$\frac{\text{Net Income}}{\text{Net Sales}}$$	Measure of net income produced by each dollar of sales
Asset turnover	$$\frac{\text{Net Sales}}{\text{Average Total Assets}}$$	Measure of how efficiently assets are used to produce sales
Return on assets	$$\frac{\text{Net Income}}{\text{Average Total Assets}}$$	Measure of overall earning power or profitability
Return on equity	$$\frac{\text{Net Income}}{\text{Average Stockholders' Equity}}$$	Measure of the profitability of stockholders' investments
Long-Term Solvency Ratios		
Debt to equity ratio	$$\frac{\text{Total Liabilities}}{\text{Stockholders' Equity}}$$	Measure of capital structure and leverage
Interest coverage ratio	$$\frac{\text{Income Before Income Taxes + Interest Expense}}{\text{Interest Expense}}$$	Measure of creditors' protection from default on interest payments
Cash Flow Adequacy Ratios		
Cash flow yield	$$\frac{\text{Net Cash Flows from Operating Activities}}{\text{Net Income}}$$	Measure of the ability to generate operating cash flows in relation to net income
Cash flows to sales	$$\frac{\text{Net Cash Flows from Operating Activities}}{\text{Net Sales}}$$	Measure of the ability of sales to generate operating cash flows
Cash flows to assets	$$\frac{\text{Net Cash Flows from Operating Activities}}{\text{Average Total Assets}}$$	Measure of the ability of assets to generate operating cash flows
Free cash flow	Net Cash Flows from Operating Activities – Dividends – Net Capital Expenditures	Measure of cash generated or cash deficiency after providing for commitments
Market Strength Ratios		
Price/earnings (P/E) ratio	$$\frac{\text{Market Price per Share}}{\text{Earnings per Share}}$$	Measure of investor confidence in a company
Dividends yield	$$\frac{\text{Dividends per Share}}{\text{Market Price per Share}}$$	Measure of a stock's current return to an investor

Test your knowledge of the chapter by choosing the best answer for each of the following items.

1. A general rule in choosing among alternative investments is that the higher the risk involved, the
   a. greater the return expected.
   b. lower the profits expected.
   c. lower the potential expected.
   d. greater the price of the investment.

2. Which of the following is the most useful in evaluating whether a company has improved its position in relation to its competitors?
   a. Rule-of-thumb measures
   b. A company's past performance
   c. A company's past performance and current financial position
   d. Industry averages

3. One of the best places to look for early signals of change in a firm's profitability is the firm's
   a. interim financial statements.
   b. year-end financial statements.
   c. annual report sent to stockholders.
   d. annual report sent to the SEC.

4. Cash flow yield equals net cash flows from operating activities divided by
   a. average stockholders' equity.
   b. net income.
   c. average total assets.
   d. net sales.

5. In trend analysis, each item is expressed as a percentage of the
   a. net income figure.
   b. retained earnings figure.
   c. base year figure.
   d. total assets figure.

6. In a common-size balance sheet for a wholesale company, which of the following could represent the 100 percent figure?
   a. Merchandise inventory
   b. Total current assets
   c. Total property, plant, and equipment
   d. Total assets

7. The best way to study the changes in financial statements between two years is to prepare
   a. common-size statements.
   b. a trend analysis.
   c. a horizontal analysis.
   d. a ratio analysis.

8. A common measure of liquidity is
   a. return on assets.
   b. profit margin.
   c. inventory turnover.
   d. interest coverage ratio.

9. Asset turnover is most closely related to
   a. profit margin and return on assets.
   b. profit margin and debt to equity ratio.
   c. interest coverage ratio and debt to equity ratio.
   d. earnings per share and profit margin.

10. Which of the following describes the computation of the interest coverage ratio?
    a. Net income minus interest expense divided by interest expense
    b. Net income plus interest expense divided by interest expense
    c. Income before income taxes plus interest expense divided by interest expense
    d. Net income divided by interest expense

TESTING YOUR KNOWLEDGE

Matching*

Match each term with its definition by writing the appropriate letter in the blank.

_____ 1. Financial performance evaluation

_____ 2. Portfolio

_____ 3. Diversified companies (conglomerates)

_____ 4. Interim financial statements

_____ 5. Horizontal analysis

_____ 6. Base year

_____ 7. Trend analysis

_____ 8. Index number

_____ 9. Vertical analysis

_____ 10. Common-size statement

_____ 11. Ratio analysis

_____ 12. Operating cycle

a. The time it takes to sell and collect for products sold

b. A group of investments or loans

c. A means of identifying significant relationships between the components of financial statements

d. A statement produced by vertical analysis in which components of a total figure are stated as percentages of that total

e. Statements presenting financial information for periods of less than a year

f. The first year considered in horizontal analysis

g. All the techniques used to show important relationships in financial statements and to relate them to important financial objectives

h. A technique for showing percentage changes in specific items over several years

i. A number used in trend analysis to show changes in related items over time

j. A technique for showing dollar and percentage changes in specific items between two years

k. A technique that uses percentages to show the relationships of individual items on a financial statement to a total within the statement

l. Large companies that operate in many unrelated industries

Short Answer

Use the lines provided to answer each item.

1. List four ratios that measure profitability.

   _____

   _____

   _____

   _____

2. Briefly distinguish between horizontal analysis and vertical analysis.

   _____

   _____

   _____

3. List the three standards that decision makers use in assessing a company's performance.

   _____

   _____

   _____

4. It is usually wiser to acquire a portfolio of small investments than to make one large investment. Why is this so?

   _____

   _____

   _____

Note to student: The matching quiz might be completed more efficiently by starting with the definition and searching for the corresponding term.

Financial Performance Evaluation

5. List four measures of cash flow adequacy.

_____

_____

_____

_____

True-False

Circle T if the statement is true, F if it is false. Provide explanations for the false answers, using the blank lines below.

T F   **1.** Horizontal analysis is applicable to both an income statement and a balance sheet.

T F   **2.** Common-size statements show the dollar amount of changes in specific items from one year to the next.

T F   **3.** A company with a 2.0 current ratio experiences a decline in the current ratio when it pays a short-term liability.

T F   **4.** Inventory is not a component in the computation of the quick ratio.

T F   **5.** Inventory turnover equals average inventory divided by cost of goods sold.

T F   **6.** The price/earnings ratio must be computed before earnings per share can be determined.

T F   **7.** In computing return on equity, interest expense is added back to net income.

T F   **8.** When a company has no debt, its return on assets equals its return on equity.

T F   **9.** A company with a low debt to equity ratio is a high-risk investment.

T F   **10.** Receivable turnover measures the time taken to collect an average receivable.

T F   **11.** A low interest coverage ratio would be of concern to a company's bondholders.

T F   **12.** Average days' inventory on hand is a liquidity ratio.

T F   **13.** Dividends yield is a profitability ratio.

T F   **14.** On a common-size income statement, net income is set at 100 percent.

T F   **15.** Interim financial statements may provide early signals of significant changes in a company's earnings trend.

T F   **16.** _The Wall Street Journal_ is the most complete financial newspaper in America.

T F   **17.** Return on assets equals the profit margin times asset turnover.

T F   **18.** The higher the payables turnover is, the longer the average days' payable is.

T F   **19.** The Sarbanes-Oxley Act prohibits auditors from acting as consultants for the companies they audit.

_____

_____

_____

_____

_____

_____

_____

_____

Multiple Choice

Circle the letter of the best answer.

1. Which of the following is a measure of long-term solvency?
   a. Current ratio
   b. Interest coverage ratio
   c. Asset turnover
   d. Profit margin

2. Short-term creditors would probably be *most* interested in which of the following ratios?
   a. Current ratio
   b. Average days' inventory on hand
   c. Debt to equity ratio
   d. Quick ratio

3. Net income is irrelevant in computing which of the following ratios?
   a. Cash flow yield
   b. Return on assets
   c. Asset turnover
   d. Return on equity

4. A high price/earnings ratio indicates
   a. investor confidence in future earnings.
   b. that the stock is probably overvalued.
   c. that the stock is probably undervalued.
   d. lack of investor confidence in future earnings.

5. Index numbers are used in
   a. trend analysis.
   b. ratio analysis.
   c. vertical analysis.
   d. common-size statements.

6. The principal internal users of financial statements are
   a. SEC administrators.
   b. managers.
   c. investors.
   d. creditors.

7. Using industry norms to evaluate a company's financial performance is complicated by
   a. the existence of diversified companies.
   b. the use of different accounting procedures by different companies.
   c. the fact that companies in the same industry usually differ in some respect.
   d. all of the above.

8. A low receivable turnover indicates that
   a. few customers are defaulting on their debts.
   b. the company's inventory is moving slowly.
   c. the company is slow in making collections from its customers.
   d. a small proportion of the company's sales are credit sales.

9. In a common-size income statement, net income is set at
   a. 0 percent.
   b. the percentage that it is in relation to net sales.
   c. the percentage that it is in relation to operating expenses.
   d. 100 percent.

10. Which of the following is a measure of cash generated or cash deficiency after providing for commitments?
    a. Cash flows to assets
    b. Cash flow yield
    c. Free cash flow
    d. Cash flows to sales

APPLYING YOUR KNOWLEDGE

Exercises

1. Complete the horizontal analysis for the comparative income statements shown below. Round percentages to the nearest tenth of a percent.

	20x6	20x5	Increase (Decrease) Amount	Percentage
Sales	$250,000	$200,000		
Cost of goods sold	144,000	120,000		
Gross margin	$106,000	$ 80,000		
Operating expenses	62,000	50,000		
Income before income taxes	$ 44,000	$ 30,000		
Income taxes	16,000	8,000		
Net income	$ 28,000	$ 22,000		

2. The following is financial information for Norton Corporation for 20xx. Current assets consist of cash, accounts receivable, marketable securities, and inventory.

Average accounts receivable	$100,000
Average (and ending) inventory	180,000
Cost of goods sold	350,000
Current assets, Dec. 31	500,000
Current liabilities, Dec. 31	250,000
Market price, Dec. 31, on 21,200 shares	40/share
Net income	106,000
Net sales	600,000
Average stockholders' equity	480,000
Average total assets	880,000
Net cash flows from operating activities	75,000

Compute the following ratios as of December 31. Round off to the nearest tenth of a whole number.

a. Current ratio = _____

b. Quick ratio = _____

c. Inventory turnover = _____

d. Average days' inventory on hand = _____

e. Return on assets = _____

f. Return on equity = _____

g. Receivable turnover = _____

h. Average days' sales uncollected = _____

i. Profit margin = _____

j. Cash flow yield = _____

k. Cash flows to sales = _____

l. Cash flows to assets = _____

m. Asset turnover = _____

n. Price/earnings ratio = _____

Crossword Puzzle
for Chapters 13, 14, and 15

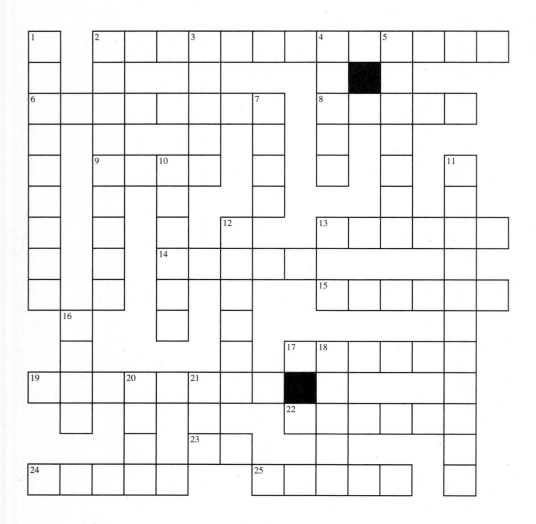

ACROSS

2. Ratio indicating investor confidence in a company (2 words)

6. Analysis resulting in 15-Across

8. The "T" of TQM

9. _____ cash flow

13. _____ Application Prize

14. Number used in trend analysis

15. _____-size statement

17. The "S" of MIS

19. Malcolm _____ Quality Award

22. _____ on assets

23. The "O" of ROQ

24. Internal failure _____

25. The "A" of CAD

DOWN

1. _____ turnover

2. Group of investment or loans

3. Operating _____

4. Current _____

5. Quarterly financial statements, e.g.

7. Purchase order _____ time

10. Return on _____

11. Costs of _____ (prevention and appraisal costs)

12. Nonvalue-_____ activity

16. Base _____

18. Dividends _____

20. _____ to equity ratio

21. _____ 9000 (quality management guidelines) activities

ANSWERS

Chapter 1

Self-Test

1. d	(LO 1)		**5.** d	(LO 3)
2. c	(LO 1)		**6.** a	(LO 4)
3. c	(LO 1)		**7.** a	(LO 6)
4. c	(LO 1			

Matching

1. f		**4.** g		**7.** a		**10.** h
2. b		**5.** e		**8.** j		
3. c		**6.** i		**9.** d		

Short Answer

1. (LO 2) The planning, executing, reviewing, and reporting stages
2. (LO 3) A just-in-time operating philosophy mandates a production environment in which personnel are hired and raw materials and facilities are purchased and used only as needed; emphasis is on the elimination of waste.
3. (LO 7) Competence, confidentiality, integrity, and objectivity
4. (LO 5) Why is the report being prepared? For whom is the report intended? What information should be provided? When is the report due?

True-False

1. F (LO 1) The management accountant provides management with the information needed for decision making.
2. T (LO 1)
3. F (LO 1) The reverse is true.
4. T (LO 1)
5. T (LO 1)
6. F (LO 1) Financial accounting reports must be prepared at regular, equal intervals.
7. F (LO 6) It relates most closely to integrity.
8. F (LO 6) It relates most closely to competence.
9. T (LO 3)
10. T (LO 4)
11. T (LO 3)
12. T (LO 1)
13. F (LO 1) Planning is the first stage; executing is the second stage.
14. T (LO 3)
15. F (LO 3) The *customer*, not the manufacturer, must perceive value in the product.

Multiple Choice

1. d (LO 6) Management accountants are expected to stay abreast of new methods and knowledge in the accounting field so that they can perform their duties as skillfully and competently as possible. Integrity means avoiding conflicts of interest, objectivity refers to fair and complete disclosure of information, and confidentiality forbids the unethical or illegal disclosure of proprietary information.

2. a (LO 6) To maintain their integrity, management accountants may not accept any gift or favor that would prejudice their actions.

3. b (LO 1) The timeliness of the information is important in both financial and management accounting reports because it enhances the usefulness of the schedules, reports, and statements that are prepared from that information. The other choices listed are areas in which the two types of accounting may differ.

4. d (LO 3) JIT, TQM, and ABM all strive for perfection, which is the goal of continuous improvement. Companies that adhere to this concept are never satisfied with what is; they constantly seek a better method, product, service, process, or resource. Although no company ever attains perfection, having it as a goal contributes to a firm's continual improvement.

5. c (LO 1) Management accounting reports are generated to assist managers in the decision-making process. Users' needs are therefore the driving force in their creation.

6. a (LO 1) Much of the work of management accounting is based on allocations, forecasts, and projections, for which there is no exact information; reports and analyses are therefore often based on estimates.

7. c (LO 1) After planning and executing a decision, managers review the expected performance established at the planning stage. Any significant differences are then identified for further analysis.

8. b (LO 4, LO 5) Operating budgets, which are used to plan a company's future, are based on financial data relating to the company's performance in the past. All the other choices listed are based on nonfinancial data.

Exercises

1. (LO 1)

	Financial Accounting	Management Accounting
1.	e	c
2.	g	l
3.	m	b
4.	i	n
5.	a	h
6.	k	f
7.	d	j

2. (LO 5)

Employee	Number of Pizzas Served per Hour	Employee Rating
P. Sanchez	22	Excellent
S. Wang	18	Good
R. Scotti	13	Lazy
E. Butterfield	16	Average
B. Jolita	19	Good
B. Warner	15	Average
G. Cohen	9	The Pits

3. (LO 3)
  1. b
  2. b
  3. a
  4. a
  5. b

Chapter 2

1. a (LO 3)   **6.** d (LO 7)
2. d (LO 3)   **7.** d (LO 5)
3. d (LO 5)   **8.** a (LO 5)
4. b (LO 4)   **9.** b (LO 6)
5. a (LO 4)   **10.** b (LO 8)

Matching

1. h   **5.** g   **9.** m   **13.** e
2. c   **6.** d   **10.** f   **14.** n
3. b   **7.** j   **11.** o   **15.** i
4. a   **8.** k   **12.** l

Short Answer

1. (LO 4) Materials Inventory, Work in Process Inventory, and Finished Goods Inventory
2. (LO 3) Direct materials, direct labor, and manufacturing overhead
3. (LO 3) A materials cost is considered direct when it can be conveniently and economically traced to a specific product or other cost object.
4. (LO 1) For profit or loss determination, product pricing, inventory valuation, and planning and cost control
5. (LO 5)
   Beginning balance, materials inventory
   + Direct materials purchased
   = Cost of direct materials available for use
   − Ending balance, materials inventory
   = Cost of direct materials used
6. (LO 5)
   Cost of direct materials used
   + Direct labor costs
   + Total manufacturing overhead costs
   = Total manufacturing costs

7. (LO 5)
   Total manufacturing costs
   + Beginning balance, work in process inventory
   = Total cost of work in process during the period
   − Ending balance, work in process inventory
   = Cost of goods manufactured
8. (LO 7) Estimated manufacturing overhead is divided by total estimated cost driver activity (e.g., direct labor hours)
9. (LO 6) Overapplied overhead is the amount by which applied manufacturing overhead costs exceeds actual manufacturing overhead costs.
10. (LO 4) Cost of goods manufactured is the total cost of all units completed and moved to finished goods storage during an accounting period.

True-False

1. T (LO 5)
2. T (LO 2, LO 4)
3. T (LO 8)
4. T (LO 3)
5. T (LO 4)

6. F (LO 5, LO 9) A service firm has no direct materials cost.
7. T (LO 8)
8. F (LO 4) The purchase request is prepared first.

9. F (LO 3) They are classified as indirect labor costs (i.e., as manufacturing overhead).

10. F (LO 5) It must be prepared *before* the income statement is prepared.

11. T (LO 5)

12. T (LO 5)

13. F (LO 5) The opposite is true.

14. T (LO 5)

15. T (LO 8)

16. T (LO 6)

17. F (LO 3) The smaller a cost object, the more difficult it is to trace.

18. F (LO 3) It is part of manufacturing overhead and is thus an indirect cost.

Multiple Choice

1. c (LO 3) A direct materials cost can easily be traced to the item manufactured. Other than the legs for the chair, each cost described is not distinctly traceable to the product.

2. c (LO 4) Goods must first be requested, then ordered, then received, then used.

3. a (LO 2) Salespeople are not involved in the manufacture of products. Thus, their salaries are treated as period costs, not product costs.

4. d (LO 4) The proper document to use when buying goods is a purchase order.

5. a (LO 4) A materials request form documents goods released to production.

6. c (LO 8) Activities are what "drive" the costs in an ABC system.

7. b (LO 8) With ABC costing, costs are accumulated for a given activity pool and applied via a cost driver.

8. a (LO 7) One of the criticisms of the traditional method is that it uses a single plantwide cost driver (e.g., direct labor hours) to apply manufacturing overhead to a product cost.

9. d (LO 1) Managers use product cost information in all the stages in the management cycle listed, as well as in the reporting stage.

Exercises

1. (LO 5)

Finished Goods, Jan. 1	$ 75,000
Add Cost of Goods Manufactured	450,000
Cost of Goods Available for Sale	$525,000
Less Finished Goods, Dec. 31	80,000
Cost of Goods Sold	$445,000

2. (LO 8)

Activity Pool	Estimated Activity Pool Amount	Cost Driver	Cost Driver Level	Activity Cost Rate
Setup	$10,000	Number of setups	200 setups	$50
Inspection	6,000	Number of inspections	300 inspections	$20
Building	8,000	Machine hours	4,000 machine hours	$2
Packaging	4,000	Packaging hours	1,000 packaging hours	$4
	$28,000			

	Activity Cost Rate	Product A Cost Driver Level	Product A Cost Applied	Product B Cost Driver Level	Product B Cost Applied
Activity Pool	Activity Cost Rate	Cost Driver Level	Cost Applied	Cost Driver Level	Cost Applied
Setup	$50	70	$ 3,500	30	$ 1,500
Inspection	20	250	5,000	150	3,000
Building	2	1,500	3,000	2,000	4,000
Packaging	4	300	1,200	700	2,800
Total			$12,700		$11,300
÷ by Number of Units			1,000		2,000
= Manufacturing Overhead Cost per Unit			$12.70		$5.65

3. (LO 5)

Specialty Company		
Statement of Cost of Goods Manufactured		
For the Year Ended December 31, 20xx		
Direct materials used		
Materials Inventory, Jan. 1	$ 8,700	
Add direct materials purchased (net)	168,300	
Cost of direct materials available for use	$177,000	
Less Materials Inventory, Dec. 31	32,600	
Cost of direct materials used		$144,400
Direct labor costs		142,900
Manufacturing overhead costs		
Depreciation, factory building and equipment	$ 31,800	
Factory insurance	2,300	
Factory utilities expense	26,000	
Indirect labor	42,800	
Other factory costs	12,600	
Total manufacturing overhead costs		115,500
Total manufacturing costs		$402,800
Add Work in Process Inventory, Jan. 1		34,200
Total cost of work in process during the year		$437,000
Less Work in Process Inventory, Dec. 31		28,700
Cost of goods manufactured		$408,300

4. (LO 3)

a. OH	d. DM	g. DM
b. DL	e. OH	h. OH
c. OH	f. DL	i. OH

Solution to Crossword Puzzle
(Chapters 1 and 2)

		¹P					²R						³R	
	⁴P	U	R	C	H	A	S	E	O	⁵R	D	E	R	
⁶W		O					T			E		Q		
O	⁷I	N	D	I	R	E	C	T		C		U		
R		U					⁸D	E	B	I	T		
K	⁹O	¹⁰C	O	S	T	O	¹¹F		I		S		
I	V	T					I		V		I		
N	E	C		¹²P	L	A	N		I		T		
¹³P	E	R	I	O	D		I		¹⁴N	A	I	L	
R	H	S	¹⁵T		S	G		O			
O	E	T	I	¹⁶W	H	O		N			
C	A	M		E	¹⁷R					
E	¹⁸D	R	I	V	E	R	¹⁹D	I	R	E	C	T	
S				N					
²⁰S	T	A	N	D	A	R	D	²¹T	O	T	A	L	

Chapter 3

Self-Test

1. a (LO 2)		**6.** c (LO 5)	
2. a (LO 2)		**7.** d (LO 6)	
3. b (LO 3)		**8.** d (LO 1)	
4. c (LO 4)		**9.** a (LO 6)	
5. a (LO 3)		**10.** c (LO 1)	

Matching

1. c	**4.** b	**6.** e
2. g	**5.** d	**7.** a
3. f		

Short Answer

1. (LO 5) Labor, materials and supplies, and service overhead
2. (LO 3) Direct materials, direct labor, and applied manufacturing overhead
3. (LO 4) The costs on the job order cost card are totaled, and the total costs are then divided by the number of goods units produced.
4. (LO 2) Railroad cars, bridges, wedding invitations, or any other unique or special-order products

True-False

1. T (LO 2)
2. T (LO 2, LO 4)
3. F (LO 3) Indirect costs are charged to Work in Process Inventory through applied overhead.
4. T (LO 4)
5. F (LO 4) The job must be completed and all costs recorded on the job order cost card before the product unit cost can be calculated.
6. T (LO 3)
7. F (LO 3) The decrease is to Finished Goods Inventory.
8. T (LO 2)
9. T (LO 4)
10. T (LO 1)
11. F (LO 5) Services are not associated with a physical product that can be inventoried and valued.
12. F (LO 6) Project costing links many different job orders and processes by transferring costs from one job or process to another, collecting and summarizing costs in a variety of ways, and providing appropriate internal controls.
13. T (LO 2)

1. c (LO 2) A job order costing system is used if the goods manufactured are unique. A supersonic jet is unique because it is manufactured to the specifications of the buyer.

2. b (LO 3) Manufacturing overhead is applied to specific jobs by increasing the Work in Process Inventory and reducing the Manufacturing Overhead account.

3. a (LO 3) Actual factory overhead costs are entered into the Manufacturing Overhead account; they do not flow through the Work in Process Inventory account.

4. b (LO 3) The Manufacturing Overhead account decreases when the manufacturing overhead costs are assigned to the Work in Process Inventory account.

5. b (LO 2) A process costing system accumulates product costs by process, department, or work cell, not by job or batch of products.

6. d (LO 3) When materials are issued into production, Work in Process Inventory and Manufacturing Overhead are increased, and Materials Inventory is decreased.

7. d (LO 1) During the reviewing stage, managers compare budgeted costs with actual costs to evaluate performance, identify problems and recommend changes.

8. a (LO 3) Costs of a manufactured product include materials, labor, and manufacturing overhead; a factory foreperson's salary would be among the indirect costs included in overhead.

Exercises

1. (LO 5)

```
┌─────────────────────────────────────────────────┐
│              Job Order Cost Card                  │
│         Melvin's Septic Service Company           │
│                                                   │
│  Customer:         Gonzales                       │
│  Contract Type:    Cost-plus                      │
│  Type of Service:  Septic Services                │
│                                                   │
│  Cost Summary:                                    │
│  Costs Charged to Job               Total         │
├─────────────────────────────────────────────────┤
```

Costs Charged to Job	Total
Septic design	
Beginning balance	$ 5,270
Design labor	500
Service overhead (30% of	
design labor)	150
Totals	$ 5,920
Septic tank installation	
Beginning balance	$28,500
Materials and supplies	4,300
Installation labor	12,800
Service overhead (50% of	
installation labor)	6,400
Totals	$52,000
Job site cleanup	
Beginning balance	$ 150
Janitorial service cost	1,050
Totals	$ 1,200
Totals	$59,120
Cost of job	$59,120
Markup (25% of cost)	14,780
Amount billed	$73,900

2. (LO 3)

Materials Inventory			
12/23	2,950	850	12/26
	2,100		

Accounts Payable			
		2,950	12/23

Work In Process Inventory			
12/26	800	3,900	12/29
12/27	1,200		
12/27	3,600		
	1,700		

Manufacturing Overhead			
12/26	50	3,600	12/27
12/26	1,200		
12/27	300		
12/31	2,500		
	450		

Factory Payroll			
		1,500	12/27

Cash			
		1,200	12/26

Finished Goods Inventory			
12/29	3,900	2,000	12/30
	1,900		

Cost of Goods Sold			
12/30	2,000	2,500	12/31
		500	

Sales			
		3,400	12/30

Accounts Receivable			
12/30	3,400		

Chapter 4

Self-Test

1. b (LO 1)		**6.** b (LO 5)	
2. c (LO 3)		**7.** d (LO 5)	
3. a (LO 4)		**8.** a (LO 5)	
4. c (LO 4)		**9.** c (LO 5)	
5. d (LO 5)		**10.** a (LO 6)	

Matching

1. d	**3.** f	**5.** g	**7.** e
2. h	**4.** c	**6.** b	**8.** a

Short Answer

1. (LO 5) Account for physical units, account for equivalent units, account for costs, compute the cost per equivalent unit, assign costs

2. (LO 5)

   Units in beginning inventory × (100% − percentage of completion)

   + Units started and completed × 100%

   + Units in ending inventory × percentage of completion

   = Equivalent units

3. (LO 5) Costs of units completed and transferred out and ending work in process

4. (LO 5)

   Costs attached to units in beginning inventory

   + Costs necessary to complete units in beginning inventory

   + Costs of units started and completed during the period

   = Costs of goods completed and transferred

True-False

1. F (LO 3) A Work in Process Inventory account is maintained for each process, department, or work cell.
2. T (LO 3)
3. T (LO 2)
4. T (LO 3, LO 4)
5. F (LO 4) Units started and completed are only part of the computation.
6. T (LO 4)
7. F (LO 5) A combined unit cost (conversion cost) is computed for direct labor and manufacturing overhead.

8. F (LO 6) Beginning inventory is multiplied by 100 percent.
9. T (LO 5).
10. F (LO 5) Equivalent units for materials and conversion costs must be multiplied by their respective unit costs.
11. T (LO 5)
12. T (LO 1)
13. T (LO 2)

1. b (LO 4, LO 5) Equivalent production for conversion costs would be 14,100 units, or the sum of (a) the 10,000 units started and completed during the period, (b) ending equivalent units of 2,100 (7,000 units × 30% complete), and (c) beginning equivalent units of 2,000 (5,000 units × 40% remaining to complete).

2. c (LO 4, LO 6) Average costing treats all units in beginning inventory as if they were started and completed during the period. Thus, equivalent production for conversion costs would be 17,100 units, or the sum of (a) beginning inventory of 5,000 units, (b) the 10,000 units started and completed during the period, and (c) ending equivalent units of 2,100 (7,000 units × 30% complete).

3. d (LO 3, LO 5) The costs necessary to complete ending inventory are costs of a future period.

4. a (LO 5) Equivalent units account for efforts expended; Step 1 accounts for physical units.

5. c (LO 4, LO 6) Using average costing, equivalent production would be 17,600 units, or the sum of (a) beginning inventory of 5,000 units, (b) 12,000 units started and completed, and (c) 600 ending equivalent units (2,000 units × 30% complete).

6. b (LO 4) Conversion costs are the costs incurred to convert raw materials into finished products. They include both direct labor costs and manufacturing overhead.

7. b (LO 5) Step 5 assigns costs to finished goods and ending work in process.

8. b (LO 5) Step 5 assigns costs to finished goods and ending work in process.

9. b (LO 1) Forecasting unit costs and budgeting are two of the uses of process costing information in the planning stage of the management cycle.

10. c (LO 1) A firm that produces custom-made suits would use a job order costing system.

Exercises

1. (LO 5)

Jaquette Manufacturing Company
Process Cost Report: FIFO Costing Method
For the Month Ended May 31, 20xx

	Physical Units	*Equivalent Units*	
Beginning inventory	2,000		
Units started this period	24,000		
Units to be accounted for	26,000		
		Direct Materials	*Conversion*
Beginning inventory	2,000	—	1,400 (70%)
Units started and completed	17,000	17,000	17,000
Ending inventory	7,000	7,000 (100%)	2,100 (30%)
Units accounted for	26,000	24,000	20,500
	Total Costs		
Beginning inventory	$ 15,000	$ 12,000	$ 3,000
Current costs	144,750	114,000	30,750
Total costs	$159,750		
Current Costs ÷ Equivalent units		$114,000 ÷ 24,000	$30,750 ÷ 20,500
Cost per equivalent unit		$4.75	$1.50

Cost of goods manufactured and transferred out:

From beginning inventory	$ 15,000	= $12,000 + 3,000
Current costs to complete	2,100	= 0 + (1,400 x $1.50)
Units started and completed	106,250	= (17,000 x $4.75) + 17,000 x $1.50)
Cost of goods manufactured	$123,350	
Ending inventory	36,400	= (7,000 x $4.75) + (2,100 x $1.50)
Total costs	$159,750	

Solution to Crossword Puzzle
(Chapters 3 and 4)

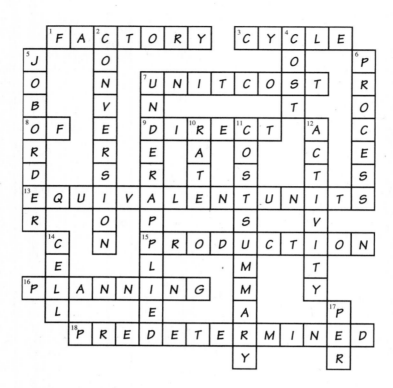

Chapter 5

1. c	(LO 5)	**6.** c	(LO 7)
2. a	(LO 5)	**7.** c	(LO 3)
3. d	(LO 5)	**8.** a	(LO 4)
4. c	(LO 3)	**9.** b	(LO 6)
5. d	(LO 1)	**10.** c	(LO 7)

Matching

1. i	**5.** d	**8.** c	**11.** k
2. a	**6.** f	**9.** h	**12.** m
3. g	**7.** e	**10.** j	**13.** l
4. b			

Short Answer

1. (LO 5) A basic concept of the just-in-time operating philosophy is that all resources—materials, personnel, and facilities—should be acquired and used only as needed.

2. (LO 4)

   Identify and classify each activity.

   Estimate the cost of resources for each activity.

   Identify a cost driver for each activity and estimate the quantity of each cost driver.

   Calculate an activity cost rate for each activity.

   Assign costs to cost objects based on the level of activity required to make the product or provide the service.

3. (LO 3) Process value analysis (PVA) is a method of identifying all activities and relating them to the events that prompt the activities and to the resources that the activities consume. PVA is helpful to managers because it forces them to look critically at all phases of their operations. It improves cost traceability and results in significantly more accurate product costs, which in turn improves management decisions and increases profitability.

4. (LO 5, LO 6) Just-in-time is an operating philosophy, not an inventory system. One of its goals is to minimize inventory. Unlike the traditional manufacturing approach, which requires that inventory be kept on hand to meet customer demands, JIT uses customer orders to trigger production runs. Throughput time is much more important than in traditional manufacturing environments.

True-False

1. F (LO 8) The primary goals of both ABM and JIT are to eliminate waste, reduce costs, improve product or service quality, and enhance an organization's efficiency and productivity.
2. T (LO 5)
3. T (LO 5)
4. T (LO 5)
5. T (LO 5)
6. F (LO 5, LO 6) Machine operators inspect products on a continuous basis.
7. F (LO 6) Queue time is the time a product waits to be worked on after it arrives at the next operation or department.

8. T (LO 6)
9. T (LO 4)
10. F (LO 4) The cost hierarchy of a service organization has four levels: the unit, batch, service, and operations levels.
11. F (LO 4) A bill of activities is used in activity-based costing. It is a list of activities and related costs that is used to compute the costs assigned to activities and the product unit cost.
12. T (LO 7)
13. T (LO 3)
14. T (LO 3)
15. T (LO 1)

Multiple Choice

1. c (LO 4) Batch-level activities are performed each time a batch of goods is produced. Installation of a vehicle's engine is an example of a unit-level activity. Unit-level activities are performed each time a unit is produced.
2. c (LO 5) Variance analysis is a method used to identify causes of differences between expected and actual results of operations. Emphasis on direct labor variance analysis could be found in any production environment.
3. b (LO 5) In pull-through production, the production process begins when a customer places an order.
4. a (LO 5) Because inventory is delivered as needed in a JIT environment and not kept on hand in advance of being needed, the resources traditionally used to store, count, maintain, and move inventories are reduced or eliminated.
5. b (LO 5) Quick and inexpensive machine setups result in cost savings. None of the other choices guarantees that a company will ultimately save money.

6. d (LO 6) Decision time precedes the start of production. Production time begins with the requisition of raw materials and ends with the transfer of the product to finished goods.
7. c (LO 3) A value-adding activity increases the market value of a product or service—for example, using a higher-quality material that increases the value of the product in the eyes of the customer. Recording the daily receipts would not add to the market value of the pizza; thus, it would be a nonvalue-adding activity.
8. a (LO 7) In a JIT environment in which backflush costing is used, the direct materials costs and the conversion costs (direct labor and manufacturing overhead) are immediately charged to the Cost of Goods Sold account.
9. a (LO 1) In the planning stage, an activity-based system can help managers estimate product costs, as well as identify value-adding activities and determine the resources required for such activities.
10. b (LO 6) Processing time is the actual amount of time spent working on a product.

Exercises

1. a. (LO 4)

Direct materials cost	$28,645
Cost of purchased parts	38,205
Direct labor cost (660 × $7.00)	4,620
Manufacturing overhead (1.6 × $4,620)	7,392
Total cost of the order	**$78,862**
Product unit cost ($78,862/350 units)	**$225.32**

b.

Activity	Activity Cost Rate	Cost Driver Level	Activity Cost
Unit level:			
Parts production	$19 per machine hour	190 machine hours	$ 3,610
Assembly	$9.50 per direct labor hour	42 direct labor hours	399
Packaging/shipping	$13 per unit	350 units	4,550
Batch level:			
Work cell setup	$45 per setup	8 setups	360
Product level:			
Product design	$31 per engineering hour	38 engineering hours	1,178
Product simulation	$45 per testing hour	14 testing hours	630
Facility level:			
Building occupancy	125% of direct labor costs	$4,620 direct labor costs	5,775
Total Activity Costs			$16,502
Cost Summary			
Direct materials		$28,645	
Cost of purchased parts		38,205	
Direct labor cost		4,620	
Activity costs		16,502	
Total cost of order		**$87,972**	
Product unit cost		**$251.35**	

2. (LO 5, LO 6) In both traditional and JIT settings, direct labor and raw materials are classified as direct costs, and a president's salary and plant fire insurance are classified as indirect costs.

Costs that are classified as indirect in a traditional setting and direct in a JIT environment are depreciation, machinery; product design costs; small tools; operating supplies; setup labor; rework costs; supervisory salaries; and utility costs, machinery. All these costs are traceable to a JIT work cell, whereas in a traditional setting, they are included in a plantwide or departmental overhead cost pool.

3. (LO 5, LO 6)

Work in Process Inventory			Finished Goods Inventory			Cost of Goods Sold	
4,890	32,750		32,750	17,880		17,880	
13,300							

Accounts Payable			Accounts Receivable			Sales	
	4,890		28,608				28,608
	13,330						

Chapter 6

Self-Test

1. b	(LO 1)	**6.** a	(LO 4)
2. c	(LO 2)	**7.** c	(LO 5)
3. a	(LO 2)	**8.** b	(LO 5)
4. b	(LO 2)	**9.** b	(LO 4)
5. d	(LO 4)	**10.** c	(LO 2)

Matching

1. d	**4.** k	**7.** i	**10.** c
2. g	**5.** j	**8.** a	**11.** e
3. h	**6.** b	**9.** f	

Short Answer

1. (LO 4) Sales = Variable Costs + Fixed Costs, or Sales − Variable Costs − Fixed Costs = 0

2. (LO 2) A mixed cost is any cost that has both fixed and variable elements. Examples include telephone expense, electricity expense, and water expense.

3. (LO 2) The high-low method breaks down a mixed cost into its fixed and variable components.

4. (LO 4) *Sales* refers to the gross proceeds realized on the sale of a product. *Contribution margin* refers to the portion of sales remaining after all variable costs have been deducted from sales. It is the amount available to cover fixed costs and earn a profit.

5. (LO 4)

Sales	$XX
− Variable Costs	XX
= Contribution Margin	$XX
− Fixed Costs	XX
= Profit	$XX

6. (LO 5)
Estimate service overhead costs.
Determine the breakeven point.
Determine the effect of a change in operating costs.
Compute targeted profit.

True-False

1. T (LO 2)

2. T (LO 4)

3. T (LO 2)

4. F (LO 2) It is a fixed cost because it does not change with volume.

5. F (LO 2) Normal capacity is the most realistic measure.

6. T (LO 4)

7. F (LO 4) A contribution margin is realized on the sale of the very first unit.

8. T (LO 4)

9. T (LO 2)

10. T (LO 3)

11. T (LO 2)

12. F (LO 4) The horizontal (x) axis represents volume, such as units of output.

13. T (LO 4)

14. F (LO 4) Unless the selling price or variable cost per unit changes, the contribution margin per unit will remain the same.

15. T (LO 4)

16. F (LO 5) Service businesses can use C-V-P analysis.

Multiple Choice

1. c (LO 2) Because part of the fare varies according to activity level and part is fixed, it is a mixed cost.
2. c (LO 4) Breakeven in units is calculated by dividing total fixed costs by the contribution margin per unit; contribution margin per unit is the selling price less variable costs per unit. Thus, $10,000 \div (\$10 - \$8) = 5,000$ units.
3. b (LO 2) Variable costs are directly associated with production levels. If production is zero, variable costs are also zero.
4. a (LO 4) Total contribution margin is the contribution margin per unit multiplied by the number of units sold. When profits (losses) are zero, the total contribution margin equals total fixed costs.
5. d (LO 4) The total-cost line includes all fixed and variable costs. The slope of the total-cost line is determined by the variable costs per unit. Therefore, where the total-cost line intercepts the total-revenue line, revenues equal costs.
6. a (LO 2) When preparing cost analyses and forecasting sales, managers assume normal operating capacity.
7. d (LO 2) When volume decreases, the number of units divided into the (same) fixed cost decreases, increasing the fixed cost per unit.
8. d (LO 4) When the selling price and variable cost per unit both increase by the same amount, the contribution margin per unit remains the same, and thus the breakeven point remains the same.
9. d (LO 5) Solve the following equation to obtain the correct answer: $\$50X - \$35X - \$30,000 = \$45,000$.
10. a (LO 5) Solve the following equation to obtain the correct answer: $10,000(X - \$10) - \$40,000 = \$26,000$.
11. b (LO 4) The weighted-average contribution margin is computed by multiplying the contribution margin for each product by the product's percentage of the sales mix. This, in turn, is used to calculate the weighted-average breakeven point.
12. d (LO 5) Calculating the breakeven point in service businesses requires a thorough analysis of each cost component and a reliable estimate of activity.

Exercises

1. (LO 4, LO 5)
   a. 20,000 units
   b. $260,000
   c. $32,000 loss
   d. 32,500 units

2. (LO 4)

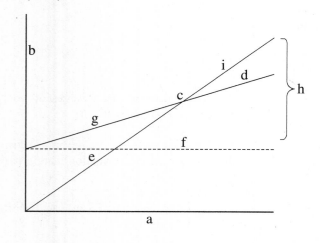

3. (LO 2)
   a. Total cost = $800 + $.25/mile
   b. $4,800

4. (LO 5)
   a. $20,000 loss
   b. $10.00
   c. $50,000

Solution to Crossword Puzzle
(Chapters 5 and 6)

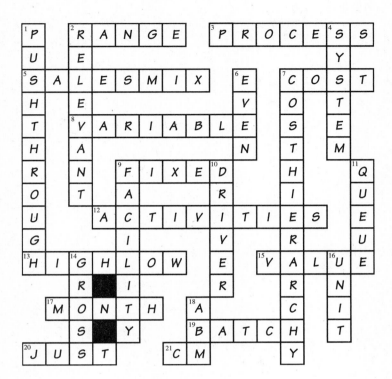

Chapter 7

Self-Test

1. d	(LO 2)	**6.** a	(LO 2)
2. d	(LO 1)	**7.** d	(LO 2, LO 3)
3. a	(LO 3)	**8.** c	(LO 4)
4. c	(LO 4)	**9.** a	(LO 1)
5. d	(LO 4)	**10.** b	(LO 3)

Matching

1. k	**4.** f	**7.** d	**10.** e
2. g	**5.** i	**8.** c	**11.** a
3. j	**6.** h	**9.** b	

Short Answer

1. (LO 1) Budgeting is the process of identifying, gathering, summarizing, and communicating financial and nonfinancial information about an organization's future activities.
2. (LO 2) A master budget consists of a set of operating budgets and a set of financial budgets. The operating budgets are plans used in daily operations. They are the basis for preparing the financial budgets, which are projections of financial results for an accounting period.
3. (LO 4) In addition to providing an estimate of the ending cash balance, the cash budget enables managers to anticipate periods of high or low cash availability and to plan for short-term investments or loans during those periods.
4. (LO 3) The three steps are to (a) calculate the total units of direct materials needed for production, (b) calculate the total units of direct materials to be purchased, and (c) calculate the total cost of direct materials to be purchased.

True-False

1. F (LO 2) A master budget usually covers a one-year period.
2. F (LO 2) A master budget represents an entire organization's budget.
3. T (LO 3)
4. T (LO 2)
5. F (LO 4) Depreciation expense does not represent a cash outflow and is therefore not included in the cash budget.
6. T (LO 1)
7. T (LO 4)
8. F (LO 4) Only cash collected from sales (including prior months' sales) are included as cash receipts.
9. F (LO 3, LO 4) The reverse is true.
10. T (LO 3)
11. F (LO 3) External factors, such as the state of the local and national economies, the state of the industry's economy, and the nature of the competition, are important factors in forecasting sales.
12. T (LO 3)
13. F (LO 4) Preparing the budgeted balance sheet is the final step in the development of the master budget.

Multiple Choice

1. d (LO 2, LO 3) The detailed operating budgets serve as the basis for preparing the financial budgets. Operating budgets are prepared at the departmental level and represent the expectations of the managers responsible for each segment of a firm.
2. c (LO 3) The production budget is the basis for preparing the other three budgets.
3. b (LO 4) The cash budget shows anticipated cash inflows and outflows. Once it has been prepared, certain account balances on the balance sheet can be forecasted (Cash, Accounts Receivable, Notes Payable, etc.). Thus, the cash budget must be prepared before the pro forma balance sheet.
4. d (LO 3) Forecasted sales would appear on the sales budget, not on the direct labor budget.
5. a (LO 4) The sales budget would provide information about the projected *inflows* of cash.
6. d (LO 4) The cash budget consists of the items listed in **a, b,** and **c** plus the beginning cash balance.
7. a (LO 3) Requirements for production in the second quarter are 72,000 pounds (24,000 units × 3 pounds). Add 10 percent of the requirement for the third quarter, or 6,300 pounds (21,000 units × 3 pounds × .10). Subtract materials on hand at the beginning of the second quarter, or 7,200 pounds (24,000 units × 3 pounds × .10). The amount that should be purchased for the second quarter is 71,100 pounds.
8. d (LO 3) A manufacturing organization would prepare a direct materials budget.
9. c (LO 4) (40% × $15,000) + (60% × $10,000) + $20,000 = $32,000
10. d (LO 3) The first step in preparing the direct labor budget is to estimate the total direct labor hours by multiplying the estimated direct labor hours per unit by the anticipated units of production. The second step is to calculate the total budgeted direct labor cost by multiplying the estimated total direct labor hours by the estimated direct labor cost per hour.

Exercises

1. (LO 3)

Donlevy Company
Production Budget
For the Quarter Ended June 30, 20xx

	April	May	June
Expected sales	10,000 units	12,000 units	15,000 units
Add ending inventory	1,200	1,500	900
Units needed	11,200	13,500	15,900
Less beginning inventory	1,000	1,200	1,500
Units to produce ending inventory	10,200 units	12,300 units	14,400 units

2. (LO 4)

Monahan Enterprises
Cash Budget
For the Month Ended June 30, 20xx

Cash receipts		
Sales—May	$52,000	
Sales—June	18,000	
Proceeds from loan*	1,000	
Total receipts		$71,000
Cash disbursements		
General and administrative expenses	$22,000	
Inventory purchases—May	20,000	
Inventory purchases—June	15,000	
Purchase of office furniture	3,000	
Selling expenses	14,000	
Total disbursements		74,000
Cash increase (decrease)		$(3,000)
Cash balance, June 1		7,000
Cash balance, June 30		$ 4,000

*Amount must be derived.

---

3. (LO 3)

Jeppo Titanium Company
Direct Labor Budget
For the Year Ended December 31, 20xx

	Product	Product	Year
	X	Y	
Bending department			
Total production units	10,000	20,000	
× Direct labor hours per unit	1	.6	
Total direct labor hours	10,000	12,000	
× Direct labor cost per hour	$10	$10	
Total direct labor cost	$100,000	$120,000	$220,000
	Product	Product	
	X	Y	
Welding department			
Total production units	10,000	20,000	
× Direct labor hours per unit	2	3	
Total direct labor hours	20,000	60,000	
× Direct labor cost per hour	$15	$15	
Total direct labor cost	$300,000	$900,000	$1,200,000
Total firmwide direct labor cost			$1,440,000

4. (LO 1) During the planning stage of the management cycle, budgeting helps managers relate long-term strategic goals to short-term activities, distribute resources and workloads, communicate responsibilities, select performance measures, and set standards for bonuses and rewards.

In the executing stage, managers use budget information to communicate expectations, measure performance and motivate employees, coordinate activities, and allot resources.

In the reviewing stage, budgets help managers evaluate performance, including its timeliness; find variances between planned and actual performance; and create solutions to any significant variances that they detect.

To provide continuous feedback about an organization's operating, investing, and financing activities, managers prepare and distribute reports based on budget information throughout the year.

Chapter 8

1. d (LO 1)		**6.** a (LO 2)
2. b (LO 5)		**7.** d (LO 2)
3. c (LO 6)		**8.** c (LO 4)
4. c (LO 4)		**9.** a (LO 5)
5. b (LO 2)		**10.** b (LO 3)

Matching

1. j	**5.** i	**8.** d	**11.** h
2. k	**6.** g	**9.** f	**12.** e
3. l	**7.** b	**10.** a	**13.** c
4. m			

Short Answer

1. (LO 1) Managers use standard costs to develop budgets in the planning stage, to control costs as they occur during the executing stage, for comparison with actual costs and the computation of variances in the reviewing stage, and to prepare and distribute reports on operations and managerial performance in the reporting stage.

2. (LO 6) A favorable fixed overhead volume variance exists when the overhead costs budgeted for the level of production achieved is less than the fixed overhead applied to production using the standard variable and fixed overhead rates.

3. (LO 2) The six standards are the direct materials price standard, direct materials quantity standard, direct labor rate standard, direct labor time standard, standard variable overhead rate, and standard fixed overhead rate.

4. (LO 4) A favorable direct materials quantity variable exists when a smaller quantity of direct materials is used than was expected for a particular level of outcome.

5. (LO 5) An unfavorable direct labor rate variance exists when a higher wage is paid than is standard for an employee doing a particular job.

True-False

1. F (LO 2) They are used in establishing direct labor time standards.
2. T (LO 2)
3. F (LO 1, LO 3) It is part of the control function.
4. T (LO 4)
5. T (LO 3)
6. T (LO 5)
7. F (LO 6) The standard overhead rate has two parts: the standard variable rate and the fixed overhead rate.
8. F (LO 5) The total direct labor cost variance is the sum of the direct labor rate and direct labor efficiency variances.

9. T (LO 7)
10. F (LO 3) A flexible budget is also referred to as a *variable budget.*
11. T (LO 6)
12. F (LO 3) Computing a variance is important; however, identifying the *reason* for a variance is critical if corrective actions are to be taken.
13. T (LO 3)

1. a (LO 5) The amount of wages paid is used to calculate the actual direct labor cost.

2. d (LO 4) The direct materials price variance is the difference between the standard price and the actual price multiplied by the actual quantity used. Thus, each of the responses could lead to such a variance.

3. d (LO 6) A static budget forecasts sales and costs for just one level of production.

4. a (LO 6) When the standard overhead applied is less than the actual overhead, a company has an unfavorable overhead variance.

5. b (LO 2) The total budgeted cost would be as follows:

Direct materials:	10,000 units	×	$4.00	=	$ 40,000
Direct labor:	10,000 units	×	1.00	=	10,000
Variable M.O.H.	10,000 units	×	3.00	=	30,000
Fixed M.O.H.					20,000
					$100,000

6. a (LO 2) The total budgeted cost would be as follows:

Direct materials:	20,000 units	×	$4.00	=	$ 80,000
Direct labor:	20,000 units	×	1.00	=	20,000
Variable M.O.H.	20,000 units	×	3.00	=	60,000
Fixed M.O.H.					20,000
					$180,000

7. a (LO 4, LO 7) Because a purchasing manager is responsible for purchasing materials, a favorable or unfavorable direct materials price variance could be used to evaluate his or her performance.

8. d (LO 5) If actual direct labor hours times standard labor rate is greater than standard direct labor hours times standard labor rate, an organization has an unfavorable direct labor efficiency variance.

9. a (LO 3) A flexible budget shows changes in budgeted amounts given different levels of activity. Fixed manufacturing overhead would be constant throughout the relevant range.

10. d (LO 1, LO 7) Standard costing can be used for all these reasons and in every stage of the management cycle.

Exercises

1. (LO 2)

Porcelain	$ .40
Red paint	.05
Blue paint	.02
Molding department wages	.12
Painting department wages	.30
Variable manufacturing overhead	
(.08 hr. x $3/hr.)	.24
Fixed manufacturing overhead	
(.08 hr. x $2/hr.)	.16
Standard cost of one dish	$1.29

2. (LO 3)

Sturchio Company
Flexible Budget
For the Year Ended December 31, 20xx

	Unit Levels of Activity			Variable Cost
Cost Item	10,000	15,000	20,000	per Unit
Direct materials	$ 12,500	$ 18,750	$ 25,000	$1.25
Direct labor	45,000	67,500	90,000	4.50
Variable manufacturing overhead	27,500	41,250	55,000	2.75
Total variable costs	$ 85,000	$127,500	$170,000	$8.50
Fixed manufacturing overhead	50,000	50,000	50,000	
Total costs	$135,000	$177,500	$220,000	

Flexible budget formula: ($8.50 × units produced) + $50,000

3. (LO 4, LO 5)

a. $13,140 \text{ F} = \left(\$.60 - \dfrac{\$381,060}{657,000}\right) \times 657,000$

b. $\$4,200 \text{ U} = (657,000 - 650,000) \times \$.60$

c. $\$1,105 \text{ U} = \left(\dfrac{\$100,555}{22,100} - \$4.50\right) \times 22,100$

d. $\$11,700 \text{ U} = [22,100 - (65,000 \times .3)] \times \$4.50$

Solution to Crossword Puzzle
(Chapters 7 and 8)

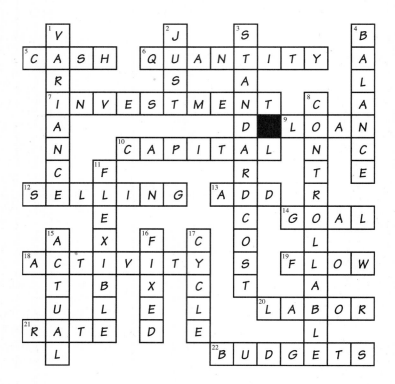

Chapter 9

Self-Test

1. c	(LO 1)	**6.** d	(LO 4)
2. b	(LO 3)	**7.** b	(LO 4)
3. c	(LO 4)	**8.** a	(LO 5)
4. a	(LO 5)	**9.** c	(LO 6)
5. a	(LO 3)		

Matching

1. g	**4.** e	**7.** c	**10.** d
2. h	**5.** b	**8.** i	
3. f	**6.** a	**9.** j	

Short Answer

1. (LO 5) Economic Value Added = After-Tax Operating Income − Cost of Capital in Dollars, or Economic Value Added = After-Tax Operating Income − [Cost of Capital × (Total Assets − Current Liabilities)]
2. (LO 3) Cost center, discretionary cost center, revenue center, profit center, and investment center
3. (LO 4) A traditional income statement assigns all manufacturing costs to cost of goods sold. A variable costing income statement uses only direct materials, direct labor, and variable manufacturing overhead to compute variable cost of goods sold. Fixed manufacturing overhead is considered a period cost.
4. (LO 1) The purpose of a balanced scorecard is to provide a framework that links the perspectives of an organization's four basic stakeholder groups with the organization's mission and vision, performance measures, strategic plan, and resources.

True-False

1. T (LO 3)
2. F (LO 3) In a discretionary cost center, the relationship between the cost of resources and the products or services produced is *not* well defined.
3. F (LO 5) Return on investment is equal to profit margin multiplied by asset turnover.
4. F (LO 3) Performance reports should contain only costs, revenues, and resources that the manager can control.
5. T (LO 4)
6. F (LO 1) The four basic stakeholder groups are investors, employees, internal business processes, and customers.
7. F (LO 5) Asset turnover is the ratio of sales to average assets invested.
8. T (LO 3)
9. F (LO 1) The reports should enable managers to monitor and evaluate performance measures that add value for stakeholders.

Multiple Choice

1. a (LO 4) Fixed manufacturing overhead does not change within a relevant range of volume or activity.
2. c (LO 4) The total variable cost per unit is multiplied by the number of units of output: $8 × 20,000 = $160,000. The fixed overhead costs of $20,000 are added to the $160,000 to equal $180,000.
3. a (LO 1) The four basic stakeholder groups are investors, employees, internal business processes, and customers.
4. a (LO 5) The equation for computing return on investment is operating income divided by assets invested.
5. b (LO 5) Profit margin is the ratio of operating income to sales.

6. c (LO 3) A revenue center is accountable primarily for revenue, and its success is based on its ability to generate revenue.
7. c (LO 4) To evaluate profit, all variable costs are subtracted from sales to arrive at the center's contribution margin. All fixed costs are then subtracted from contribution margin to determine operating income.
8. b (LO 3) The five types of responsibility centers are a cost center, a discretionary cost center, a revenue center, a profit center, and an investment center.
9. a (LO 5) The asset turnover ratio indicates the productivity of assets, or the number of sales dollars generated by each dollar invested in assets.

Exercises

1. (LO 4)

Corwin Company
Flexible Budget
For the Year Ended December 31, 20xx

Variable budget:	
Direct materials (350,000 × $1.80)	$ 630,000
Direct labor (350,000 × $.35)	122,500
Variable manufacturing overhead	
(350,000 × $.60)	210,000
Total variable budget	$ 962,500
Fixed manufacturing overhead	135,000
Total flexible budget	$1,097,500

2. (LO 3)
   a. Budgeted sales of $120,000 compared with actual sales of $125,000 results in a favorable variance of $5,000.
   b. Budgeted net income of $20,000 compared with actual net income of $18,000 results in an unfavorable variance of ($2,000).
   c. The cost of goods sold is budgeted at $62.50 per unit, but the actual production cost was $63.20. Therefore, it cost $.70 more to produce each unit; $.70 multiplied by 1,250 (the number of units sold) results in a variance of ($875).

Chapter 10

Self-Test

1. d	(LO 1)		**6.** a	(LO 7)
2. b	(LO 2)		**7.** d	(LO 1)
3. b	(LO 2)		**8.** c	(LO 3–LO7)
4. d	(LO 3)		**9.** d	(LO 2)
5. b	(LO 4)			

Matching

1. d	**4.** b	**7.** j	**10.** e
2. f	**5.** c	**8.** g	
3. h	**6.** i	**9.** a	

Short Answer

1. (LO 1)
   Discovering a problem or need
   Identifying alternative courses of action to solve the problem or meet the need
   Analyzing the effects of each alternative on business operations
   Selecting the best alternative
2. (LO 2) Relevant decision information is information that differs among the alternatives under consideration. All other information is irrelevant.
3. (LO 3) Outsourcing can (a) reduce a company's investment in physical assets and human resources, (b) improve cash flow, and (c) increase profits.
4. (LO 3–LO 7)
   Outsourcing decisions
   Special order decisions
   Segment profitability decisions
   Product mix decisions
   Sell or process-further decisions

True-False

1. T (LO 2)
2. F (LO 2) Sunk costs are irrelevant in incremental analysis.
3. T (LO 1)
4. T (LO 2) The main concern is with the differences in revenues and costs.
5. T (LO 3)
6. T (LO 4)
7. T (LO 2)
8. F (LO 5) If a segment has a negative segment margin (i.e., if its revenue is less than its direct costs), it should be eliminated.
9. T (LO 2)
10. T (LO 7)
11. F (LO 2, LO 5) Sunk costs are costs that cannot be recovered; avoidable costs are costs that can be eliminated by dropping a segment.
12. F (LO 4, LO 6) A sales mix decision is what is being described.
13. F (LO 4) Special order decisions should also consider qualitative factors, such as the order's impact on sales to regular customers, its potential to lead the company into new sales areas, and the customer's ability to maintain an ongoing relationship with the company that includes good ordering and paying practices.

Multiple Choice

1. b (LO 6) In making a sales mix decision, a service business must analyze the contribution margin.

2. c (LO 2, LO 3) By focusing on the quantitative differences between outsourcing a product or service and producing or performing it internally, incremental analysis speeds and simplifies the decision making process.

3. d (LO 6) The contribution margins are as follows: Superior, $3 per hour; Deluxe, $4 per hour; and Standard, $5 per hour. To realize the highest operating income, the company should therefore produce all of the required Standard, followed by the Deluxe, and then the Superior, up to the amount possible with the machine hours available.

4. d (LO 3) All choices except **d** are possible benefits of outsourcing; the loss of critical information is one of its potential drawbacks.

5. a (LO 3) Decisions about whether a company should make a product itself or engage another

company to make it are outsourcing decisions, as are decisions about whether to use another company to perform an activity that could be performed in-house.

6. a (LO 2) Relevant costs are those that differ among alternatives. When decisions are based solely on cost, relevant costs are the only factors considered.

7. c (LO 7) The incremental revenues resulting from further processing must exceed the processing costs.

8. b (LO 7) The split-off point occurs at the end of joint processing. Until then, joint products are indistinguishable.

9. a (LO 5) An avoidable cost can be eliminated by dropping the segment to which the cost is traced. Relevant variable costs are always avoidable. Some fixed costs may be avoidable.

10. c (LO 7) Joint costs are incurred before the split-off point and are therefore irrelevant to the sell or process-further decision.

Exercises

1. (LO 2)

	Machine A	Machine B	Difference (A – B)
Cost of machine	$10,000	$17,000	($7,000)
Direct labor	16,000	8,000	8,000
Maintenance	300	500	(200)
Electricity savings	(50)	80	(130)
Totals	$26,250	$25,580	$ 67

The company should purchase Machine B because of its lower incremental cost: $25,580.

2. (LO 2, LO 4) $1.75 (All other costs are sunk and are therefore irrelevant.)

3. (LO 4)

Special order price		$600
Incremental costs:		
Design labor	(10 hr × $40)	(400)
Printing labor	(4 hr × $15)	(60)
Incremental gain		$140

Matt should accept the order because it will increase income by $140. Additional considerations include the special order's impact on sales to regular customers, its potential to lead the company into new sales areas, and the customer's ability to maintain an ongoing relationship with the company that includes good ordering and paying practices. The benefit to the community in which the company operates is also a consideration.

Solution to Crossword Puzzle
(Chapters 9 and 10)

```
D¹   E²   O³             S⁴        O⁵
I    C⁶ E  N  T  E  R⁷   E    T⁸ E  R  M
S    O                   E    G    A
C    N         R⁹ I¹⁰ S   M¹¹ I  X    O¹² F
R    O            N     P  E          R
E    M         A¹³ C  C  O  U  N  T  I  N  G    A
T    I            R     N  T          A
I¹⁴ N  C  O  M  E     S        J¹⁵ O¹⁶ I  N  T
O              M     I    S¹⁷    R       I
N    M¹⁸ A  K  E     B    A¹⁹ N  D       Z
A    A         N     I    L     E        A
R²⁰ E  N  T       T     L     V    R²¹ A  T  E
Y    A      C²² A  P  I  T  A  L        I
     G         L     T     G    R²³ O  I
N²⁴ E  E  D              Y    E²⁵ V  A  N
```

Chapter 11

Self-Test

1. c (LO 1)	**6.** d (LO 4)
2. d (LO 2)	**7.** c (LO 5)
3. a (LO 1)	**8.** a (LO 5)
4. a (LO 3)	**9.** b (LO 5)
5. c (LO 3)	

Matching

1. e	**4.** b	**7.** j	**10.** h
2. d	**5.** f	**8.** i	
3. g	**6.** a	**9.** c	

Short Answer

1. (LO 2) To determine the optimal price for an item, its marginal revenue and marginal cost curves must be computed and plotted. The point at which the two lines intersect is projected onto the demand curve, and a price is determined.

2. (LO 1) Any four of the following would answer the question:
   Demand for the product or service
   Number of competing products or services
   Quality of competing products or services
   Prices of competing products or services
   Customers' preferences
   Seasonal demand or continual demand

3. (LO 1) Any four of the following would answer the question:
   Cost of the product or service
   Desired return on investment
   Quality of materials and labor
   Labor-intensive or automated process
   Usage of scarce resources

4. (LO 3) The sum of the following costs yields the total billing:
   (a) Total cost of materials and parts
   (b) Materials and parts overhead percentage × (a)
   (c) Total labor cost
   (d) Labor cost overhead percentage × (c)

5. (LO 5)
   A cost-plus transfer price is the sum of costs incurred by the producing division plus an agreed-on percentage of profit.
   A market transfer price is the amount that the product would sell for on the open market.
   A negotiated transfer price is a price negotiated by managers that will benefit the entire company.

True-False

1. F (LO 1) Long-run objectives should include a pricing policy.
2. F (LO 1) It is more of an art than a science.
3. F (LO 2) The definition is of marginal revenue, not total revenue.
4. T (LO 1)
5. F (LO 1) It is a possible pricing policy objective.
6. T (LO 4)
7. T (LO 3)
8. F (LO 3) They often use the time and materials approach to pricing.
9. F (LO 5) They bargain for a negotiated transfer price.
10. T (LO 5)
11. F (LO 5) An artificial price cannot increase or decrease total company profits.

Multiple Choice

1. d (LO 1) Charging unrealistically low prices may be a pricing "strategy" to gain market share. It is not a pricing policy "objective."

2. b (LO 1) Effective price setting depends on a manager's ability to analyze the marketplace and anticipate customers' reactions to a product or service and its price. This requires both experience and creativity.

3. c (LO 2) Actual "total cost" behavior and "total revenue" behavior cannot be expected to produce straight lines. Changes in costs are influenced by volume. Changes in price per unit are influenced by competition and other market forces. The lines are therefore curved. These curves produce multiple "breakeven" points at the intersections that occur after the initial "breakeven."

4. a (LO 1) Return on investment is an internal factor that can influence a pricing decision.

5. d (LO 4) The objective of target costing is to avoid this mistake. With target costing, the product is designed so it can be produced in a profitable manner once it is known how much the market will pay for it. Any modifications to the production procedures after the product is marketed are to improve profitability, not to obtain it.

6. b (LO 3) This is the formula used in gross margin pricing.

7. c (LO 3) Service businesses often use "time and materials" to establish prices. The hourly rate, expected time required, a materials list, and an overhead rate should provide a fair estimate of a job's total costs .

8. d (LO 5) The prices that a division charges for goods and services that it provides to another division of the same organization are called *transfer prices*. When the managers of these divisions have discussed and decided on an appropriate transfer price, that price is called a *negotiated transfer price.*

9. a (LO 5) Because they include an estimated amount of profit, transfer prices can be used as a basis for measuring performance. This pricing method enables management to evaluate the contributions that individual production departments make to a company's profitability.

10. b (LO 1, LO 5) Transfer pricing and pricing products for the marketplace have similar objectives and use similar data. The art of price setting is developed through experience in dealing with customers and products. This is as true for setting transfer prices as it is for setting prices for the open market.

Exercises

1. (LO 3)

$$\text{Markup Percentage} = \frac{\text{Desired Profit} + \text{Total Selling, General, and Administrative Expenses}}{\text{Total Production Costs}}$$

$$= \frac{\$382,500 + \$238,000 + \$510,000}{\$680,000 + \$552,500 + \$204,000 + \$263,500}$$

$$= \frac{\$1,130,500}{\$1,170,000}$$

$$= \underline{\underline{66.50\%}}$$

Gross-Margin-Based Price = Total Production Costs per Unit + (Markup Percentage × Total Production Costs per Unit)

$$= (\$1,700,000 \div 850,000) + (\$1,700,000 \div 850,000 \times .665)$$

$$= \underline{\underline{\$3.33}}$$

2. (LO 3)

Zeriscape Landscaping Company

Materials and supplies	$ 46,500
Materials and supplies-related overhead ($46,500 × .4)	18,600
Total materials and supplies charges	$ 65,100
Labor charge	$ 32,800
Overhead charge ($32,800 × .6)	19,680
Total labor charges	$ 52,480
Total billing	$117,580

3. (LO 4)

a. Target cost = $575 ÷ 1.25 = $460

b. Anticipated unit cost of the workbench

Raw materials cost						$120
Purchased parts cost						80
Manufacturing labor	2 hr	×	$14	=		28
Assembly labor	4 hr	×	$15	=		60
Activity-based costs						
Materials and parts handling activity	5%	×	$200	=		10
Engineering activity	$20	×	1	=		20
Production and assembly activity	$15	×	8	=		120
Packaging and delivery activity	$33	×	1	=		33
Sales and marketing activity	$14	×	1	=		14
Total projected unit cost						$485

c. The company should not produce the workbench because its projected cost is $25.00 above the target cost, which means that it would not earn the desired 25 percent profit. The company needs to lower its profit expectations, reduce the product's overall cost, or decide against venturing into this market segment.

4. a. (LO 5)

	Volume = 20,000 units	
	Total Cost	*Unit Cost*
Direct materials	$130,000	$6.50
Direct labor	172,000	8.60
Variable overhead	90,000	4.50
Variable shipping expenses	5,000	.25
Total variable costs	$397,000	$19.85
Avoidable overhead	50,000	2.50
Incremental costs	$447,000	$22.35

b. Unless Ohms Division is willing to pay at least $22.35 per unit, Electra Division should not continue to produce this product. Incremental unit costs exceed the $20 selling price, and Electra is therefore decreasing its profits by continuing to produce the component. The division manager's contention about variable cost recovery is not valid. Revenues must recover all incremental costs, both fixed and variable, to avoid an adverse effect on profits.

Sales (20,000 × $20)	$ 400,000
Less variable costs	(397,000)
Contribution margin	$ 3,000
Avoidable fixed costs	(50,000)
Loss ($2.35 × 20,000 units)	$ 47,000

The division manager should also consider the alternative uses to which plant capacity could be applied. This opportunity cost is not included in measuring the $47,000 loss.

Chapter 12

Self-Test

1. b	(LO 1)	**6.** c	(LO 6)
2. a	(LO 4)	**7.** c	(LO 5)
3. b	(LO 3)	**8.** a	(LO 6)
4. a	(LO 3)	**9.** c	(LO 6)
5. a	(LO 5, LO 6)	**10.** b	(LO 4)

Matching

1. d	**4.** e	**7.** i	**10.** a
2. g	**5.** j	**8.** b	
3. f	**6.** c	**9.** h	

Short Answer

1. (LO 1) Identification of capital investment needs, formal requests for capital investment, preliminary screening, establishment of an acceptance-rejection standard, evaluation of proposals, final decisions on the proposals

2. (LO 2) Cost of debt, cost of preferred stock, cost of common stock, and cost of retained earnings

3. (LO 5, LO 6) Net present value method, payback period method, and accounting rate-of-return method

True-False

1. F (LO 1) Capital investment analysis does not deal with obtaining cash; it involves making decisions about capital investments.
2. F (LO 5, LO 6) The accounting rate-of-return and payback period methods are easier.
3. T (LO 6)
4. F (LO 6) It is the minimum time, not the maximum time.
5. T (LO 6)
6. F (LO 5) The desired rate of return must be known.
7. T (LO 5)
8. F (LO 3) Carrying values are past costs and are therefore irrelevant.
9. F (LO 1) They do this in the planning stage.
10. F (LO 3) They are a source of cash and are therefore relevant.

Multiple Choice

1. b (LO 6) Net income is used to calculate rate of return; net cash inflows do not equate with net income for an accounting period. Some non-cash transactions occur and affect net income, but they have no impact on the Cash account.

2. d (LO 2) The average cost of capital involves all sources of capital used to fund the business. Costs of financing through debt, common and preferred stock, and retained earnings are averaged and weighted by their proportions of the total debt and equity to arrive at the weighted cost of capital.

3. a (LO 4) When used in capital investment analysis, the time value of money restates the estimated cash flows of a capital investment in terms of present value. This analysis restates cash flows using appropriate present value interest factors for timing of the cash flows and the discount rate chosen.

4. b (LO 4) Because of the discount rate used in evaluating the value of money in today's terms, the present value per dollar shrinks as cash flows occur farther in the future. Cash flows that occur sooner are comparatively more valuable per dollar. An investment that has higher cash inflows early in its life would have a greater present value than a similar investment that had the same total cash flows later in its life.

5. a (LO 6) The payback period method shows when an initial investment in a project will be recovered in constant dollars. It is a quick and easy method of ranking investment possibilities.

6. b (LO 1) During the reviewing stage, each project undergoes a postcompletion audit to determine if it is meeting the goals and targets set forth in the planning stage.

7. d (LO 5) The net present value method uses the minimum rate of return as the discount rate.

8. c (LO 3) Estimates of future cash flows should cover the entire life of a project and be as detailed as possible. Cash flows that occur later in the life of a project may be difficult to estimate, but for complete analysis and evaluation, they should not be ignored

9. c (LO 6) The payback period is 4.0 years. It takes four years of net cash inflows to equal the $500,000 initial investment ($160,000 + $140,000 + $120,000 + $80,000 = $500,000).

Exercises

1. (LO 6)

   a. Accounting Rate of Return $= \dfrac{\$8,000}{\$70,000 \div 2} = 22.9\%$

   b. Payback Period $= \dfrac{\$70,000}{\$8,000 + \$14,000} = 3.2$ years

   (The $14,000 in the denominator is depreciation.)

   Because the minimum desired rate of return is 25 percent and the minimum payback period is three years, the company should not invest in the machine.

2. (LO 5)

Year	Net Cash Inflows		Present Value Multiplier		Present Value
1	8,000	×	.862	=	$6,896
2	6,000	×	.743	=	4,458
3	6,000	×	.641	=	3,846
4	6,000	×	.552	=	3,312
5	6,000	×	.476	=	2,856
Total					$21,368

   The company should purchase the machine because the present value of future net cash inflows is greater than the cost of the machine.

3. (LO 3, LO 5, LO 6)

   a. Depreciation = ($400,000 – $40,000) ÷ 5 = $72,000
   b. Project's average annual net income = $160,000 – $72,000 = $88,000
      Average investment cost = ([$400,000 – $40,000] ÷ 2) + $40,000 = $220,000
      Accounting rate of return = $88,000 ÷ $220,000 = 40%
   c. Payback period = $400,000 ÷ $160,000 = 2.5 years
   d. Present value factor from Table 3: 5th year at 20% return = .402
      Present value factor from Table 4: 5 years at 20% return = 2.991
      Present value = ($160,000 × 2.991) + ($40,000 × .402) = 494,640
   e. The net present value of all future cash inflows ($494,640) is greater than the $400,000 initial investment. The investment will therefore earn the minimum desired rate of return. Because of this and because the payback period of 2.5 years is less than the 3.0 maximum allowed, the company should purchase the machine.

Solution to Crossword Puzzle
(Chapters 11 and 12)

```
   C   C O M M I T T E D             L
   O               R                 O
   S   S   R   C A R R Y I N G
   T   A   E           N             G
   O   V   T   A S S E T S           I
   F   I   U   F           I         N
   C   N   R   E           M         T
   M A R G I N A L R E V E N U E
   P   S             P               R
   I       F U T U R E V A L U E
   T   M             I               S
   T A R G E T       C       C O S T
   L       R   I     D E B T       F
           M
   D E C E N T R A L I Z E D
```

Across answers:
2. COMMITTED
7. CARRYING
8. ASSETS
11. MARGINAL REVENUE
12. FUTURE VALUE
14. TARGET
16. COST
18. DEBT
19. DECENTRALIZED

Down answers:
1. COST OF CAPITAL
3. TRANSFER PRICE
5. SAVINGS
6. RETURN
10. INTERESTS

Chapter 13

Self-Test

1. d	(LO 1)		**6.** c	(LO 3)
2. b	(LO 1)		**7.** d	(LO 3)
3. c	(LO 2)		**8.** a	(LO 3)
4. a	(LO 2)		**9.** d	(LO 2)
5. d	(LO 3)		**10.** c	(LO 5)

Matching

1. b	**4.** a	**7.** i	**10.** f
2. j	**5.** g	**8.** e	
3. d	**6.** c	**9.** h	

Short Answer

1. (LO 1) An MIS database supplies managers with relevant and reliable information that they can use to formulate strategic plans, make forecasts, and develop budgets in the planning stage of the management cycle; to implement decisions about personnel, resources, and activities in the executing stage; to evaluate all major business functions in the reviewing stage, and to generate customized performance reports in the reporting stage.

2. (LO 2, LO 3) Costs of conformance include prevention costs (e.g., the costs of design review and quality training of employees) and appraisal costs (e.g., the costs of product simulation and development and of vendor audits and sample testing). Costs of nonconformance include internal failure costs (e.g., the costs of scrap, rework, and downtime) and external failure costs (e.g., the costs of warranty claims and returned goods).

3. (LO 2, LO 3) Nonfinancial measures of quality are measures of product design, vendor performance, production performance, delivery cycle time, and customer satisfaction. These nonfinancial measures supplement the cost-based measures. By focusing on them, managers can detect and correct problems early on, before they have a detrimental effect on the financial statements. Nonfinancial measures of quality thus help managers maximize the net income from operations.

True-False

1. F (LO 2) CAD is the acronym for computer-aided design.
2. F (LO 2, LO 3) Quality can be measured by using both financial measures (costs of quality) and nonfinancial measures (production performance).
3. T (LO 2)
4. F (LO 2) The costs of conformance are incurred to ensure that products do not have defects. As they increase, the costs of nonconformance, which are incurred to correct defects, should decrease.
5. F (LO 4) The description applies to process mapping, not benchmarking.

6. T (LO 2)
7. T (LO 2)
8. F (LO 2, LO 3) Reductions in delivery cycle time have a positive impact on income because they reduce nonvalue-adding activities and shorten the time between a company's payment for manufacturing inputs and its receipt of payment for the products it sells.
9. T (LO 2)
10. F (LO 5) The Malcolm Baldrige Quality Award recognizes U.S. organizations for their achievements in quality and business performance.

Multiple Choice

1. b (LO 1) An MIS not only gives managers access to historical costs; it also provides continuous, detailed records of a company's activities and provides managers with timely measures of operating results.
2. a (LO 2) Costs of conformance are the costs incurred to produce a quality product or service. The inspection of rework needed to correct a defect is a cost of nonconformance.
3. b (LO 2) Costs of nonconformance are costs incurred because of design flaws, poor materials, poor workmanship, poor machinery, or poor management. These avoidable costs increase the cost of a product or service without adding value. The objective of controlling the costs of quality is to eliminate such costs.
4. b (LO 2) $11,200 + $18,900 + $10,100 + $16,400 = $56,600
5. c (LO 2) $13,000 + $10,500 = $23,500
6. d (LO 2, LO 3) Nonfinancial measures of quality are important to TQM for all the reasons stated in **a, b,** and **c.** By focusing on these measures, managers can detect problems at an early stage (before they show up in financial statements) and take steps to correct them.

7. b (LO 2) Production cycle time is the time it takes to make a product and have it available for shipment to a customer.
8. a (LO 2) The costs of conformance are the costs incurred to produce a quality product or service. The costs of nonconformance are the costs incurred to correct defects in a product or service.
9. c. (LO 2) Delivery cycle time consists of purchase order lead time (the time it takes for materials to be ordered and received), production cycle time (the time it takes to make a product), and delivery time (the time between completion of a product and its receipt by the customer).
10. d (LO 2) Company A's conformance costs exceed its costs of nonconformance, but not by much. Company B spends less than Company A on conformance costs, but that is not always the best route to follow. However, because Company B's costs of nonconformance costs are only 20 percent of its costs of conformance it is more likely to have a higher level of product quality than Company A.

Exercises

1. (LO 2)

   a.

	20x4	20x5
Costs of conformance		
Prevention costs		
Prototype design	$38,000	$42,000
Quality training	20,000	30,000
Total prevention costs	$58,000	$72,000
Appraisal costs		
Product simulation	$ 6,000	$ 9,000
Materials testing	4,000	6,000
Total appraisal costs	$10,000	$15,000
Total costs of conformance	$68,000	$87,000

   b.

	20x4	20x5
Costs of nonconformance		
Internal failure costs		
Scrap	$ 20,000	$15,000
Rework	50,000	35,000
Total internal failure	$ 70,000	$50,000
External failure costs		
Product warranty	$ 40,000	$25,000
Total external failure	$ 40,000	$25,000
Total costs of nonconformance	$110,000	$75,000

   c. The quality improvement program was successful. In 20x4, the costs of nonconformance exceeded those of conformance by $42,000. In 20x5, the costs of conformance exceeded those of nonconformance by $12,000. In addition, the the costs of nonconformance decreased by $35,000, and conformance costs increased by only $19,000. The company is definitely moving in the right direction.

2. (LO 2, LO 3)
   a. CC
   b. CN
   c. CC
   d. CN
   e. CC
   f. CN
   g. CC

Chapter 14

Self-Test

1. c	(LO 1)		**6.** d	(LO 3)
2. d	(LO 1)		**7.** c	(LO 5)
3. a	(LO 2)		**8.** c	(LO 2)
4. a	(LO 2)		**9.** b	(LO 4)
5. b	(LO 5)		**10.** d	(LO 1)

Matching

1. b	**4.** h	**7.** c	**10.** f
2. g	**5.** i	**8.** e	
3. a	**6.** j	**9.** d	

Short Answer

1. (LO 4) *Step 1:* Calculate the allocation fraction by dividing a center's specific cost driver amount by the sum of all the other open centers' cost driver amounts. Only the cost driver amounts for the open service centers and revenue centers are used in determining the allocation fraction.

   Step 2: Determine the dollar amount to assign to each open service center and each revenue center by multiplying each service center's total costs by the corresponding service or revenue center's allocation fraction calculated in Step 1.

   Step 3: Total the costs for each revenue center.

2. (LO 3) *Step 1:* Calculate allocation fractions. An allocation fraction is a revenue center's specific cost driver amount divided by the sum of all revenue centers' cost driver amounts.

   Step 2: Determine the dollar amount to assign to each revenue center by multiplying each service center's total costs by the corresponding revenue center's allocation fraction calculated in Step 1.

   Step 3: Total the costs for each revenue center. Add the assigned service costs to the other costs incurred in the revenue center.

3. (LO 1) Managers use cost allocation reports to monitor costs and the allocation methods and bases used to assign costs.

4. (LO 2)

Branch store	2
Distribution center	1
Customer service center	1
Technology support center	1
Receptionist	1
Auto repair service	2
Physician services	2

5. (LO 2) Number of hours or minutes, number of reports processed, number of employees, number of checks processed, number of customers, number of audits

True-False

1. T (LO 1)
2. T (LO 2)
3. F (LO 3) The direct method assigns the cost of service centers only to revenue centers.
4. T (LO 4)
5. F (LO 1) The full cost includes the costs of direct materials, direct labor, and all production and nonproduction activities required to satisfy the customer.
6. T (LO 1)
7. F (LO 1) The actual amounts of service centers are allocated to other responsibility centers that use their services. The actual total costs of a company do not change.
8. T (LO 2)
9. F (LO 5) The drawback of the ability to pay method is that revenue centers that sell more are charged a higher percentage of the service centers' costs.
10. T (LO 6)
11. T (LO 2)
12. T (LO 6)

Multiple Choice

1. c (LO 1) The total costs of the company will be the total costs of all its responsibility centers.
2. c (LO 5) The full costs to the Mexican Revenue Center will be $97,500. To calculate this amount, the service center costs are totaled and then divided by 2 (two centers use the services): [$15,000 + $20,000 + $40,000] ÷ 2 = $37,500. Actual costs of $60,000 are added to this amount: $37,500 + $60,000 = $97,500.
3. a (LO 5) The ability to pay method would allocate one-third of the service costs to the U.S. Revenue Center because it contributed one-third of the total sales (assigned costs = $250,000 ÷ [$250,000 + $500,000] = $25,000 + $50,000 [actual costs] = $75,000).
4. c (LO 5) The simultaneous equation method is also called the *reciprocal method*.
5. a (LO 6) A departmental overhead rate is a single rate that includes all of a department's overhead costs. It is used to determine the full cost of a product or service.
6. d (LO 3, LO 4) When using either the direct method or the step method, the first step is to calculate the allocation fraction to be used in determining the dollar amount assigned to each responsibility center.
7. b (LO 1) During the planning stage, managers select an allocation base for measuring the usage of each activity and a method of assigning costs.
8. b (LO 2) Of the choices given, the number of customer accounts would be the most appropriate cost driver for a collection department.
9. c (LO 2) The number of employees would be an appropriate cost driver for payroll and human resources centers. The more employees a center has, the more work it has to do—for example, a payroll center would have more checks to distribute, and a human resources center would have more employee evaluations to process.
10. d (LO 1) All the choices are clear advantages of service cost allocation.
11. a (LO2) A service center is a responsibility center that provides benefits to other service centers and revenue centers.
12. a (LO 1) During the reviewing stage, managers evaluate customer profitability and product or service performance. They also review the appropriateness of the cost allocation bases and methods used, and they revise them as needed.
13. d (LO 5) If a center's revenue increases, the allocation base of that center will also increase, and the center will therefore be assigned a higher cost. Consequently, managers may feel penalized for increasing their sales.
14. c (LO 1) Common costs are mutually beneficial indirect costs that may not have a clear cause-and-effect relationship to a specific product or service because they come from a service center that benefits and supports many products and services.

Exercises

1. (LO 3, LO 4)

a. Direct method

	Allocation Fraction: Accounting	Accounting	Purchasing	MIS	Utilities	Advertising	Allocation Fraction: Car Stereos	Car Stereos	Allocation Fraction: Portable Players	Portable Players	Total
Total center costs		$ 50,000	$ 80,000	$ 30,000	$ 35,000	$ 75,000		$200,000		$350,000	$820,000
Assign Accounting costs	200/4,900	(50,000)					200/850	11,765	650/850	38,235	
Assign Purchasing costs			(80,000)				2,000/4,500	35,556	2,500/4,500	44,444	
Assign MIS costs				(30,000)			1,500/2,600	17,308	1,100/2,600	12,692	
Assign Utilities costs					(35,000)		100,000/250,000	14,000	150,000/250,000	21,000	
Assign Advertising costs						(75,000)	300/1,000	22,500	700/1,000	52,500	
Total revenue center costs after allocation								$301,129		$518,871	$820,000

b. Step method

	Allocation Fraction: Accounting	Accounting	Allocation Fraction: Purchasing	Purchasing	Allocation Fraction: MIS	MIS	Allocation Fraction: Utilities	Utilities	Allocation Fraction: Advertising	Advertising	Allocation Fraction: Car Stereos	Car Stereos	Allocation Fraction: Portable Players	Portable Players	Total
Total center costs		$ 50,000		$ 80,000		$ 30,000		$ 35,000		$ 75,000		$200,000		$350,000	$820,000
Assign Purchasing costs	200/4,900	3,265		(80,000)	75/4,900	1,224	25/4,900	408	100/4,900	1,633	2,000/4,900	32,653	2,500/4,900	40,816	
Assign Advertising costs		0								(76,633)	300/1,000	22,990	700/1,000	53,643	
Assign Accounting costs		(53,265)			8/860	495	2/860	124			200/860	12,387	650/860	40,258	
Assign Utilities costs					5,000/255,000	697		(35,532)			100,000/255,000	13,934	150,000/255,000	20,901	
Assign MIS costs						(32,417)					1,500/2,600	18,702	1,100/2,600	13,715	
		$ 0		$ 0		$ 0		$ 0		$ 0		$300,666		$519,334	$820,000

2. (LO 2)

Utilities:	f
Purchasing:	d
Human Resources:	g
Maintenance:	a
MIS:	b
Secretarial Pool:	c
Mailroom:	e

3. (LO 3, 4, 5)

a. Cosmetics: $350,000 \div 1,500,000 \times \$12,500 = \$2,917$
Housewares: $500,000 \div 1,500,000 \times \$12,500 = \$4,167$
Tools: $650,000 \div 1,500,000 \times \$12,500 = \$5,416$

b. Each revenue center would be assigned \$5,000:
$\$15,000 \div 3 = \$5,000$.

c. Cosmetics: $100 \div 850 \times \$25,500 = \$3,000$
Housewares: $500 \div 850 \times \$25,500 = \$15,000$
Tools: $250 \div 850 \times \$25,500 = \$7,500$

Chapter 15

Self-Test

1. a	(LO 1)		**6.** d	(LO 4)
2. d	(LO 2)		**7.** c	(LO 4)
3. a	(LO 3)		**8.** c	(LO 5)
4. b	(LO 5)		**9.** a	(LO 5)
5. c	(LO 4)		**10.** c	(LO 5)

Matching

1. g	**4.** e	**7.** h	**10.** d
2. b	**5.** j	**8.** i	**11.** c
3. l	**6.** f	**9.** k	**12.** a

Short Answer

1. (LO 5) Profit margin, asset turnover, return on assets, and return on equity
2. (LO 4) Horizontal analysis presents absolute and percentage changes in specific financial statement items from one year to the next. Vertical analysis, on the other hand, uses percentages to show the relationship of individual items on a financial statement to a total within the statement.
3. (LO 2) Rule-of-thumb measures, analysis of past performance of the company, and comparison with industry norms
4. (LO 1) The risk of total loss is far less with several investments than with one investment because only a rare set of economic circumstances could cause several different investments to suffer large losses all at once.
5. (LO 5) Cash flow yield, cash flows to sales, cash flows to assets, and free cash flow

True-False

1. T (LO 4)
2. F (LO 4) Common-size statements show relationships between items in terms of percentages, not dollars.
3. F (LO 5) The current ratio will increase.
4. T (LO 5)
5. F (LO 5) It equals the cost of goods sold divided by average inventory.
6. F (LO 5) The reverse is true because the price/earnings ratio depends on the earnings per share amount.
7. F (LO 5) Interest is not added back.
8. T (LO 5)
9. F (LO 5) The higher the debt to equity ratio, the greater the risk is.
10. F (LO 5) Receivable turnover measures how many times, on average, the receivables were converted into cash during the period.
11. T (LO 5)
12. T (LO 5)
13. F (LO 5) It is a market strength ratio.
14. F (LO 4) Sales are set at 100 percent.
15. T (LO 3)
16. T (LO 3)
17. T (LO 5)
18. F (LO 5) A higher payables turnover will produce a *shorter* average days' payable.
19. T (LO 1)

Multiple Choice

1. b (LO 5) The interest coverage ratio measures the degree of protection creditors have from a default on interest payments on loans.

2. d (LO 5) The quick ratio measures a company's ability to cover immediate cash requirements for operating expenses and short-term payables.

3. c (LO 5) Asset turnover is calculated using net sales as the numerator and average total assets as the denominator. It is a measure of how efficiently a company uses its assets to produce sales.

4. a (LO 5) A high price/earnings ratio indicates that investors are optimistic about a company's future earnings and growth.

5. a (LO 4) Index numbers are calculated to reflect percentage changes over several consecutive years. The base year is assigned the value of 100 percent; changes from that base are then assigned a percentage so that subsequent amounts can be compared with base amounts. This method, which is used to identify trends, eliminates differences resulting from universal changes, such as inflation.

6. b (LO 1) Of the choices given, only managers are internal users of financial statements. In setting financial performance objectives for a company and in seeing that those objectives are achieved, managers rely on the information presented in the financial statements.

7. d (LO 2) All the factors listed in **a** through **c** contribute to the complexity of comparing a company's performance with the performance of other companies in the same industry.

8. c (LO 5) The turnover of receivables is the number of times receivables are collected in relation to sales in an accounting period. A low number suggests that average accounts receivable balances are high and that credit policy is weak.

9. b (LO 4) Net income is given a percentage in relation to net sales, as are all other components of the common-size income statement. Net sales are set at 100 percent.

10. c (LO 5) Free cash flow is the cash that remains from operating activities after deducting the funds a company must commit to dividends and net capital expenditures.

Exercises

1. (LO 4)

	20x6	20x5	Increase (Decrease) Amount	Increase (Decrease) Percentage
Sales	$200,000	$250,000	$ 50,000	25.0
Cost of goods sold	120,000	144,000	24,000	20.0
Gross margin	$ 80,000	$106,000	26,000	32.5
Operating expenses	50,000	62,000	12,000	24.0
Income before income taxes	$ 30,000	$ 44,000	14,000	46.7
Income taxes	8,000	16,000	8,000	100.0
Net income	$ 22,000	$ 28,000	6,000	27.3

2. (LO 5)

    a. 2.0 ($500,000 ÷ $250,000)

    b. 1.3 $\left(\dfrac{\$500,000 - \$180,000}{\$250,000}\right)$

    c. 1.9 times ($350,000 ÷ $180,000)

    d. 192.1 days (365 ÷ 1.9)

    e. 12.0% ($106,000 ÷ $880,000)

    f. 22.1% ($106,000 ÷ $480,000)

    g. 6.0 ($600,000 ÷ $100,000)

    h. 60.8 days (365 ÷ 6.0)

    i. 17.7% ($106,000 ÷ $600,000)

    j. .7 times ($75,000 ÷ $106,000)

    k. 12.5% ($75,000 ÷ $600,000)

    l. 8.5% ($75,000 ÷ $880,000)

    m. .68 times ($600,000 ÷ $880,000)

    n. 8 times $\left(\dfrac{\$40}{\$106,000 ÷ \$21,200}\right)$

Solution to Crossword Puzzle
(Chapters 13, 14, and 15)